I0812719

IMAGES
of America

ZANESVILLE

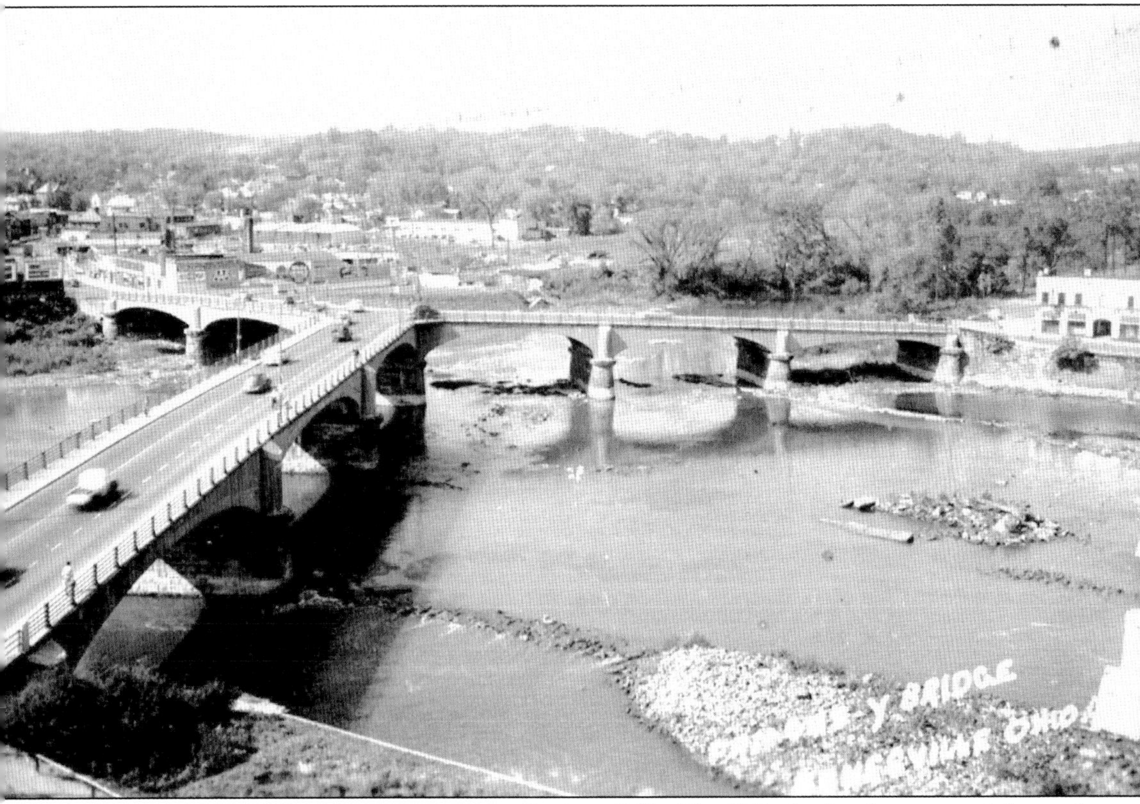

This is a view of the famous Y Bridge in the late 1950s. The Y Bridge has been one of the city's most distinctive landmarks since 1814. It is possible to cross the Y Bridge and not cross the Muskingum River. (Courtesy of Chance Brockway.)

IMAGES
of America

ZANESVILLE

Kathryn Lynch and Michael S. Sims

ARCADIA
PUBLISHING

ISBN 978-0-7385-3995-9

Published by Arcadia Publishing
Charleston, South Carolina

Printed in the United States of America

Library of Congress Catalog Card Number: 2005935036

For all general information contact Arcadia Publishing at:
Telephone 843-853-2070
Fax 843-853-0044
E-mail sales@arcadiapublishing.com
For customer service and orders:
Toll-Free 1-888-313-2665

Visit us on the Internet at www.arcadiapublishing.com

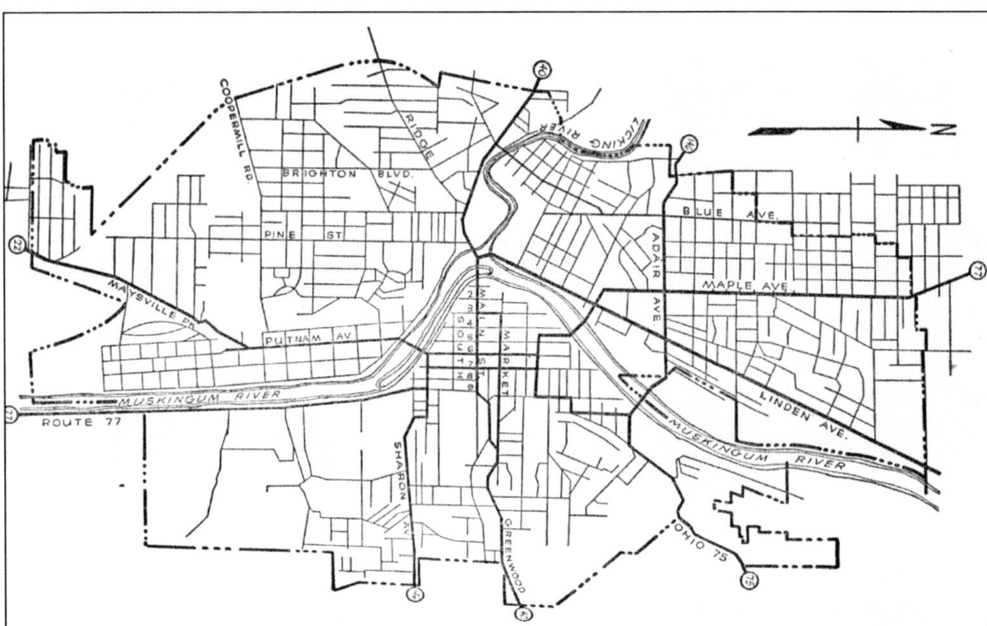

This map shows the street layout of Zanesville in the 1930s. The earliest sections of the city were laid out in a grid by John McIntire in 1798. Several neighborhoods in the Underwood section of the city were lost to urban renewal when Interstate 70 was constructed in the 1960s.

Contents

ACKNOWLEDGMENTS

It goes without saying that this book would not have been possible without the generosity and support of many people. The number of people who expressed enthusiasm and encouragement for this book made the experience of researching and writing it all the more enjoyable. It was a pleasure to sit down with everyone who came forward to share their recollections of the past.

This book is not intended to be an exhaustive photographic essay of Zanesville's historic past, but rather a broad overview of the city. Once we began our research, we discovered that Zanesville was a complex and intriguing subject. There is still much to be told about the city that could become the subject of future books.

The following people are acknowledged for their part in making this book a reality.

Chance Brockway, Tom Brown, Wayne Estep, Danny Grandstaff, Muskingum County Chapter of the Ohio Genealogy Society (MCCOGS), Mose Mesre, and Betty Ward for sharing their photograph collections.

The innovative and creative team at Pictures Plus, including Michael Carter, Diane Lantz, and Chas D. Whitcomb, for digitally scanning many of the images used in this book.

Knowledgeable local historian Jane Price offered a great deal of wisdom to this process through her narrative in the introduction of the book.

We would also like to thank Vincent Adornetto, Charlene Bargiel, Thomas Barker, Chris Crooks, Margaret Deedrick, Jill Downs, Dan Ekman, Bart and Kathleen Hagemayer, Richard Holly, Jamie Iannelli, Rose Ellen Jenkins, Pam Jones, John Kunkel, Peg Lilly, Chris Lynch, Kimberly Lynch, Jason Maddux, Kathy McLeister, Chuck Martin, Terry Martin, MCCOGS Library staff, Barbara Powers, Terra K. Schramm, Alta Sims, Richard J. Sklenar, Sharon Stemm, Susan Talbot-Stanaway, Bill Sullivan, Sandy Tubbs, Amy Underwood, and Brenda Wolfe.

Finally, to all of our family and friends, we appreciate your patience and understanding.

INTRODUCTION

After the Revolutionary War, many men were recompensed for their service with land grants in the frontier "over the mountains." Col. Ebenezer Zane contracted with the government to cut a road for settlers and mail carriers to use that would run due west from Wheeling, West Virginia, to the Muskingum River in the Ohio frontier lands and then southwest to Maysville, Kentucky. He was paid for his work with land, and he subsequently transferred a mile-square section of that land, which lay at the confluence of the Muskingum and Licking Rivers, to his brother Jonathan and son-in-law John McIntire. It was payment for their help in blazing the trail that eventually became the National Road and U.S. Route 40.

Zane and McIntire established a ferry service in 1797, and McIntire moved to the site in 1798. He immediately laid out a town plat, set up a post office, and built a place where travelers could obtain meals and beds. By the end of the year, "Zane's Town" could boast of seven log cabins and weekly mail service.

Another name bound up in the history of the area is Dr. Increase Mathews. With the help of his uncle, Gen. Rufus Putnam, Mathews established the town of Putnam across the Muskingum River from Zanesville. Most of its original citizens were New Englanders. The two towns became bitter rivals, but eventually Putnam, along with the other villages that had sprung up west of the rivers, was incorporated into Zanesville.

Zanesville has always been the seat of Muskingum County. The state legislature met in Zanesville during the years 1810 to 1812 in the second of three courthouses built in the city.

Zanesville's location has always been of primary importance to its growth. The roads that converged there provided access to the west. The Muskingum River was fully navigable and thus allowed a great deal of commercial and passenger traffic to flow between the city and landings along the Muskingum, Ohio, and Mississippi Rivers. A canal, built in 1831, connected Zanesville with Lake Erie and the Erie Canal to the north, and Portsmouth on the Ohio River to the south.

When the railroads made their way west, seven lines eventually passed through Zanesville. With the railroad came new bridges, depots, repair shops, and spur lines that served local industries. Streetcars provided transportation around the city beginning in the 1870s, and in the early 1900s, interurbans carried passengers between Zanesville and other towns in the area. Automobiles became an increasingly popular means of getting around the city after 1900. The first airplane flights over Zanesville took place in 1911.

The abundance of local natural resources including coal, clay, water, and timber enabled Zanesville to become the home of several industries that employed thousands of workers. Glass, iron, bricks, art pottery, floor and wall tiles, soap, farm wagons, cotton cultivators, plows, mining machinery, steam engines, and seamless pipe are just a few of the products once manufactured in Zanesville. These industries, along with its transportation facilities, enabled Zanesville to become a transportation hub and one of the largest cities in southeastern Ohio.

Zanesville has had many nicknames over the years including the "Clay City" and the "Y Bridge City." In 1926, the Zanesville Chamber of Commerce declared Zanesville as "America's Typical City" in an advertisement that appeared in the *Literary Digest*.

Readers of this book will be able to travel back in time and visit the Zanesville that the generations that came before them knew. Many neighborhoods throughout the city have remained intact for more than 100 years and still hold many hidden treasures waiting to be discovered. Zanesville has nearly 50 properties listed on the National Register of Historic Places, many recognized for their unique architectural style and aesthetic beauty. Our history is what makes our hometown so special.

—Jane Price

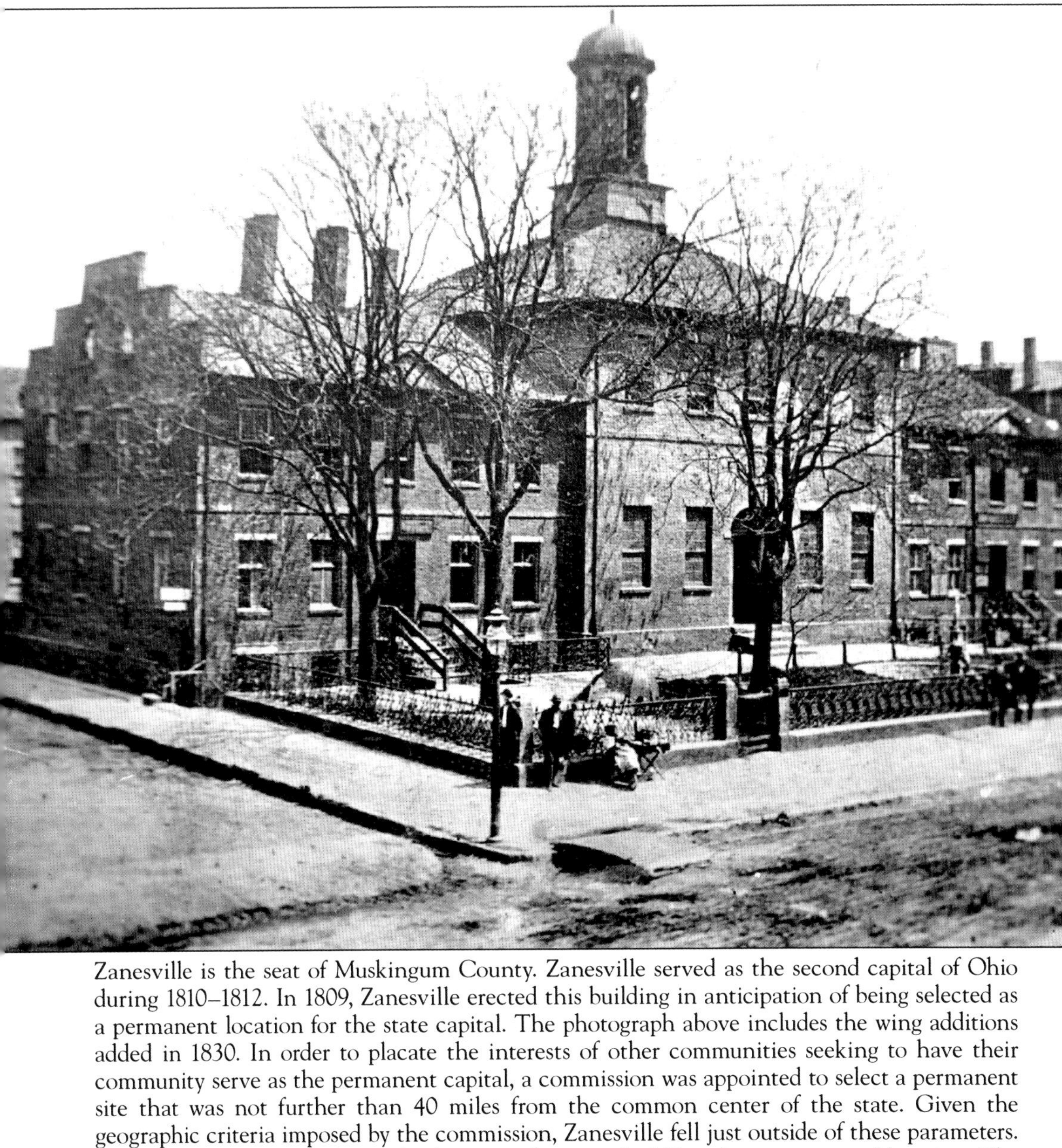

Zanesville is the seat of Muskingum County. Zanesville served as the second capital of Ohio during 1810–1812. In 1809, Zanesville erected this building in anticipation of being selected as a permanent location for the state capital. The photograph above includes the wing additions added in 1830. In order to placate the interests of other communities seeking to have their community serve as the permanent capital, a commission was appointed to select a permanent site that was not further than 40 miles from the common center of the state. Given the geographic criteria imposed by the commission, Zanesville fell just outside of these parameters. Columbus was the city ultimately chosen as the capital of Ohio due to its central location. The building then became Muskingum County's courthouse. "Old 1809," as the building came to be called, served in that capacity until 1874. (Courtesy of Mose Mesre.)

One

EARLY DAYS

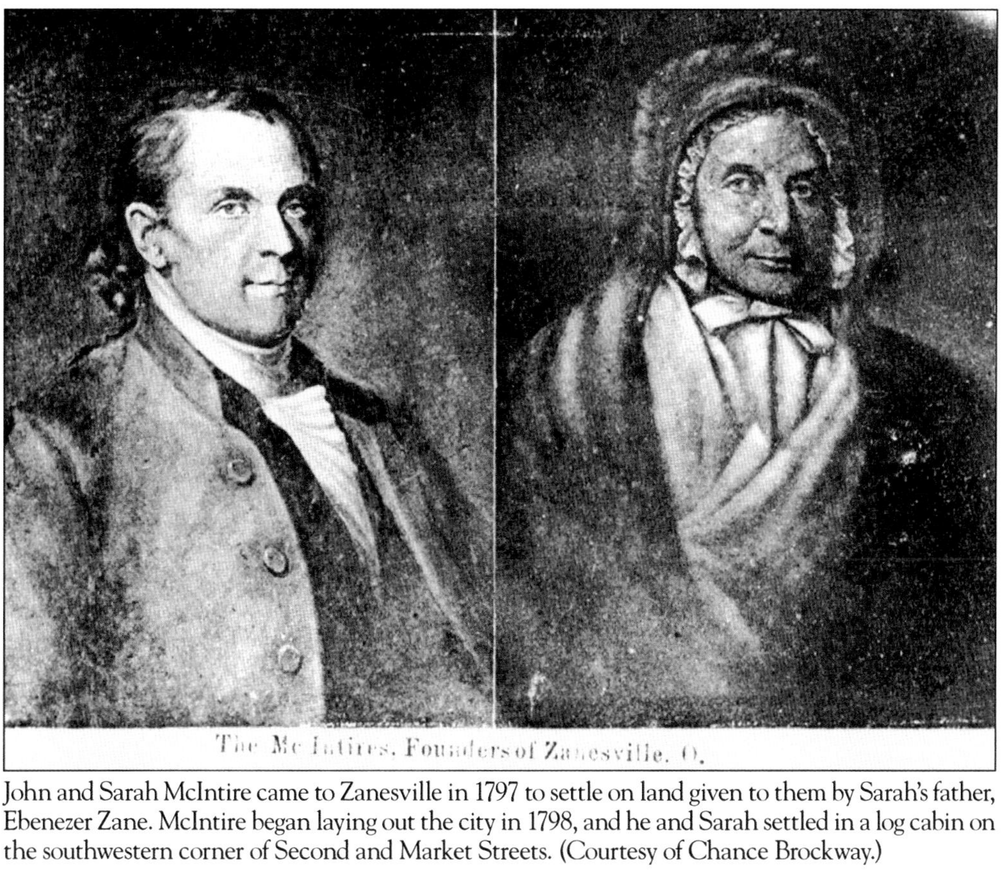

John and Sarah McIntire came to Zanesville in 1797 to settle on land given to them by Sarah's father, Ebenezer Zane. McIntire began laying out the city in 1798, and he and Sarah settled in a log cabin on the southwestern corner of Second and Market Streets. (Courtesy of Chance Brockway.)

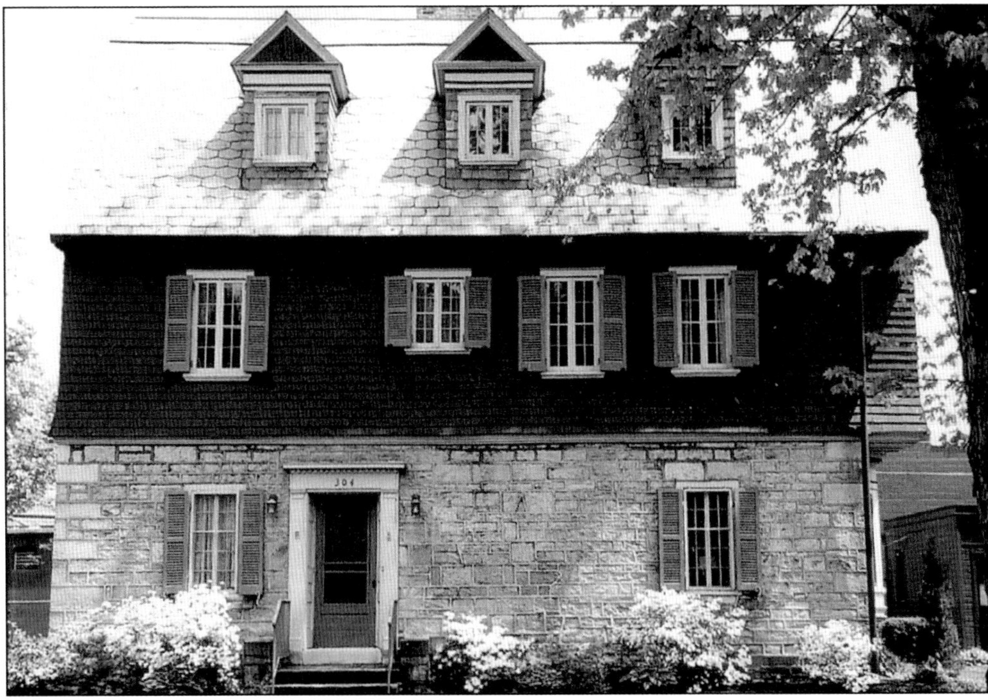

The Dr. Increase Mathews House, located at 304 Woodlawn Avenue, is the oldest structure in the Putnam District. It was built in 1805 as a one-story residence, and the two upper levels were added in 1884. (Courtesy of MCCOGS.)

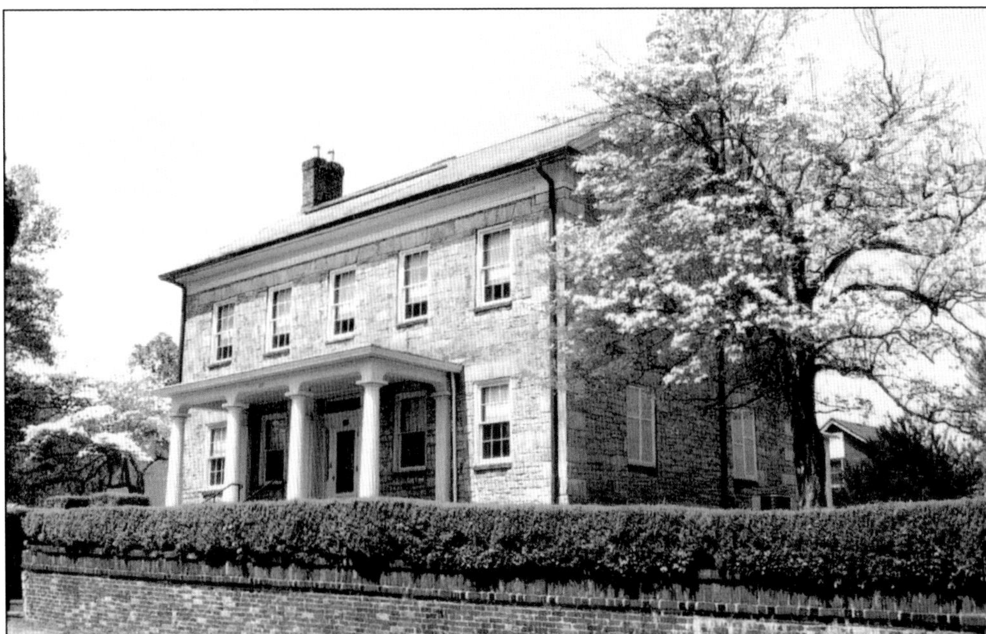

The Stone Academy was built in 1809 as a school at 115 Jefferson Street. It was frequently used for public meetings including a State Abolition Society meeting in 1839. A stone wing was added to the rear of the building in the mid-19th century.

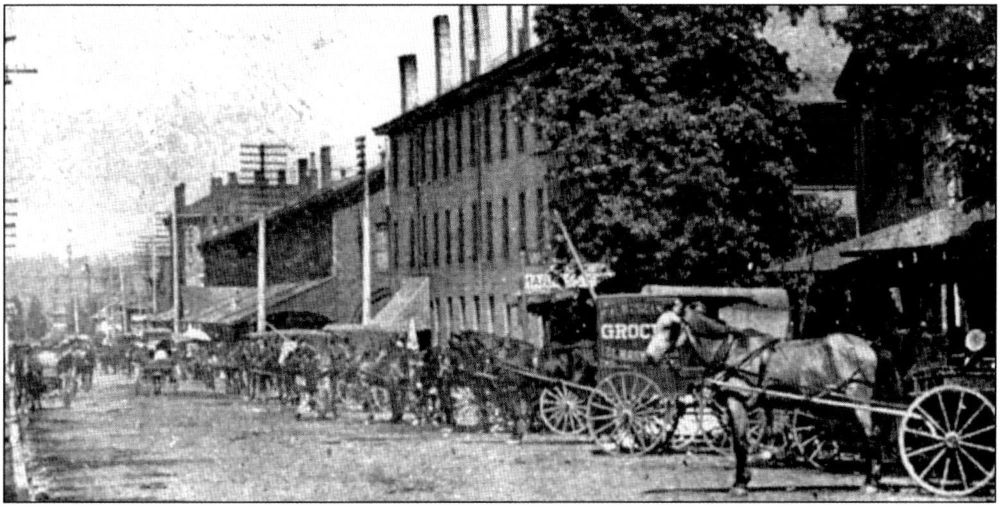

Since 1832, hundreds of farmers gathered on Wednesday and Saturday mornings each week to sell their produce, meat, and so forth to local residents and businesses at the Market House, shown in this 1895 image. During the months of September and October, the market grew so large that the overflow of gardeners and fruit growers extended eastward on Market Street along the sidewalk the length of another city block.

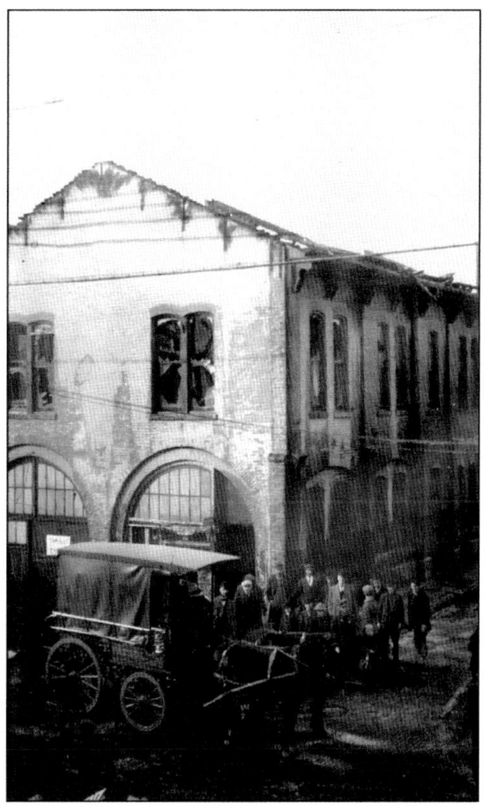

In 1912, the Market House sustained extensive damage as a result of a fire. Note the missing roof, broken windows, and scorch marks on the building. The building was repaired and served as the city's marketplace for several more years. It presently houses various city government offices. (Courtesy of Wayne Estep.)

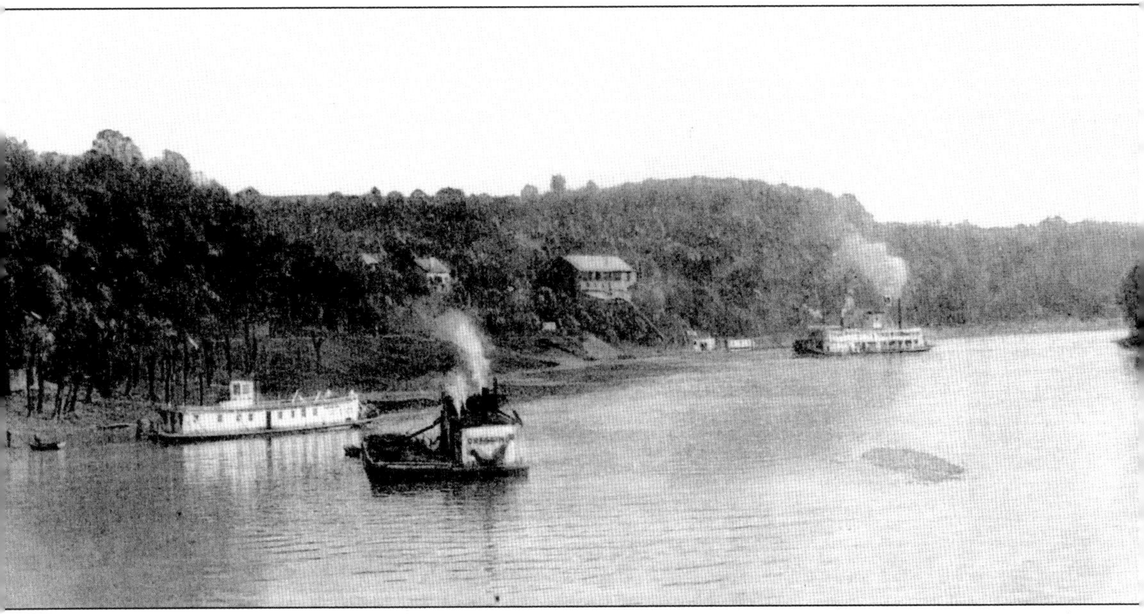

The Muskingum River brought early settlers to the banks of Zanesville and Putnam at the confluence of the Licking River. The river served as a main source of transportation from 1797 until the railroad carried its first passengers to the area in 1852. The early pottery manufacturers from Zanesville and the surrounding area depended on the Muskingum River as the main source of transporting their wares. Barges took the pottery south to the Ohio River and farther along to the Mississippi River.

Two

TWO RIVERS, A CANAL, AND FLOODS

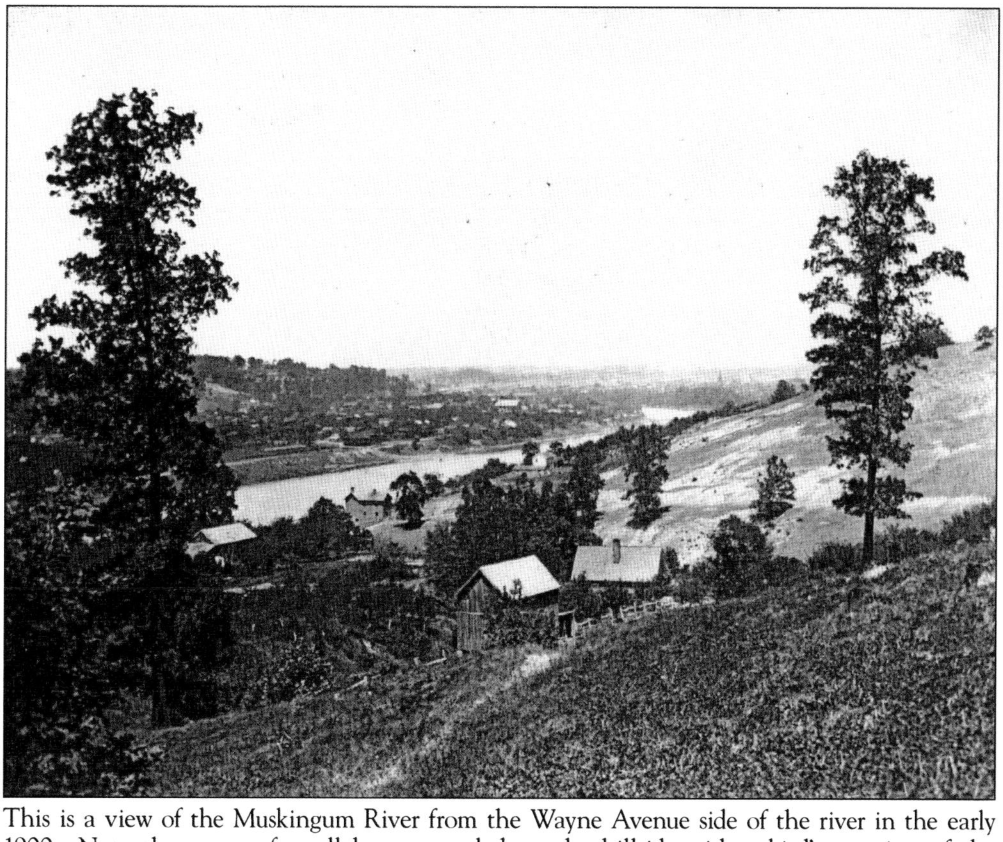

This is a view of the Muskingum River from the Wayne Avenue side of the river in the early 1900s. Note the group of small houses nestled on the hillside with a bird's-eye view of the downtown area.

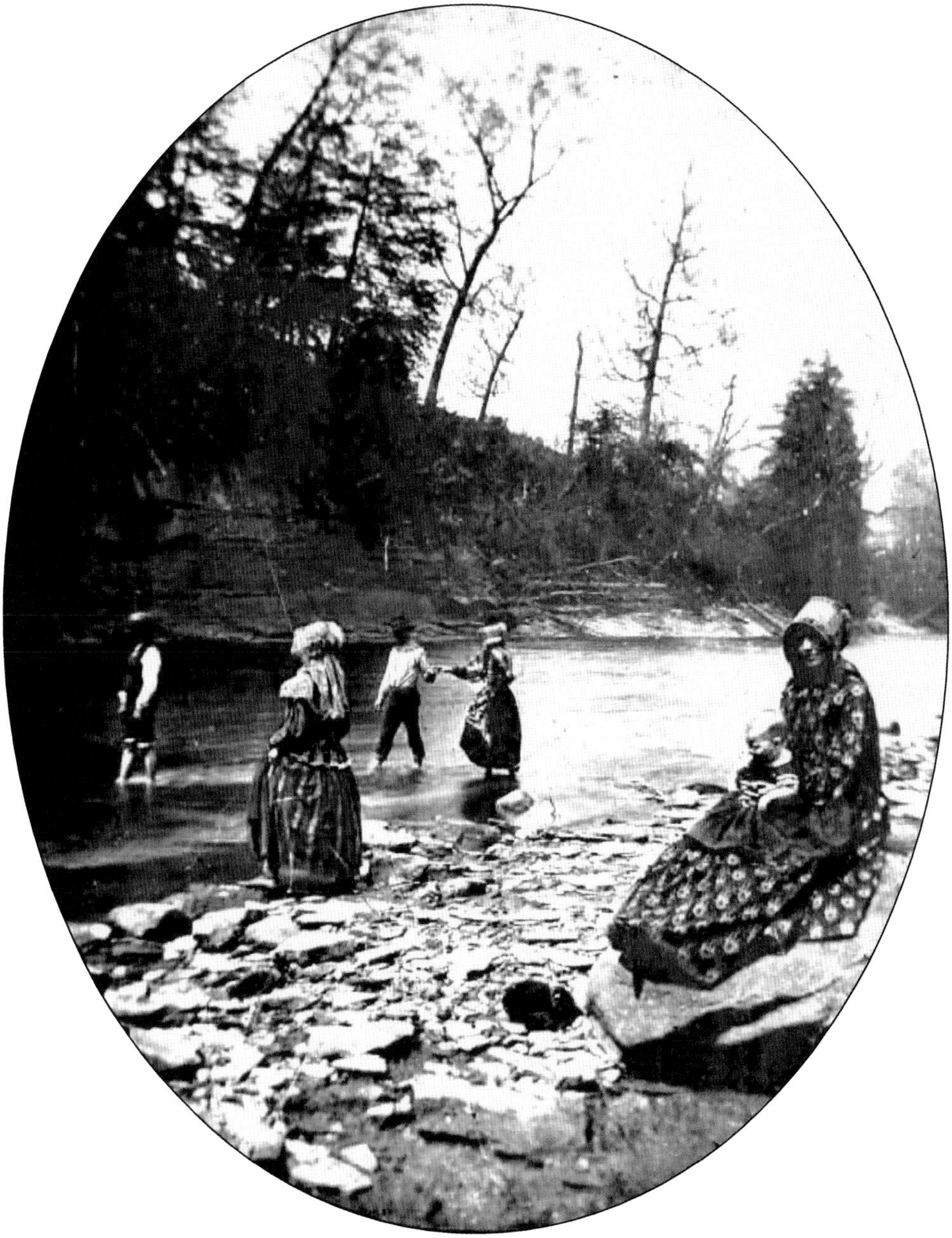

Bathers wade through ankle-deep water in the Muskingum River in the 1860s or 1870s. (Private collection.)

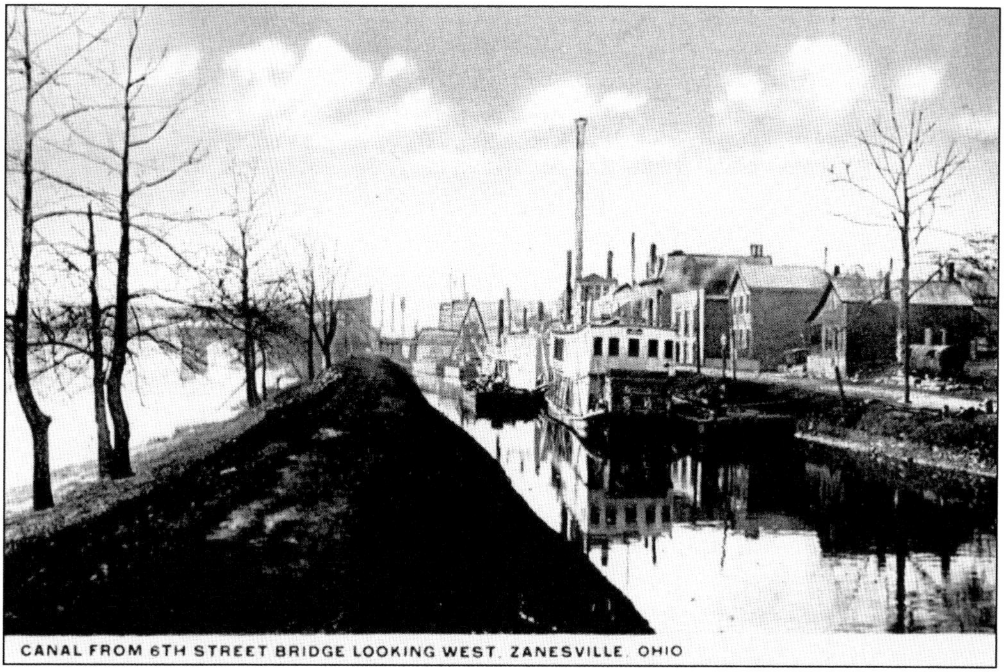

This is the Ohio Canal between the Sixth Street and Third Street Bridges in the early 1900s. Note the factories and warehouses lining the waterfront. (Courtesy of Chance Brockway.)

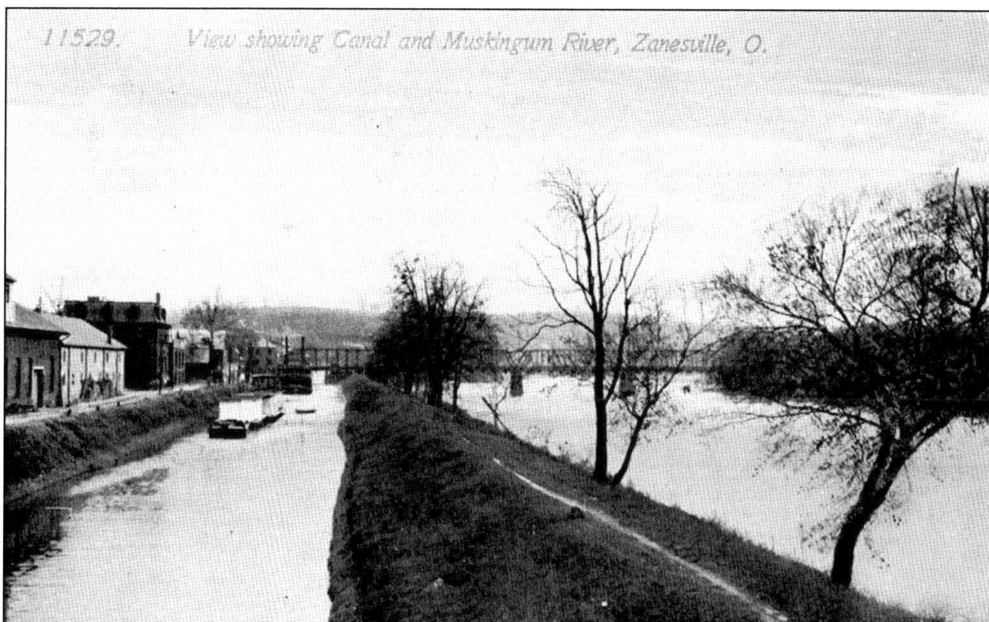

Looking eastward, this view shows the Ohio Canal with the Sixth Street Bridge in the background. (Courtesy of Chance Brockway.)

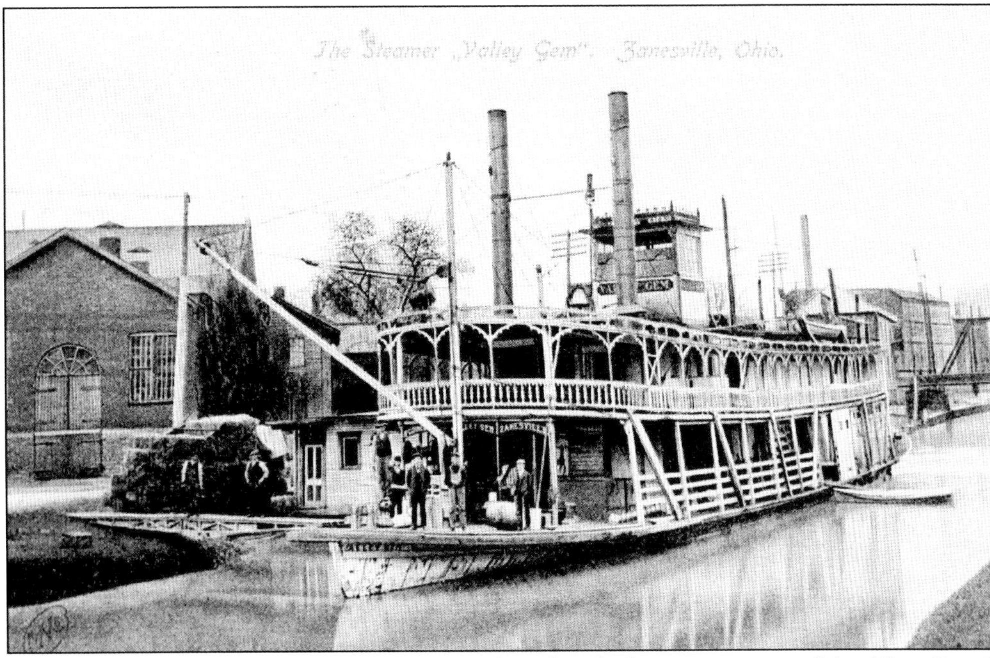

The navigability of the Muskingum River, combined with the convenience of the Ohio Canal, helped make Zanesville a transportation hub. Canal boats, flatboats, and later, steamers carried goods and passengers between Zanesville and other port cities such as Marietta, Pittsburgh, Cincinnati, and New Orleans. The *Valley Gem* is shown docked along the canal bank in the early 1900s. (Courtesy of Chance Brockway.)

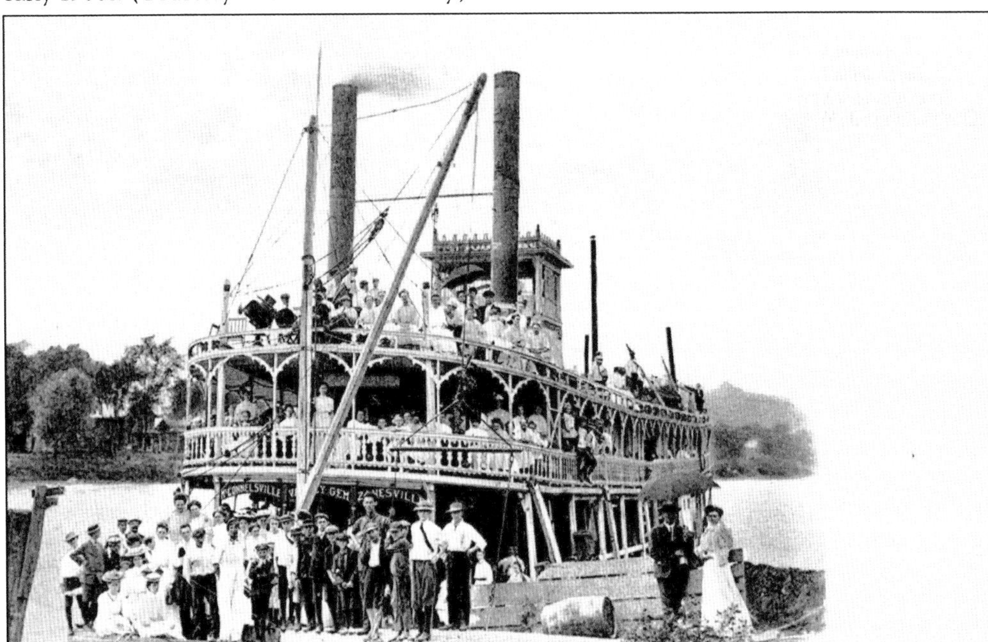

The *Valley Gem* traveled with excursion parties between Zanesville and McConnellsville from 1897 to 1917. Note the sign behind the passengers. It reads, "McConnellsville Valley Gem Zanesville." (Courtesy of Chance Brockway.)

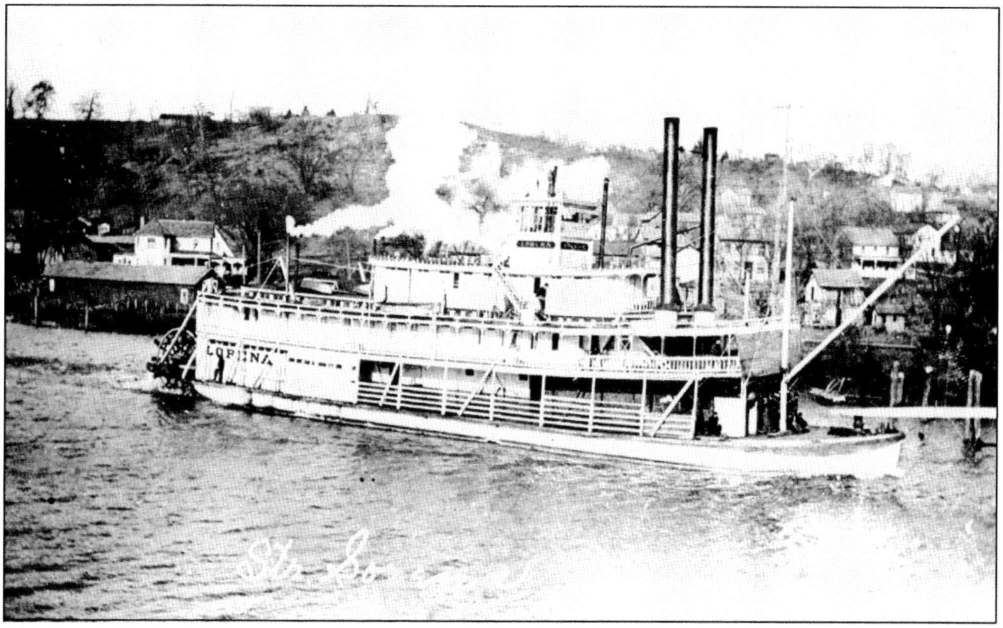

The steamer *Lorena* was named after the popular Civil War song written by Henry D. L. Webster. He was inspired to write the song after being jilted by Ella Blocksom. The *Lorena* was built in Marietta in 1895 and ran between Zanesville and Pittsburgh in the early 1900s. (Courtesy of Chance Brockway.)

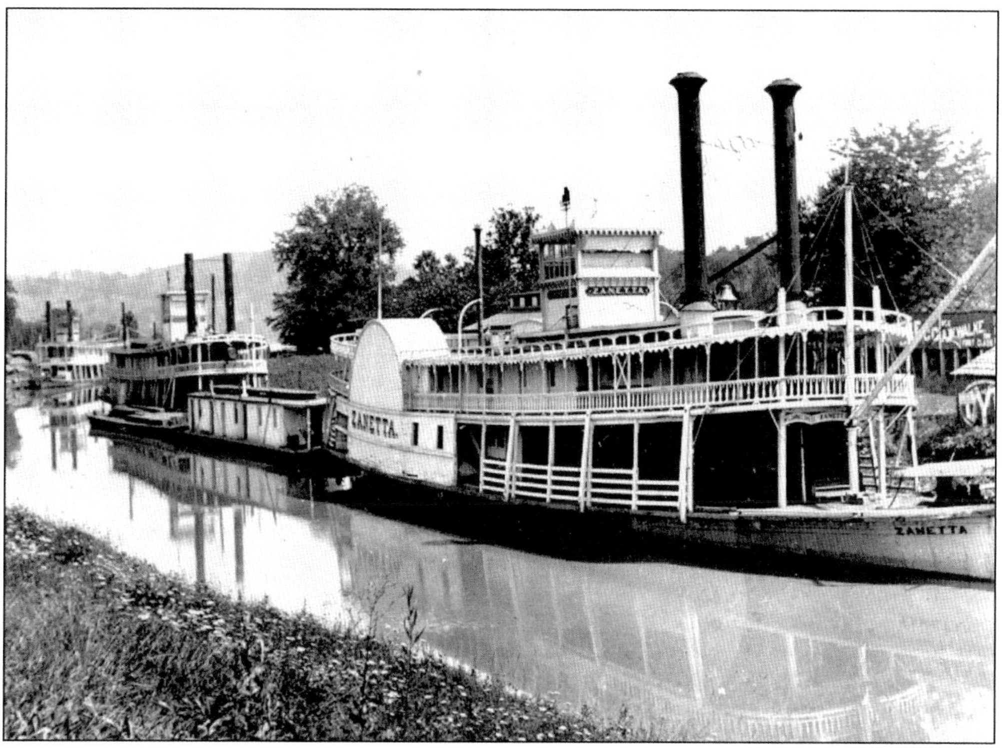

The *Zanetta*, shown here in the early 1900s, was one of the few side-wheelers on the Muskingum River. (Courtesy of Mose Mesre.)

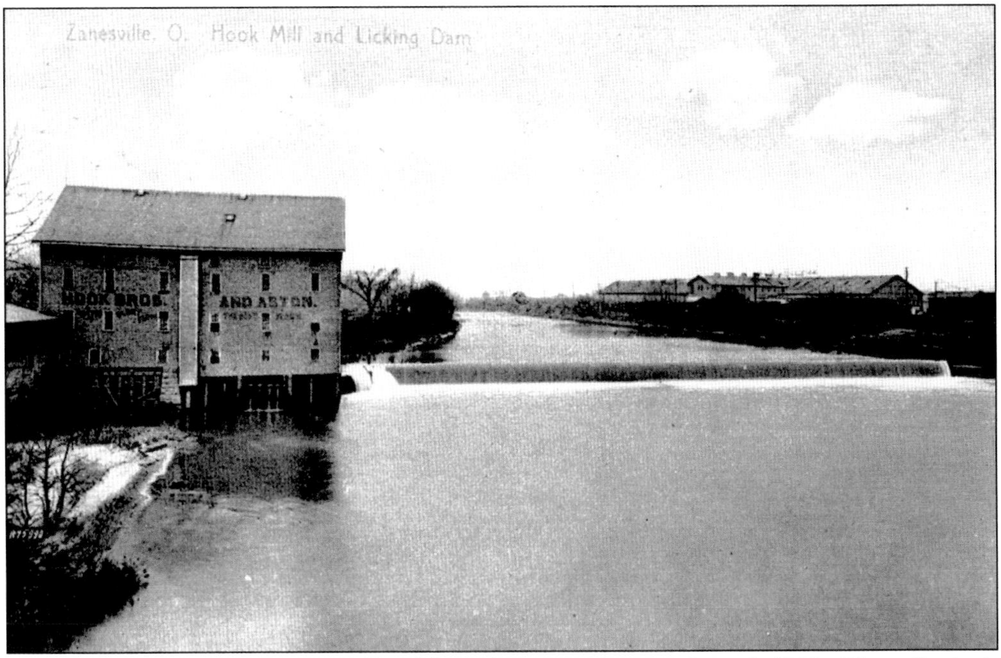

This is Hook Brothers and Aston Mill and the Licking River Dam in the early 1900s. The mill, which had operated at this location on the south bank of the Licking River since 1828, ceased operations after the Flood of 1913. The building burned down in 1923. (Courtesy of Chance Brockway.)

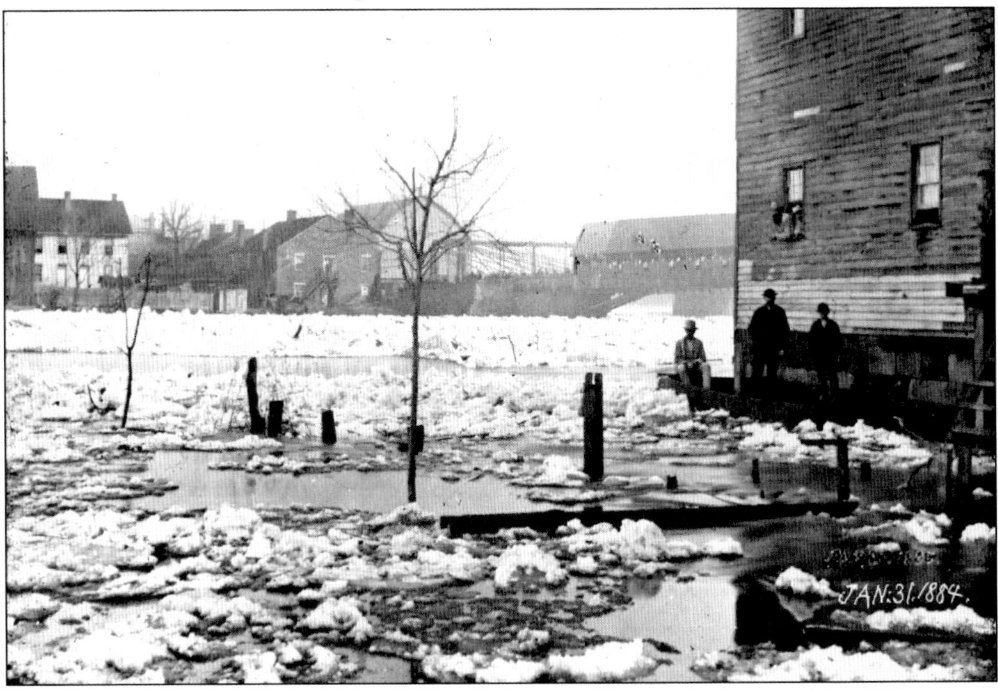

On January 31, 1884, an ice jam caused the Muskingum River to back up and flood. The water crested at 34.1 feet above flood stage on February 8, 1884. The boat shown at the lower right is alongside the Hook Brothers and Aston Mill. Note that portions of the Y and Baltimore and Ohio Railroad Bridges can be seen in the background. (Private collection.)

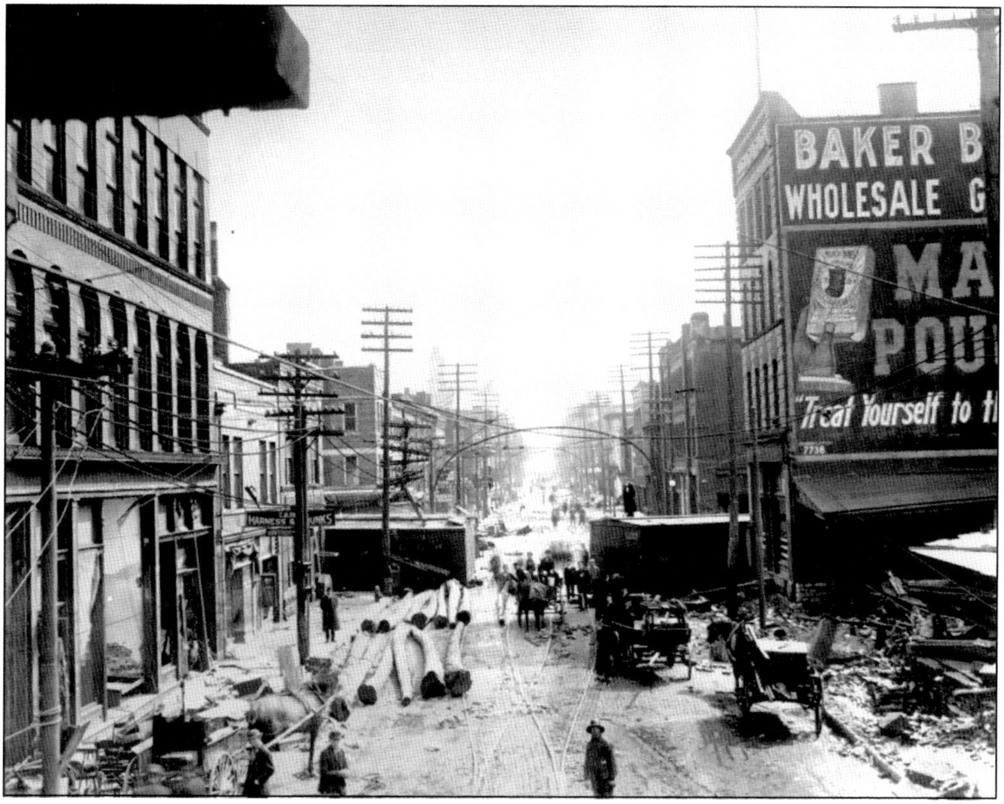

The Flood of 1913 left behind all kinds of debris, including logs and a pair of railroad cars on Main Street, just east of the Y Bridge. (Courtesy of Mose Mesre.)

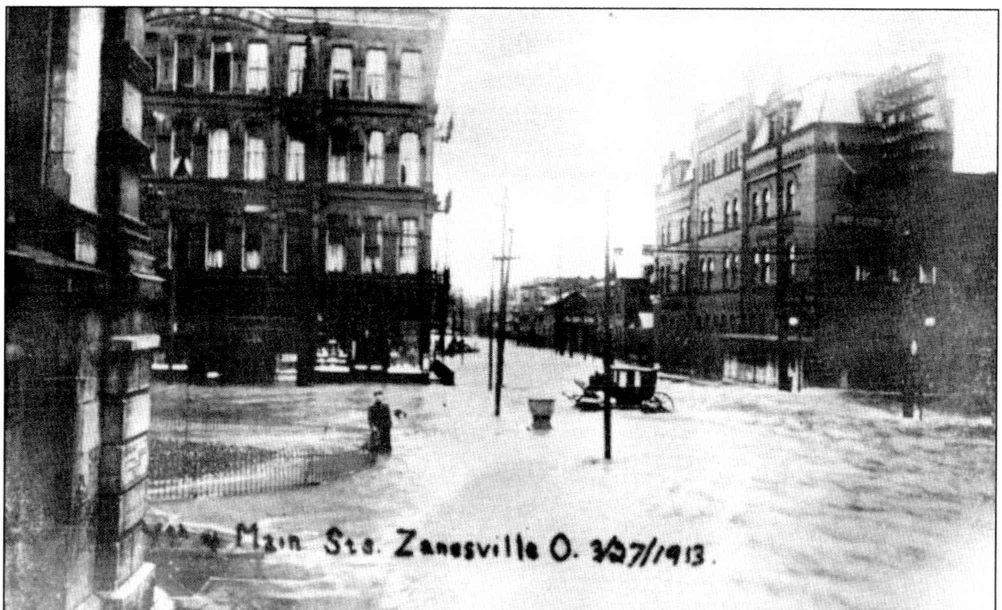

The floodwaters were just beginning to recede at the intersection of Fourth and Main Streets on March 27, 1913.

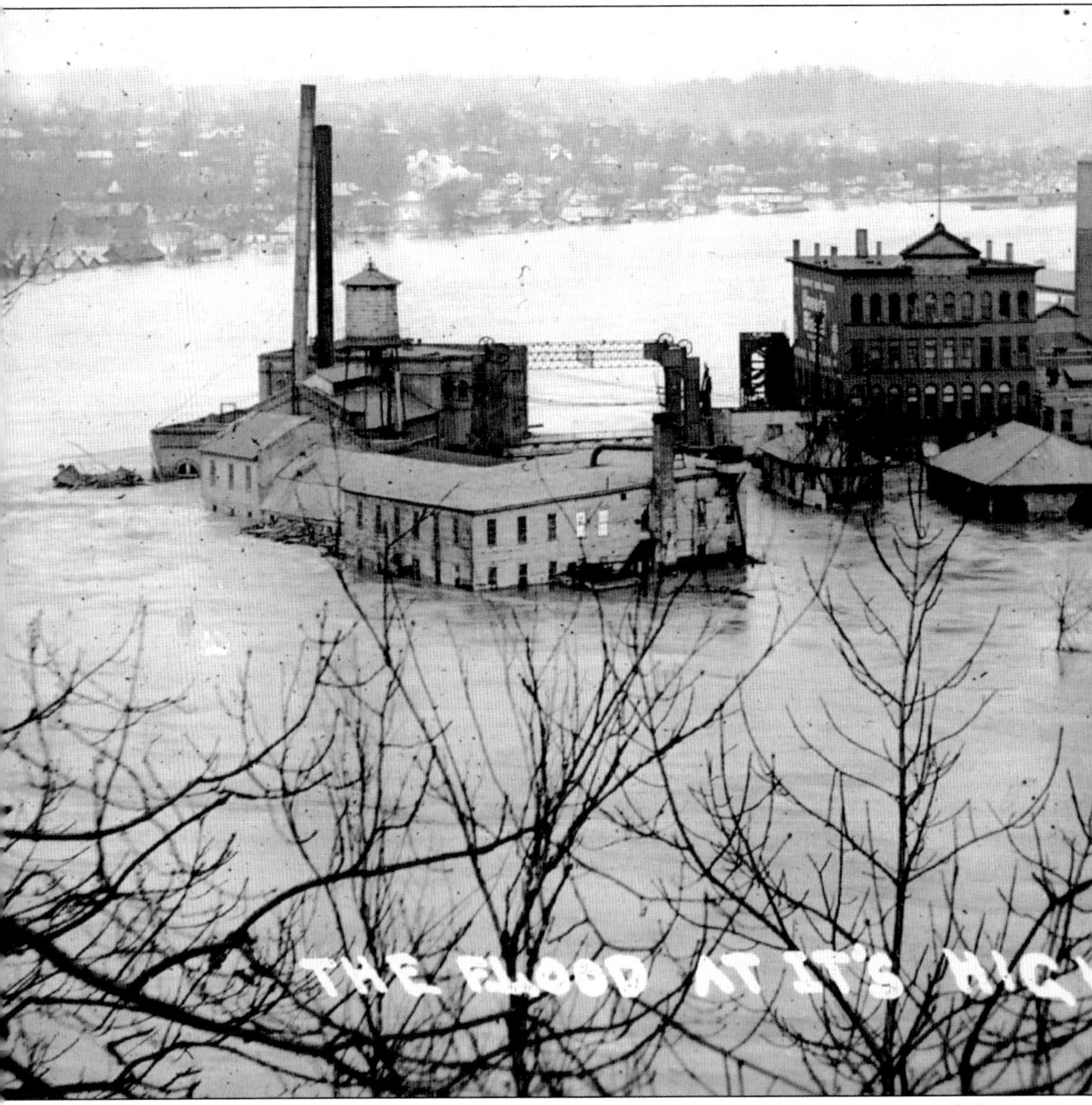

Natural disasters have struck Zanesville throughout its existence. The worst natural disaster to strike the city came in March 1913, when heavy rains caused the Muskingum and Licking Rivers to overflow their banks and flood large portions of the city. The floodwaters eventually crested at a record 51.8 feet above flood stage. The downtown area was inundated with water,

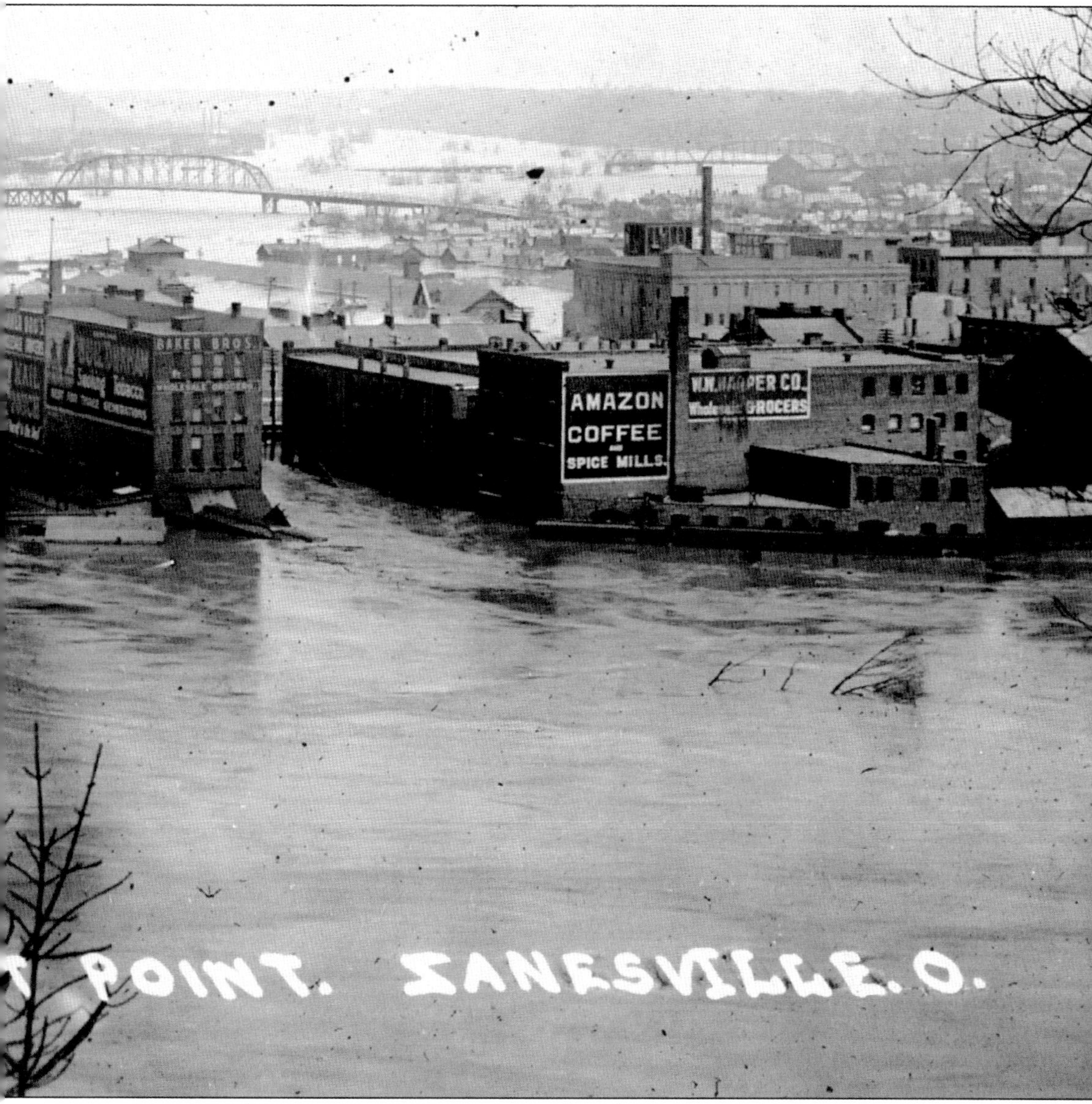

as were homes in the Putnam District. Portions of Linden Avenue were 20 feet under water. Taken from Putnam Hill, this image shows the western end of the downtown area when the floodwaters were at their crest. Note that the Ohio Canal and the end of the Y Bridge cannot be seen because they were completely submerged. (Private collection.)

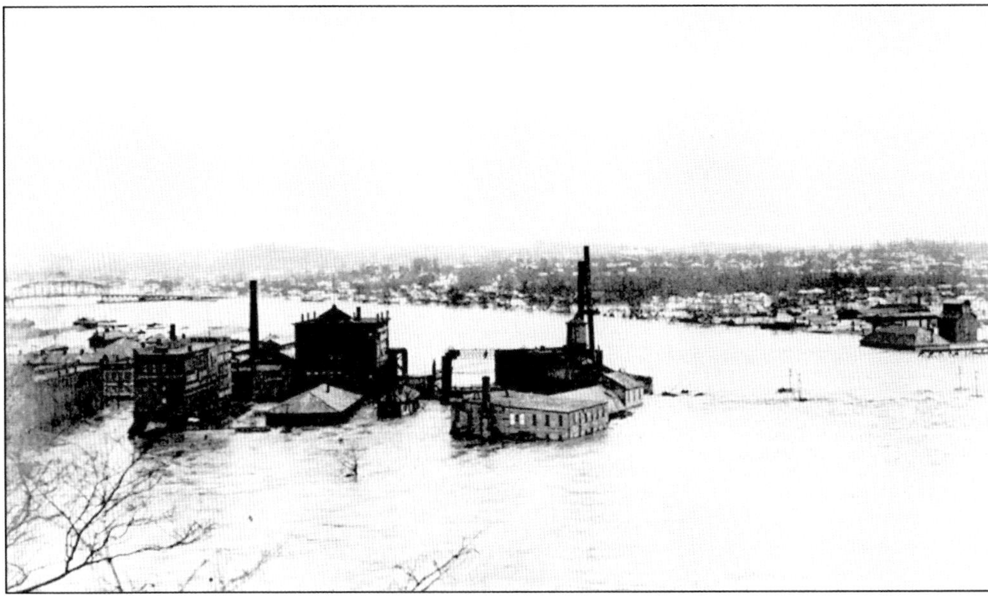

The Y Bridge lost its railings and lampposts during the flood, but its piers and span survived intact. (Courtesy of Chance Brockway.)

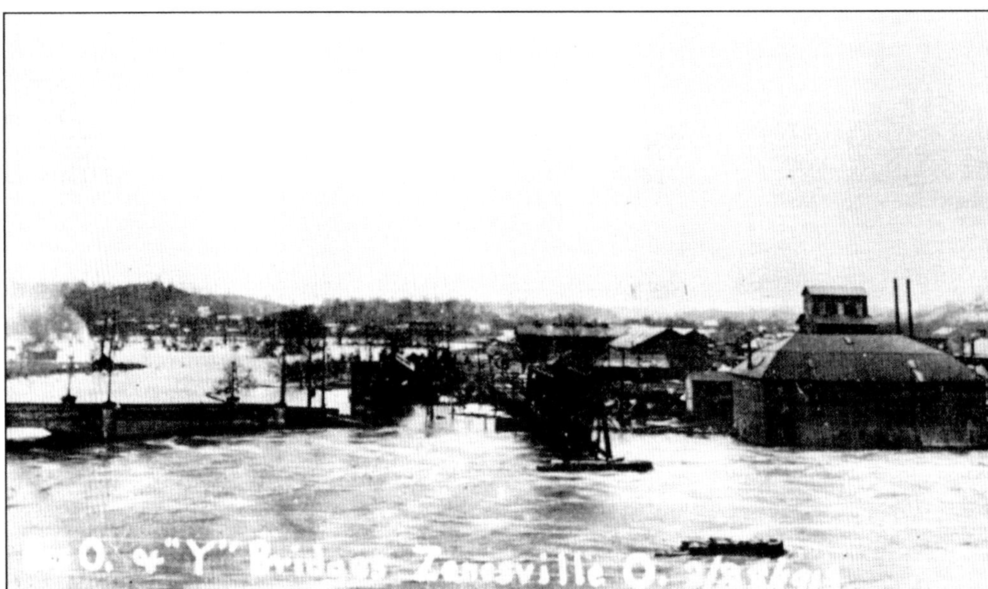

The Baltimore and Ohio and Y Bridges were still submerged in muddy water and debris on March 28, 1913.

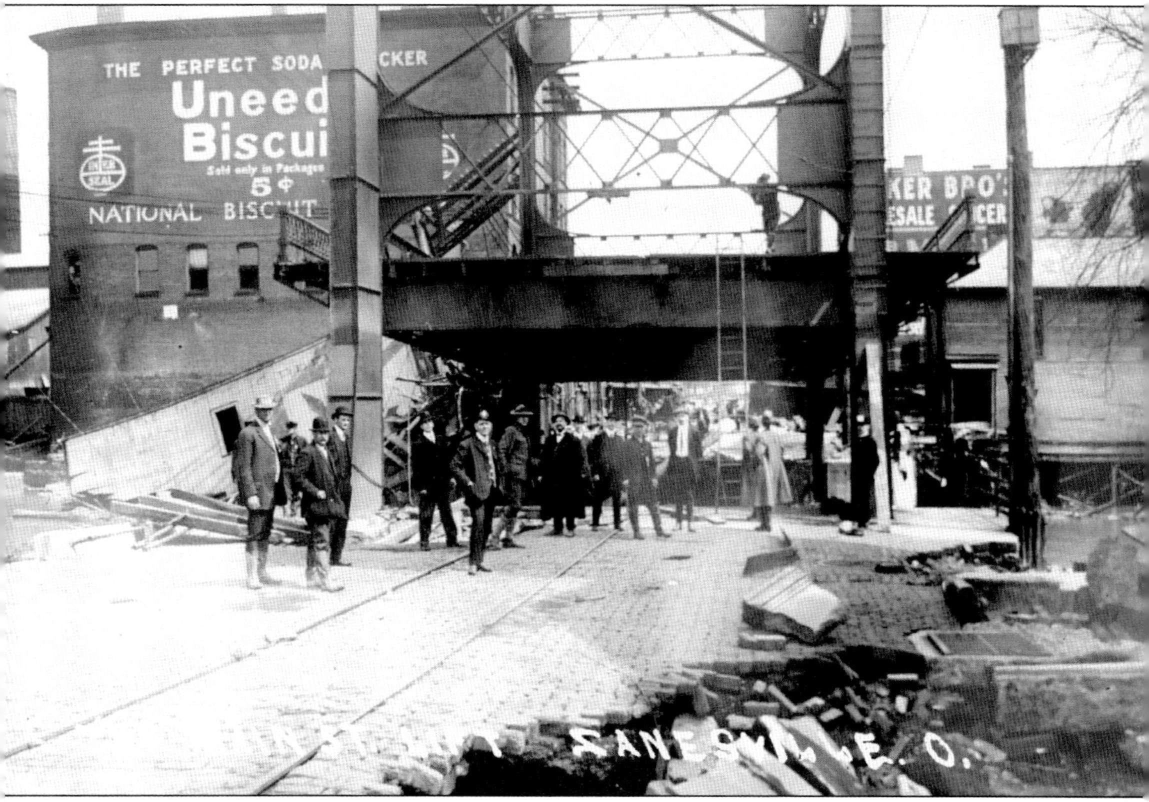

The lift span over the Ohio Canal at the Main Street end of the Y Bridge was raised before the Flood of 1913 to prevent it from becoming damaged. It got stuck in the up position, and after the flood, people wanting to cross the canal to get in and out of downtown via the Y Bridge had to climb up and down tall ladders in order to cross the jammed lift span. (Courtesy of Tom Brown.)

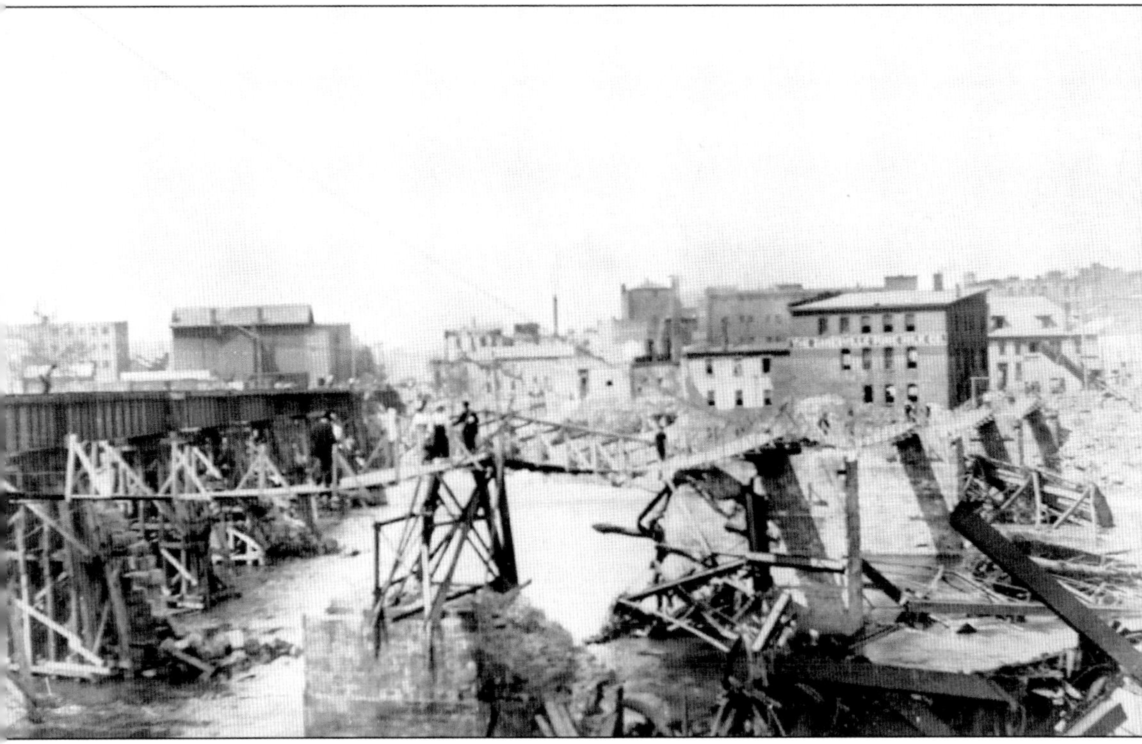

A makeshift rope and wooden plank suspension bridge was put up over the piers of the destroyed Third Street Bridge following the Flood of 1913. The temporary bridge was quickly dubbed "the Turkey Trot." Mischievous youngsters thought it great sport to make the bridge sway back and forth when nervous adults reached the middle. (Courtesy of Tom Brown.)

Three

City of Bridges

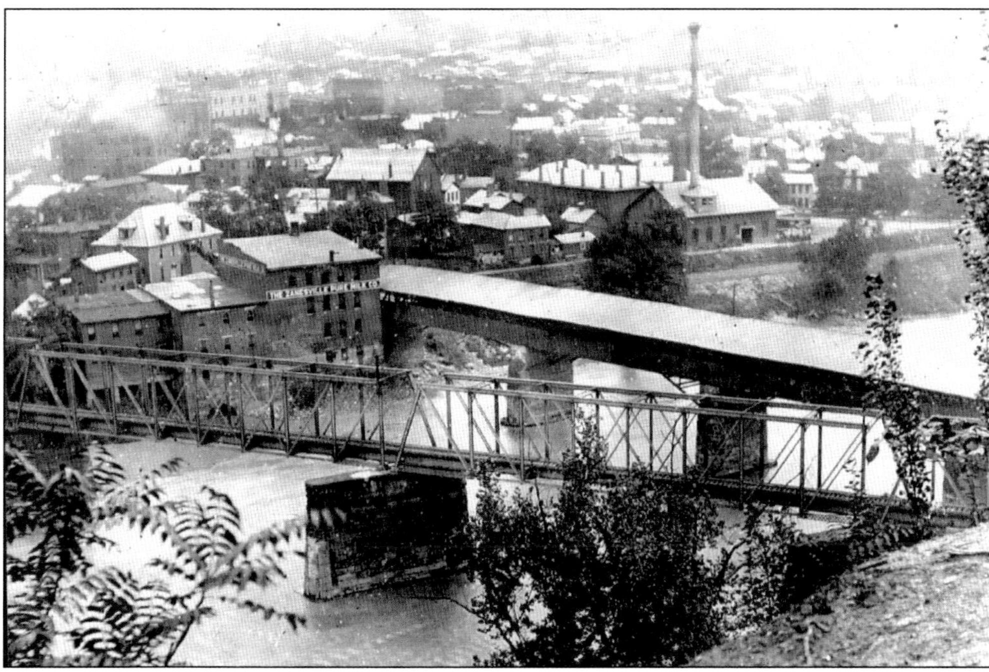

Zanesville has long been known for its many bridges. The city's first bridge, an uncovered toll bridge, was built in 1813. It spanned the Muskingum River between the foot of Third Street at the Ohio Canal and the eastern end of Dug Road. It was rebuilt in 1820 and burned all the way down to its piers in 1845. The bridge was immediately replaced with a covered bridge. The raging floodwaters of the Flood of 1913 carried this bridge away, and it was not rebuilt. (Courtesy of Wayne Estep.)

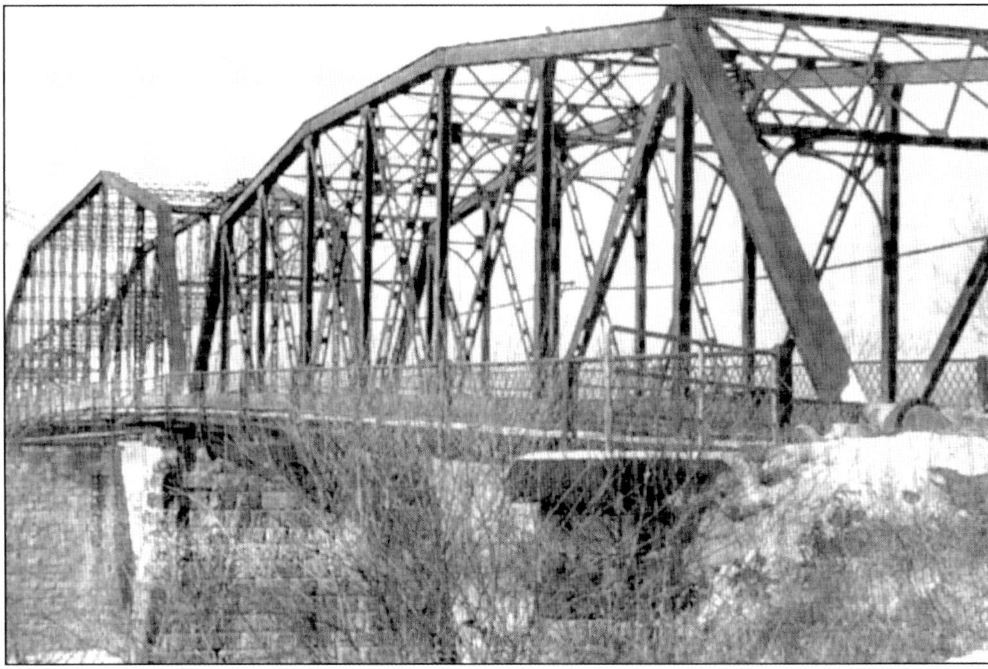

When it opened in 1890, the Monroe Street Bridge allowed residents in the north end of town to cross the river without first having to trek all the way down to the Y Bridge. (Courtesy of Wayne Estep.)

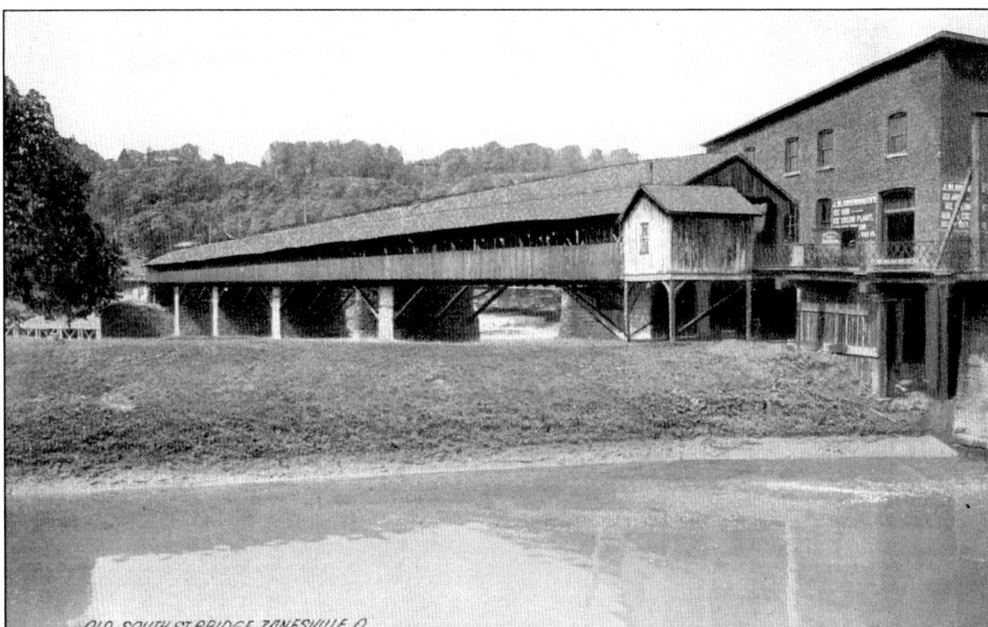

This is the old South Street Bridge from the Ohio Canal end of the bridge. (Courtesy of Tom Brown.)

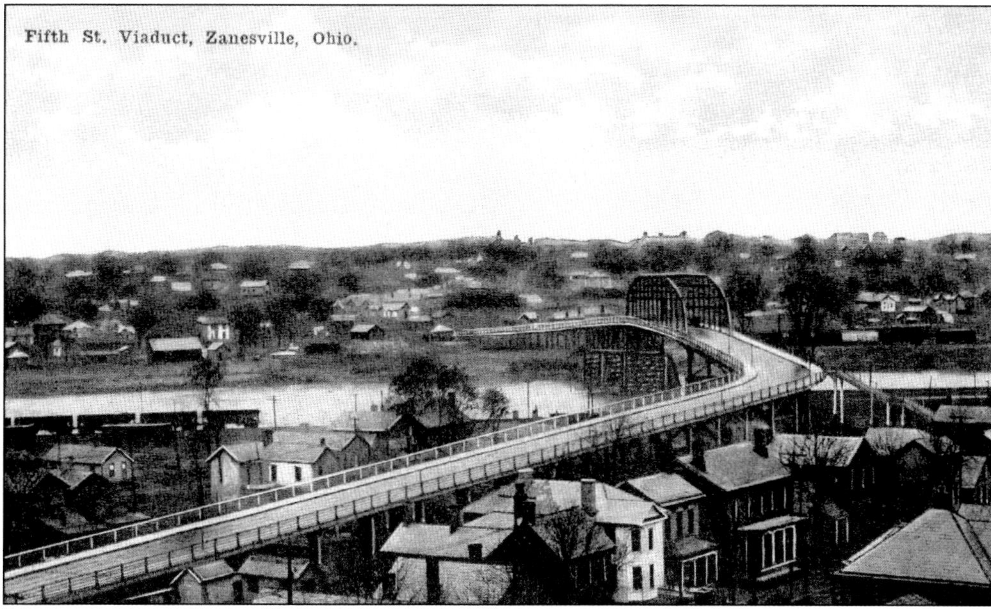

Built in 1893, the Fifth Street Bridge was found to be weak and unsafe in 1909. A new bridge, similar in appearance to the one it replaced, was built and opened for traffic in September 1912. (Courtesy of Tom Brown.)

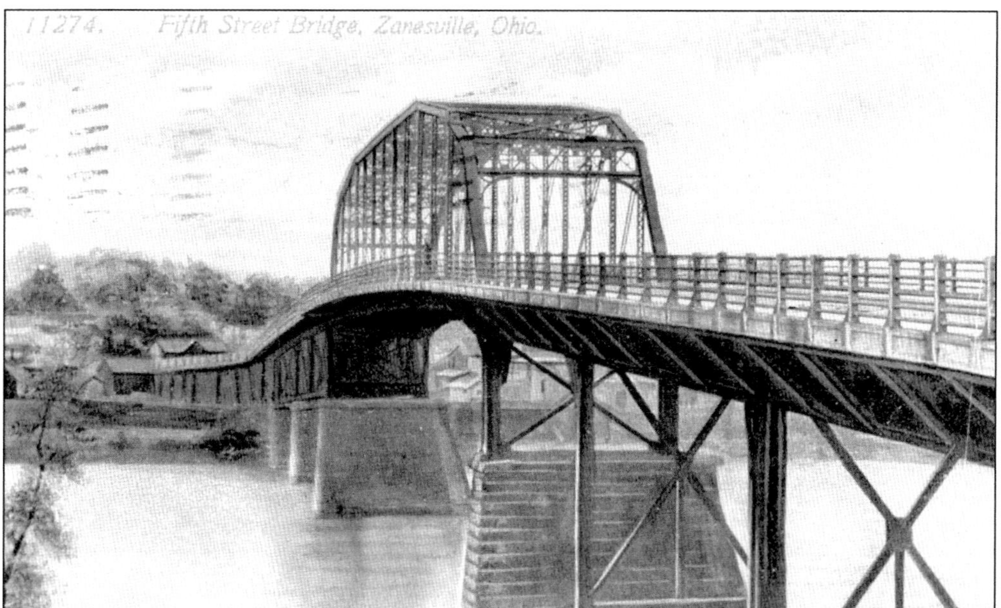

This is a close-up view of the span of the Fifth Street Bridge in the early 1900s. (Courtesy of Chance Brockway.)

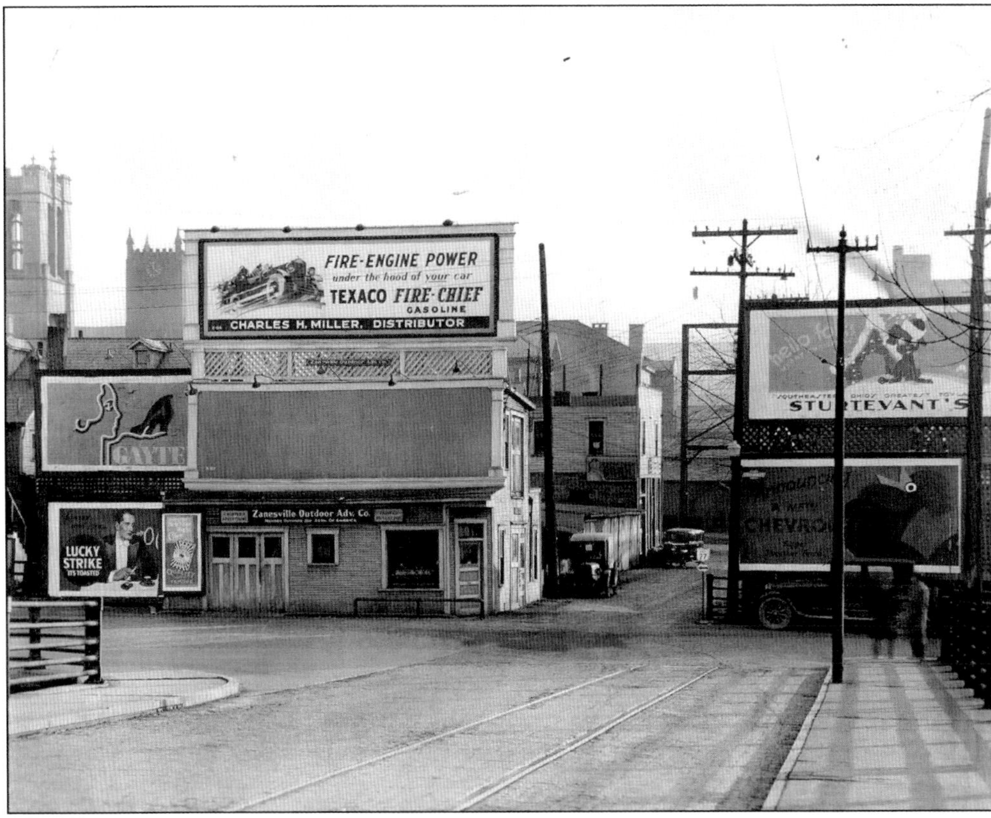

This is how motorists saw downtown Zanesville as they came off the end of the Fifth Street Bridge during the 1930s. (Courtesy of MCCOGS.)

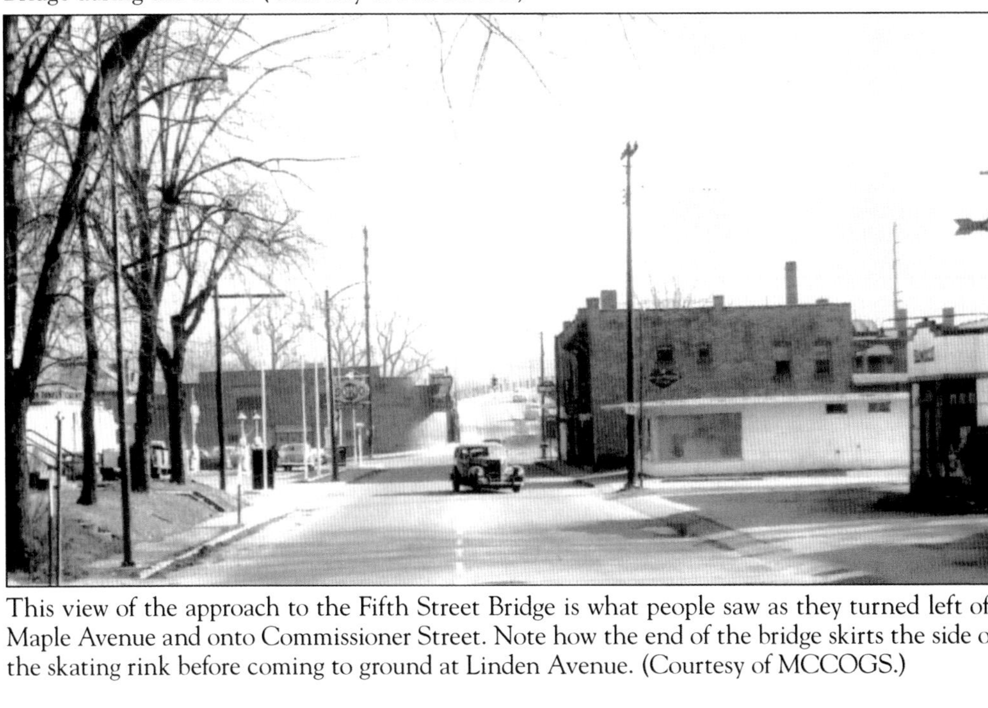

This view of the approach to the Fifth Street Bridge is what people saw as they turned left off Maple Avenue and onto Commissioner Street. Note how the end of the bridge skirts the side of the skating rink before coming to ground at Linden Avenue. (Courtesy of MCCOGS.)

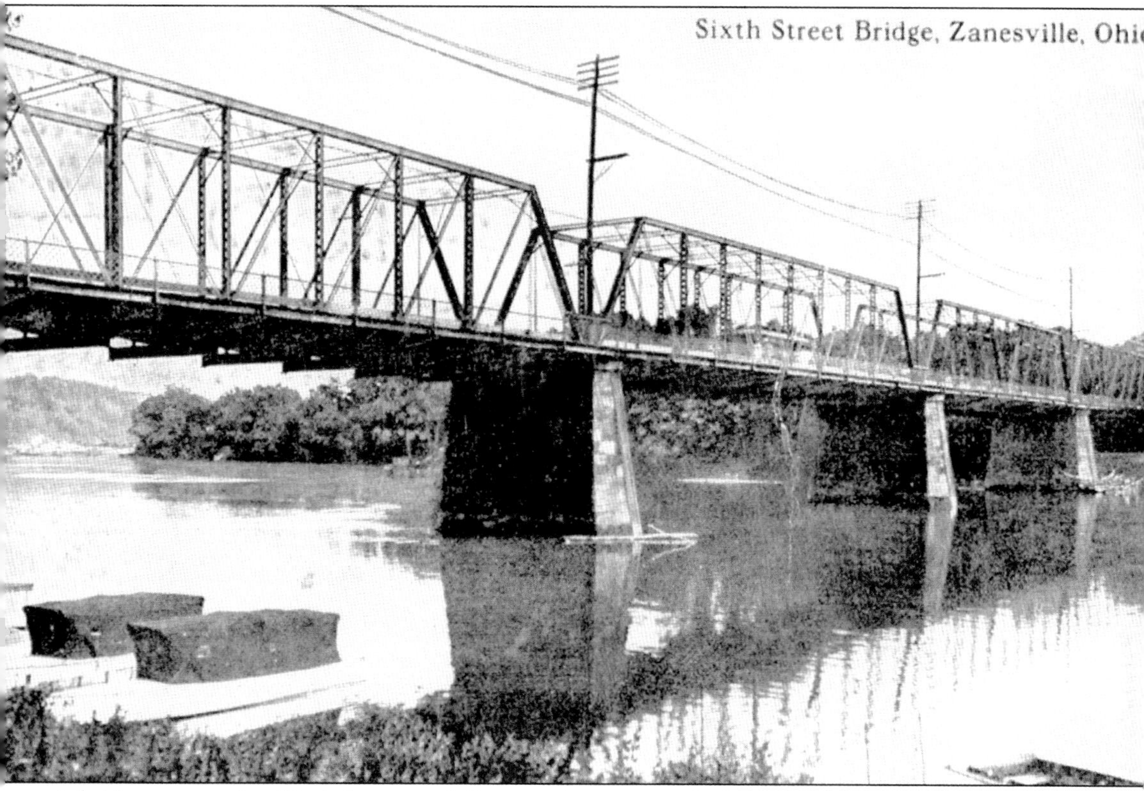

A bridge connecting Sixth Street and Putnam Avenue was built in 1895. It was carried away by the Flood of 1913 and was replaced with the bridge shown here in 1915. (Courtesy of Chance Brockway.)

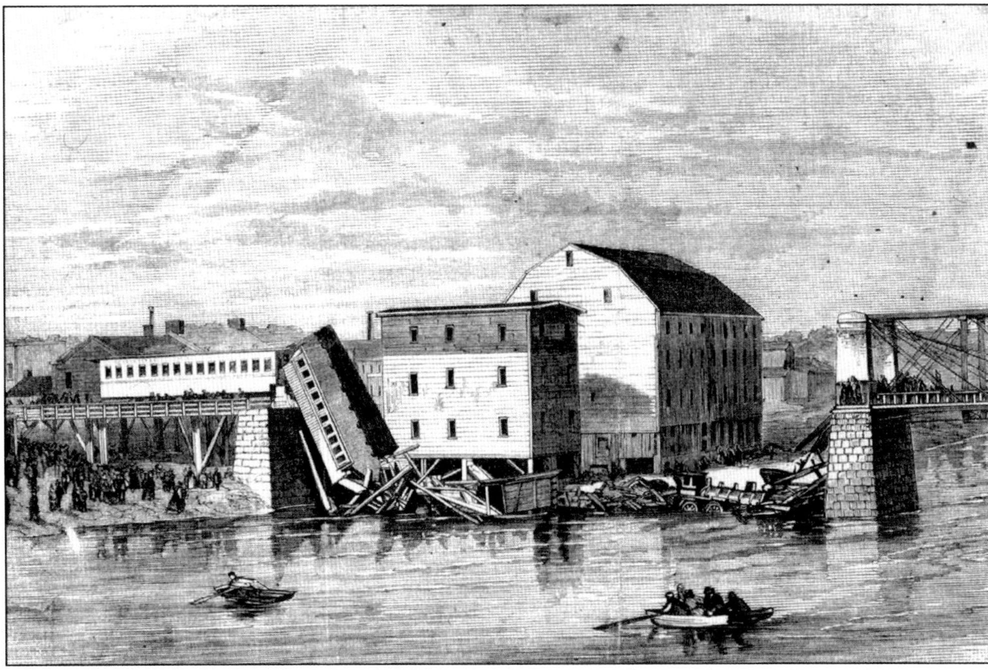

The Central Ohio Railroad built a bridge in 1851 to cross the Muskingum River. It was one of the first iron railroad bridges built in the state. In December 1866, the westernmost span of the bridge collapsed as a Baltimore and Ohio Railroad train tried to cross the river. The bridge was replaced, but was swept away during the Flood of 1913. (Courtesy of Wayne Estep.)

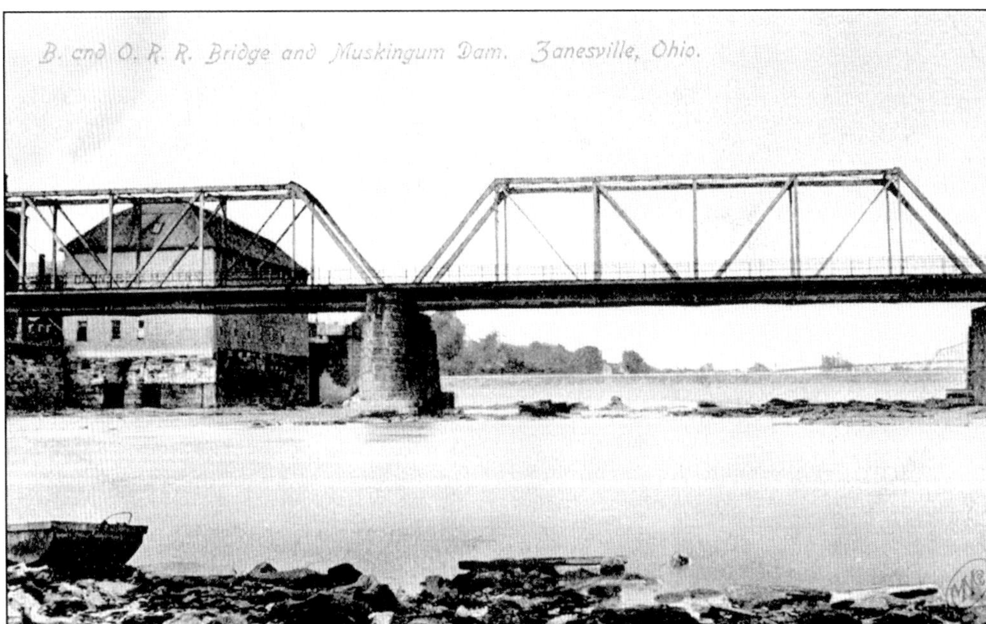

This is the Baltimore and Ohio Railroad Bridge in the early 1900s. The bridge was destroyed during the Flood of 1913. Its replacement is still in use today. (Courtesy of Chance Brockway.)

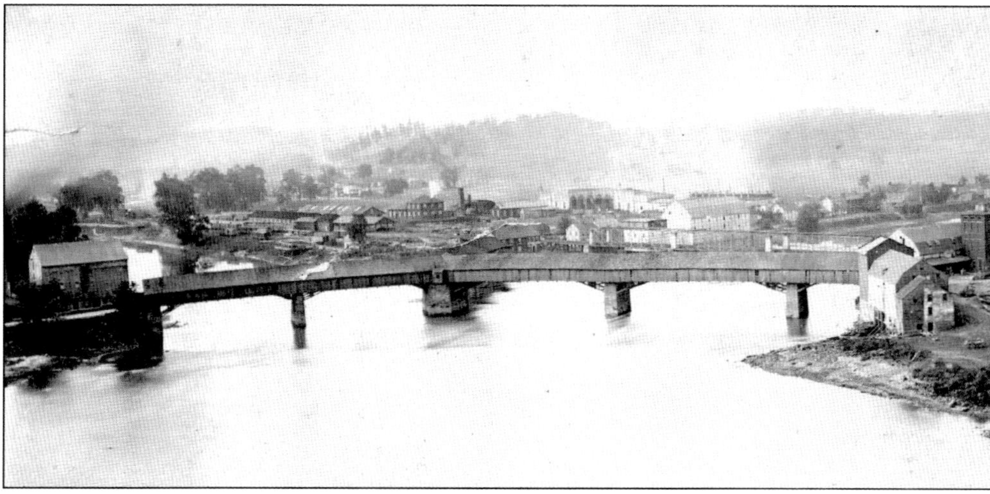

The Y Bridge has become one of the city's most distinctive landmarks over the past two centuries. The first in a series of five bridges, all constructed in the shape of a "Y," was an open wooden structure built in 1814. The second bridge, which resembled the first one, was built in 1819. The third Y Bridge, shown here in 1863, was built in 1832. Like the first two bridges before it, people crossing the bridge had to pay a toll. Note the strategically located tollbooth at the juncture of the three spans. (Courtesy of Wayne Estep.)

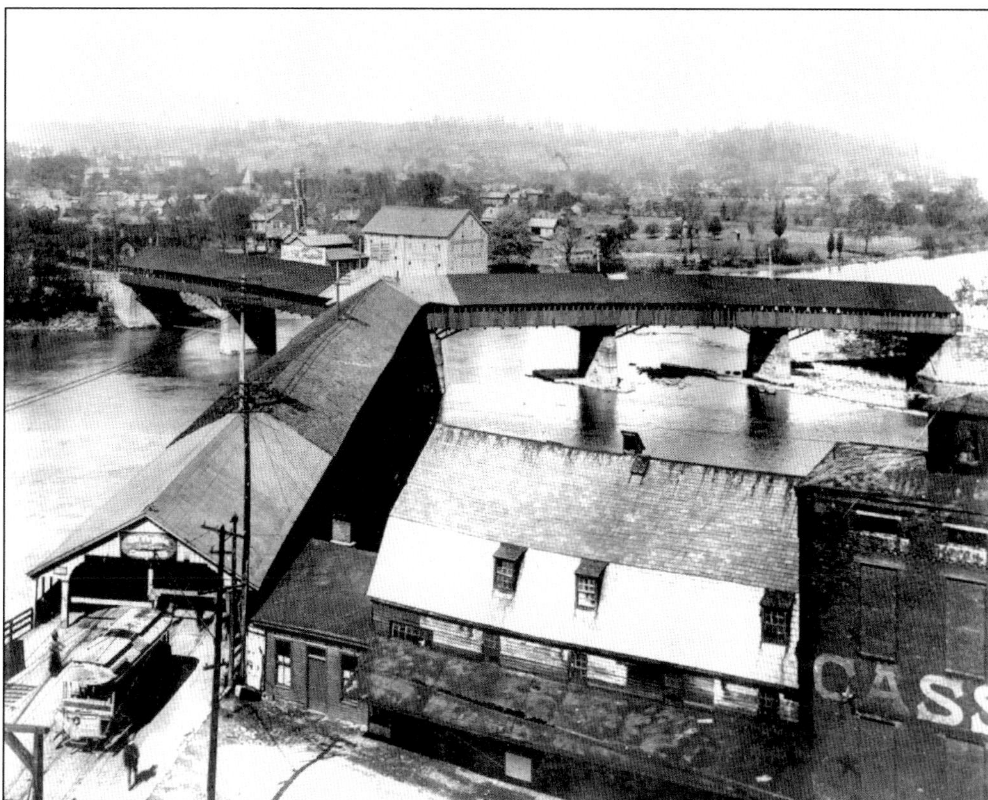

A streetcar is shown coming off the Main Street end of the third Y Bridge in the early 1900s. (Courtesy of Mose Mesre.)

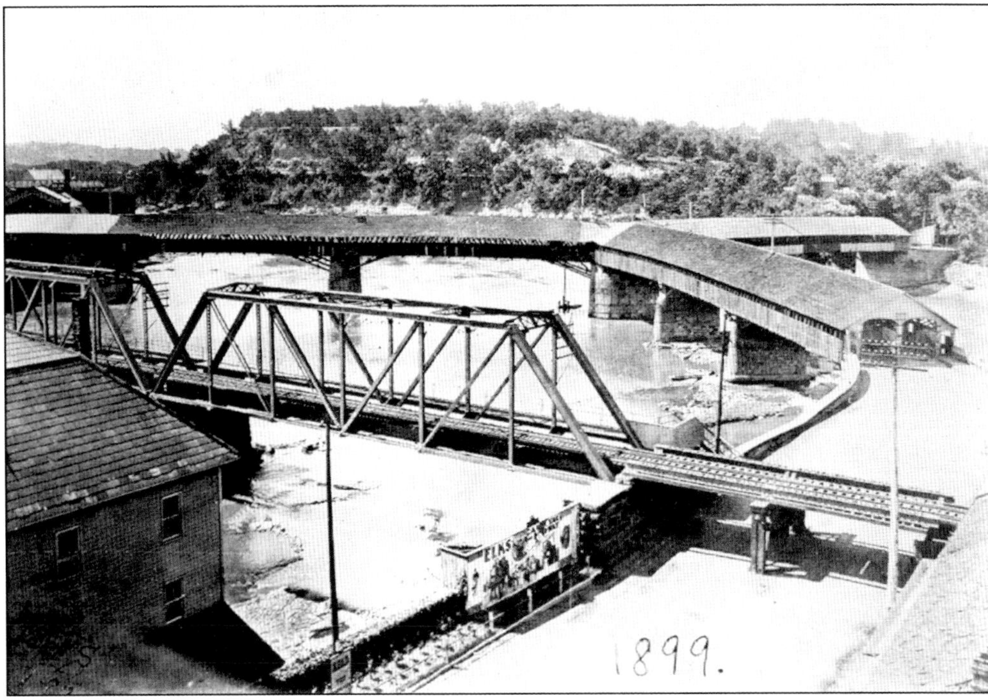

The third Y Bridge is shown from the Linden Avenue side of the river. (Courtesy of Mose Mesre.)

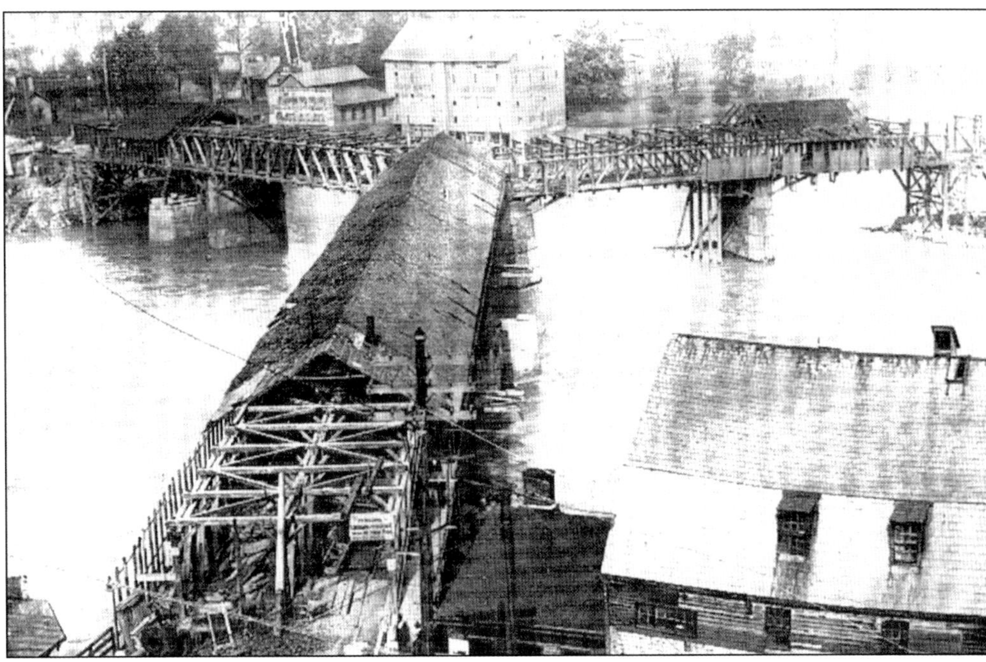

In 1900, the third Y Bridge was found to be unsafe and too deteriorated to repair. Workers are shown dismantling the wooden covered bridge in 1901. (Courtesy of Wayne Estep.)

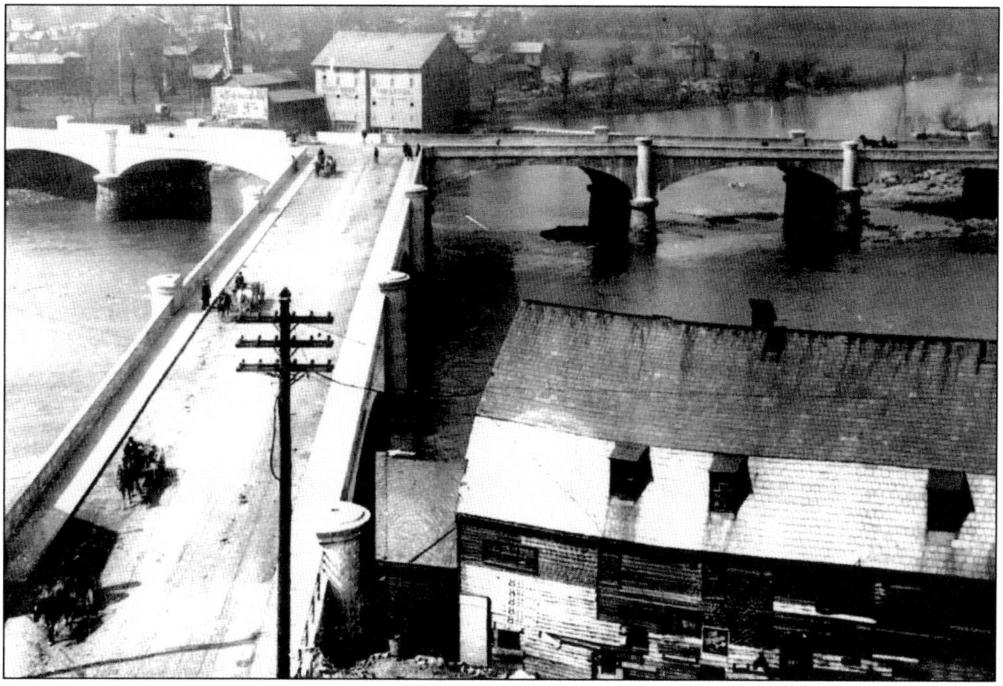

The fourth Y Bridge opened to traffic on January 4, 1902. It was an open bridge constructed of concrete. At the time of its construction, it was the largest reinforced concrete bridge in the nation. Note that the lampposts have not yet been installed (Courtesy of Wayne Estep.)

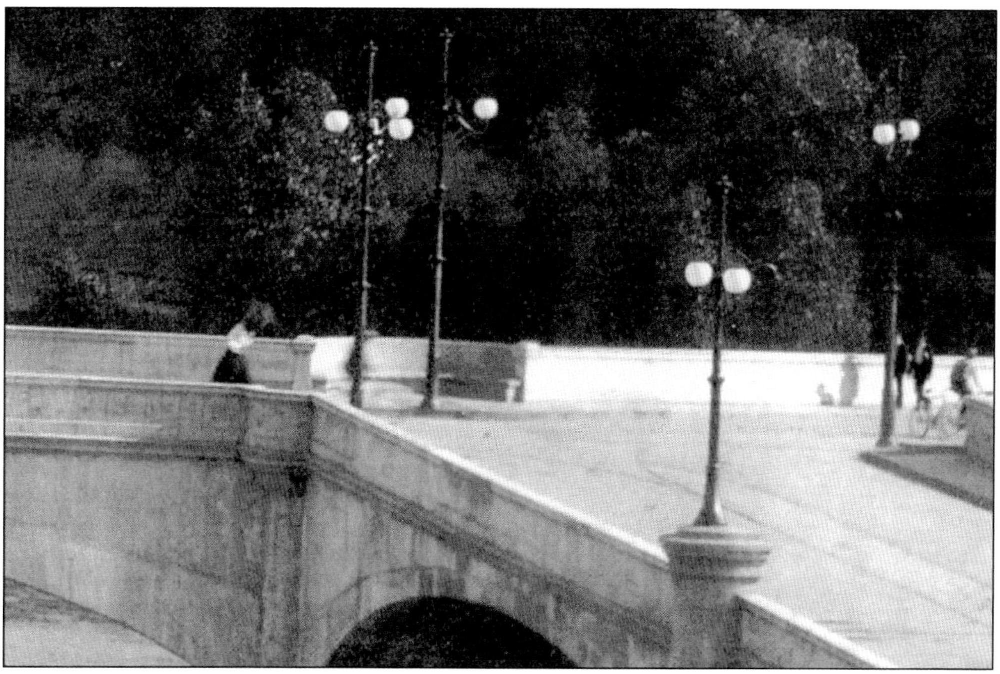

The architect of the fourth Y Bridge thought of everything. A bench alcove for pedestrians to sit on was installed in the middle of the Y span of the bridge. The bench was destroyed by the Flood of 1913 and was not replaced when the bridge was rebuilt. (Courtesy of Wayne Estep.)

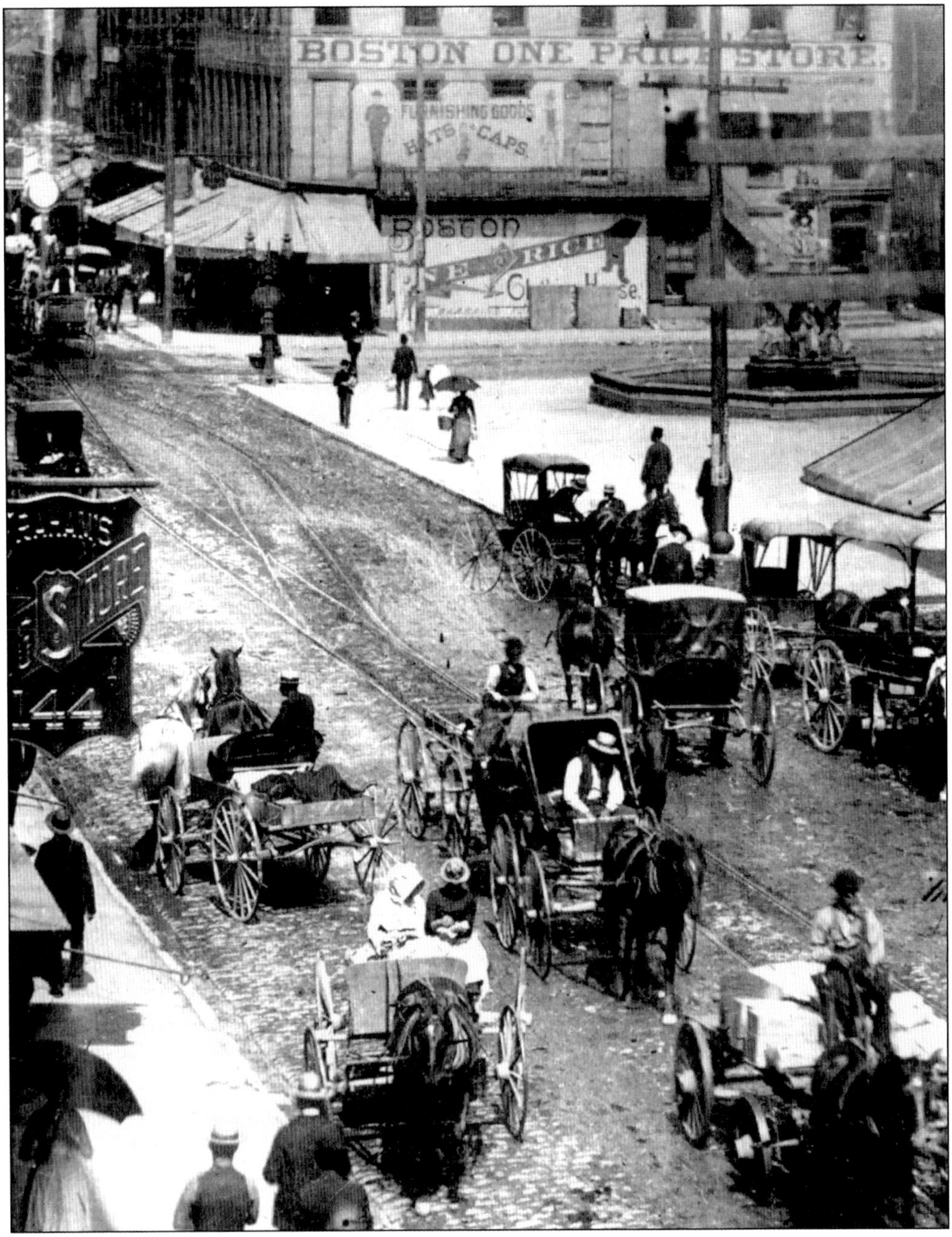

The Boston One Price House of Clothing was located at the corner of Fourth and Main Streets. A. E. Starr opened the store in 1865 and pioneered the cash and one-price system in Zanesville. Around 1900, Starr changed the name of the store to A. E. Starr. (Courtesy of Mose Mesre.)

Four

DOWNTOWN
THE HEART OF THE CITY

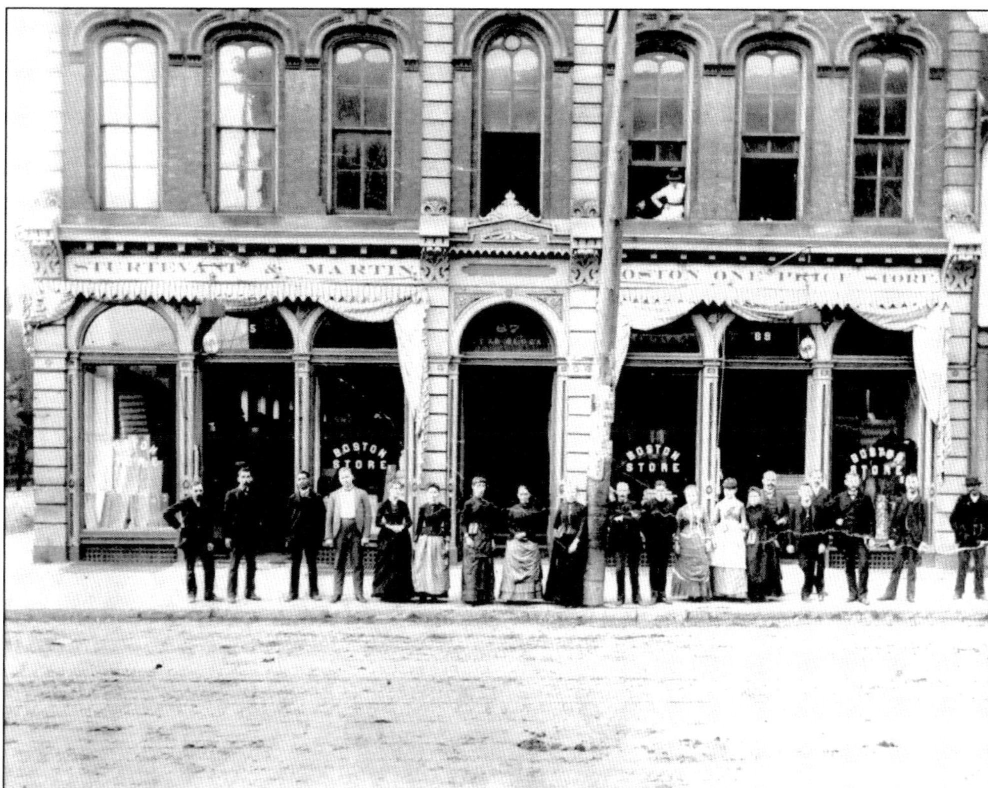

This is the Sturtevant and Martin Boston One Price Dry Goods House in the late 1880s. It was located at the northeast corner of Third and Main Streets. They sold a variety of dry goods, carpets, wallpaper, draperies, and fixtures on three floors. After 1893, the store was known as Sturtevant's and operated under that name until 1941, when the building became Bintz's department store. (Courtesy of Mose Mesre.)

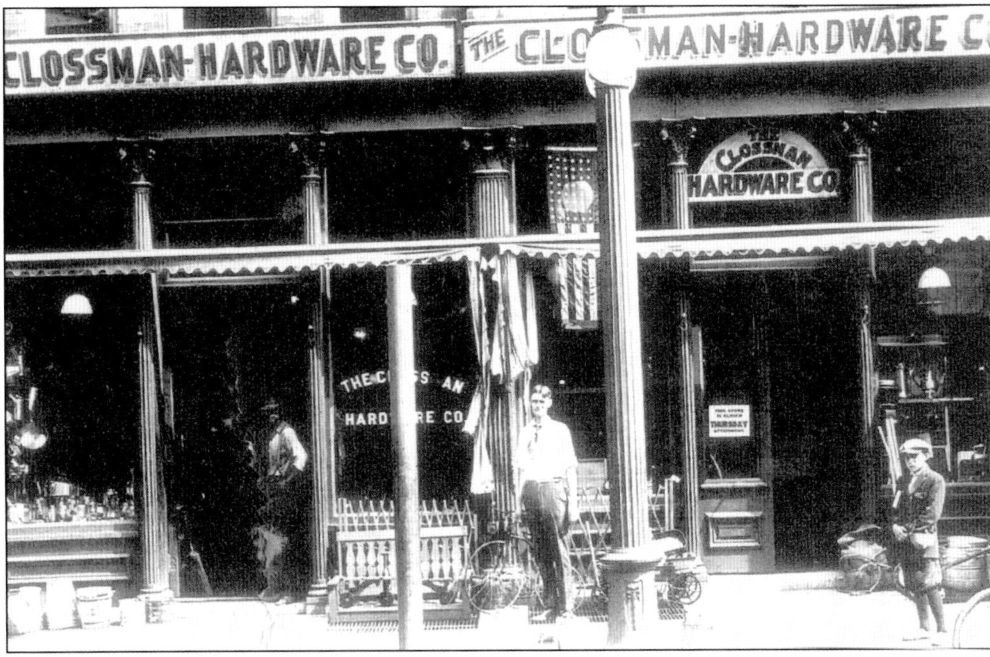

The Clossman Hardware Company opened for business in the early 1880s at 621–623 Main Street. The storefront was originally built with cast-iron columns. Architect Clarence E. Handschy redesigned it in 1922. (Courtesy of Wayne Estep.)

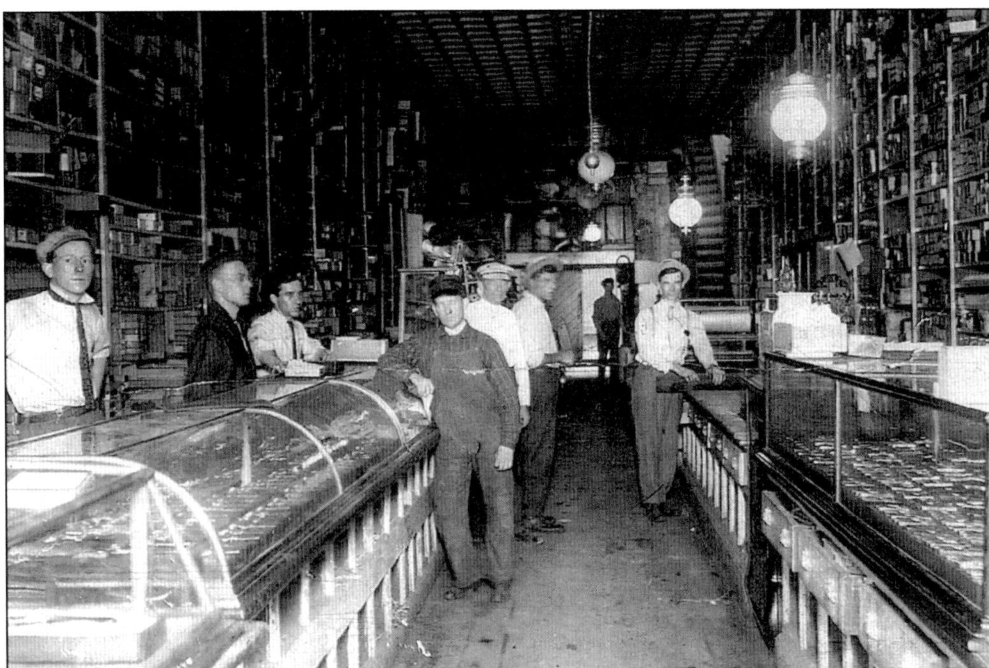

The interior of Clossman Hardware Company is pictured in the early 1900s. It has remained largely unaltered over the past 100 years. Many of the floor-to-ceiling wooden shelves and the stamped metal ceiling remain intact. (Courtesy of Wayne Estep.)

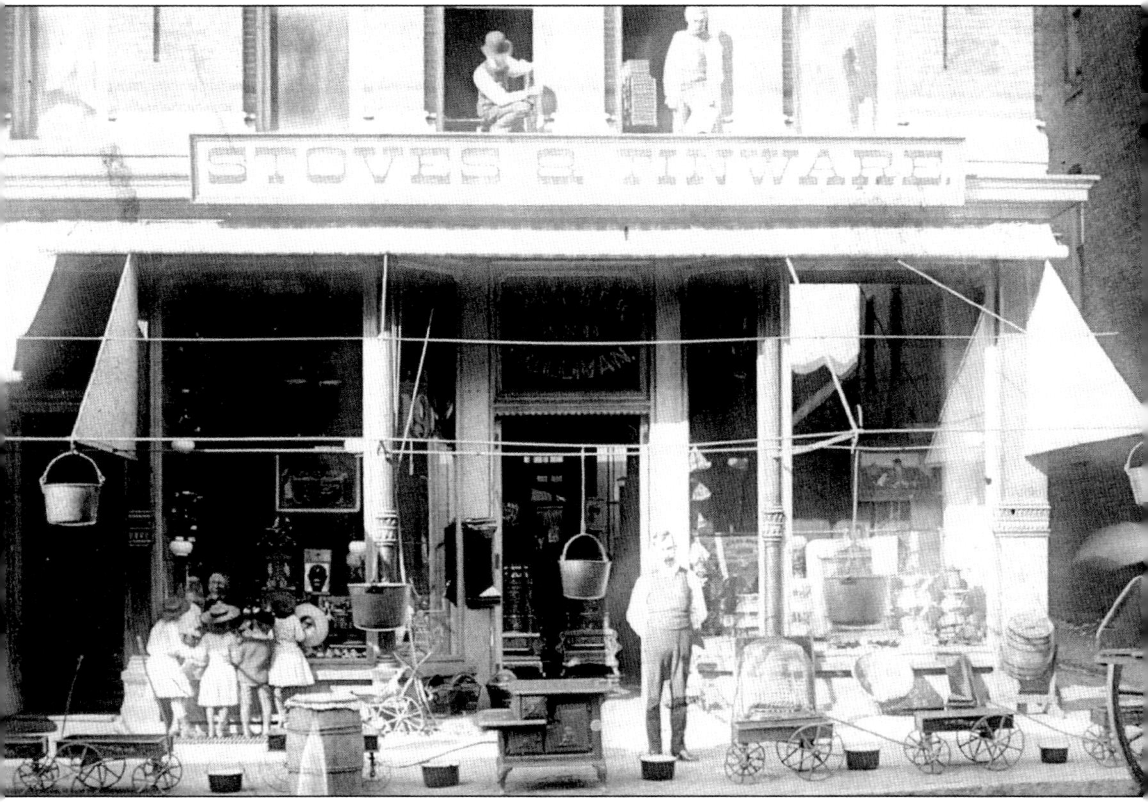

In the 1880s, Shinnick and Sullivan operated a store at 193 Main Street. The store sold a variety of home furnishings, including stoves and tinware, wagons, and children's carriages fabricated from sheets of copper, tin, and iron. Note the children looking at toys and games in the display window. (Courtesy of Wayne Estep.)

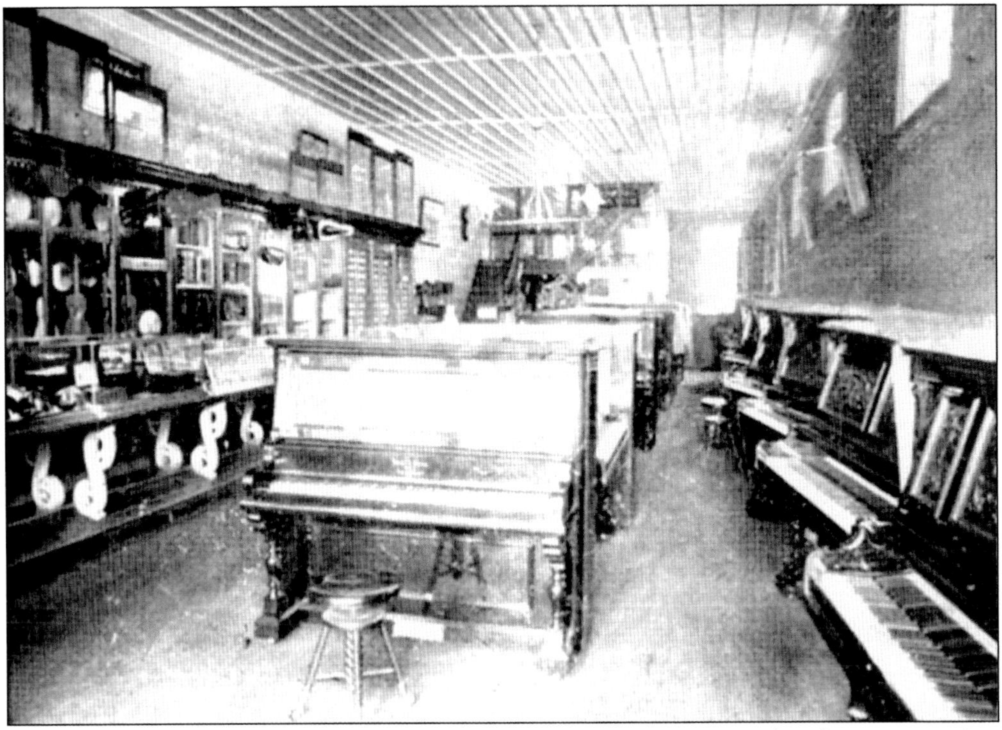

Munson's Music Company was established in 1850, and then reorganized and incorporated in 1902. Munson's was located at 302 Main Street. It supplied Zanesville with sheet music and all kinds of musical instruments. The entire front of the store was torn off during the Flood of 1913 and approximately $150,000 worth of instruments was lost.

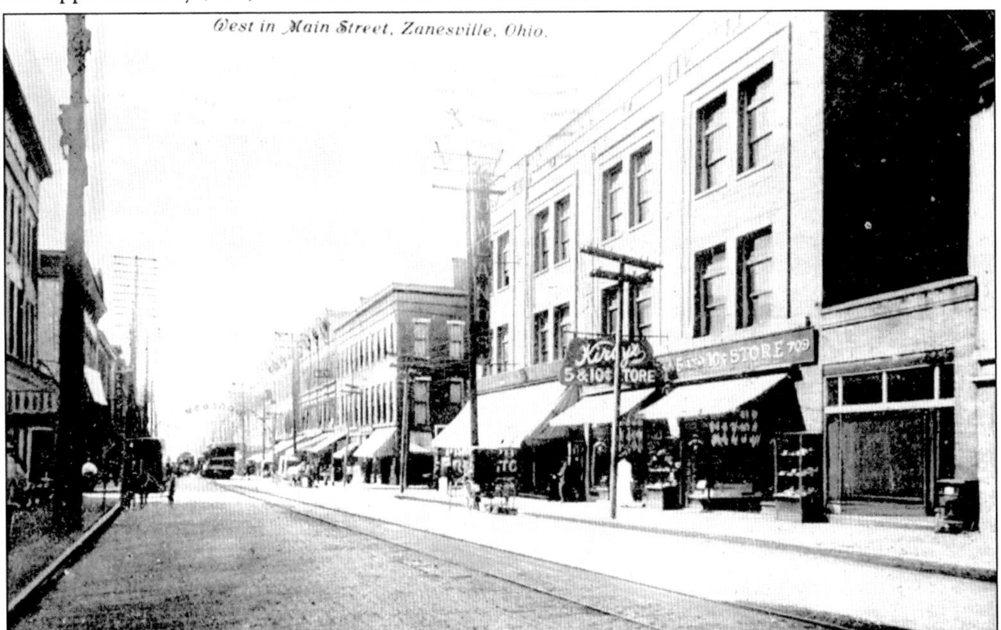

F. M. Kirby's 5 and 10 Cent Store was a popular dime store located at 709 Main Street. (Courtesy of Chance Brockway.)

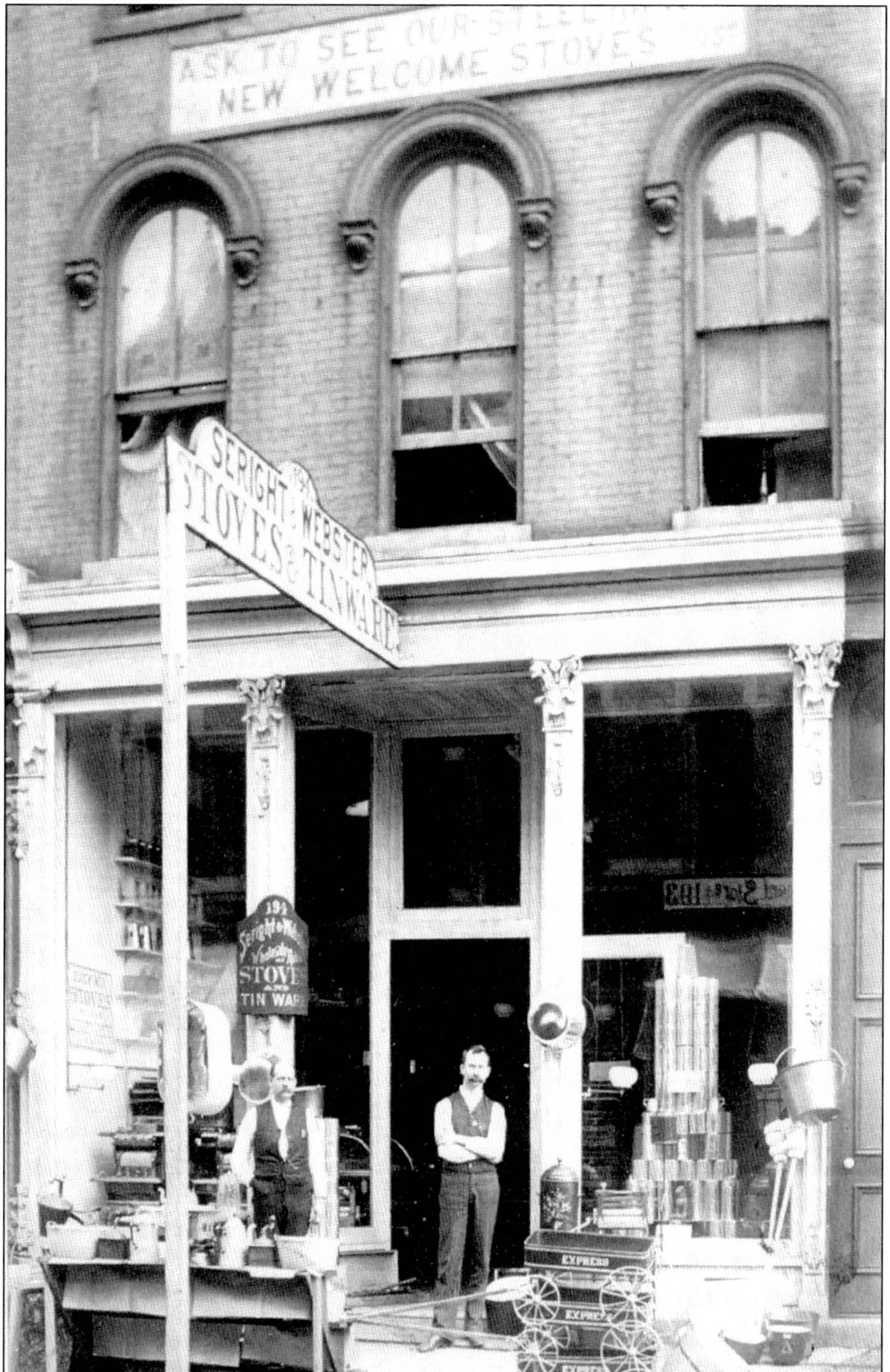

Seright and Webster sold various household items including stoves and tinware from this store at 610 Main Street. (Courtesy of Wayne Estep.)

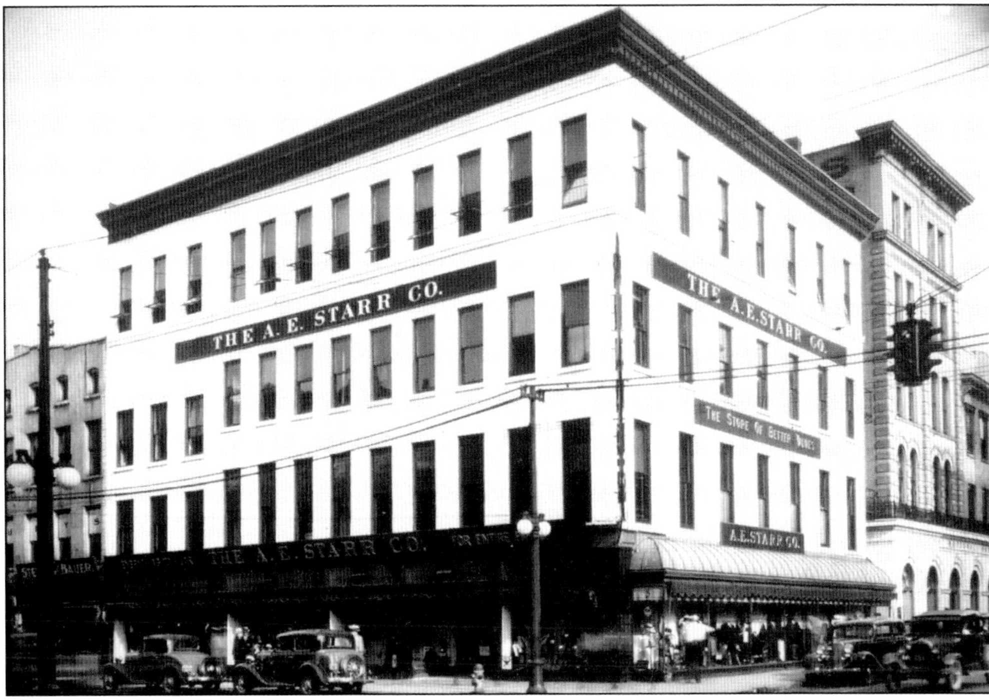

This is the A. E. Starr Company in the 1930s. It was located on the corner of Fourth and Main Streets. The building was torn down in 1974. (Courtesy of Wayne Estep.)

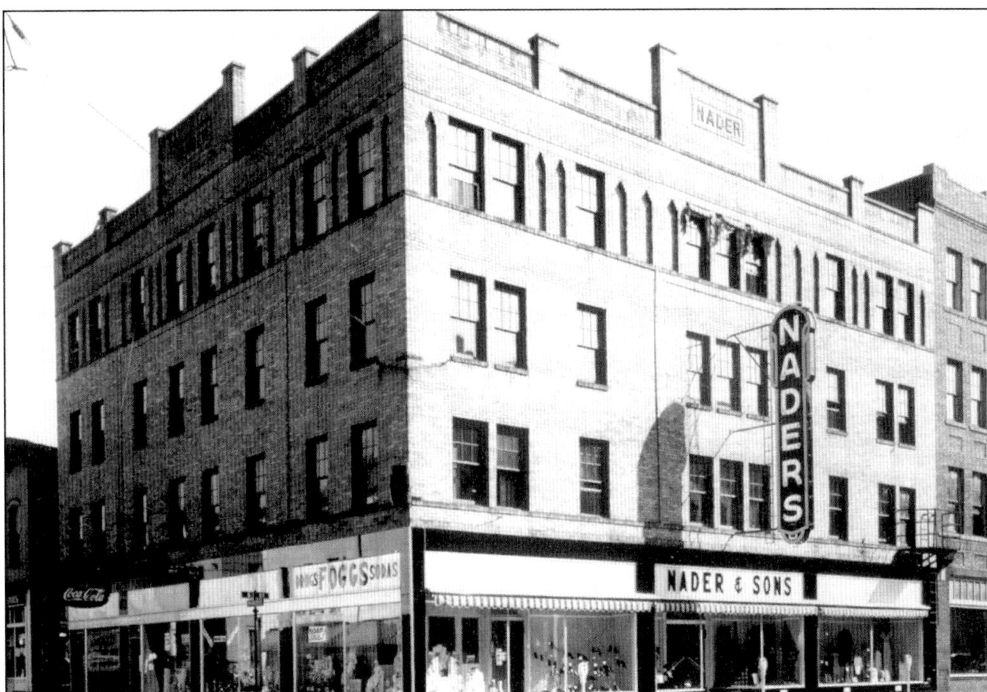

This is Nader and Sons Department Store in the 1930s. It operated at the corner of Fifth and Market Streets from 1904 to 1997. (Courtesy of Wayne Estep.)

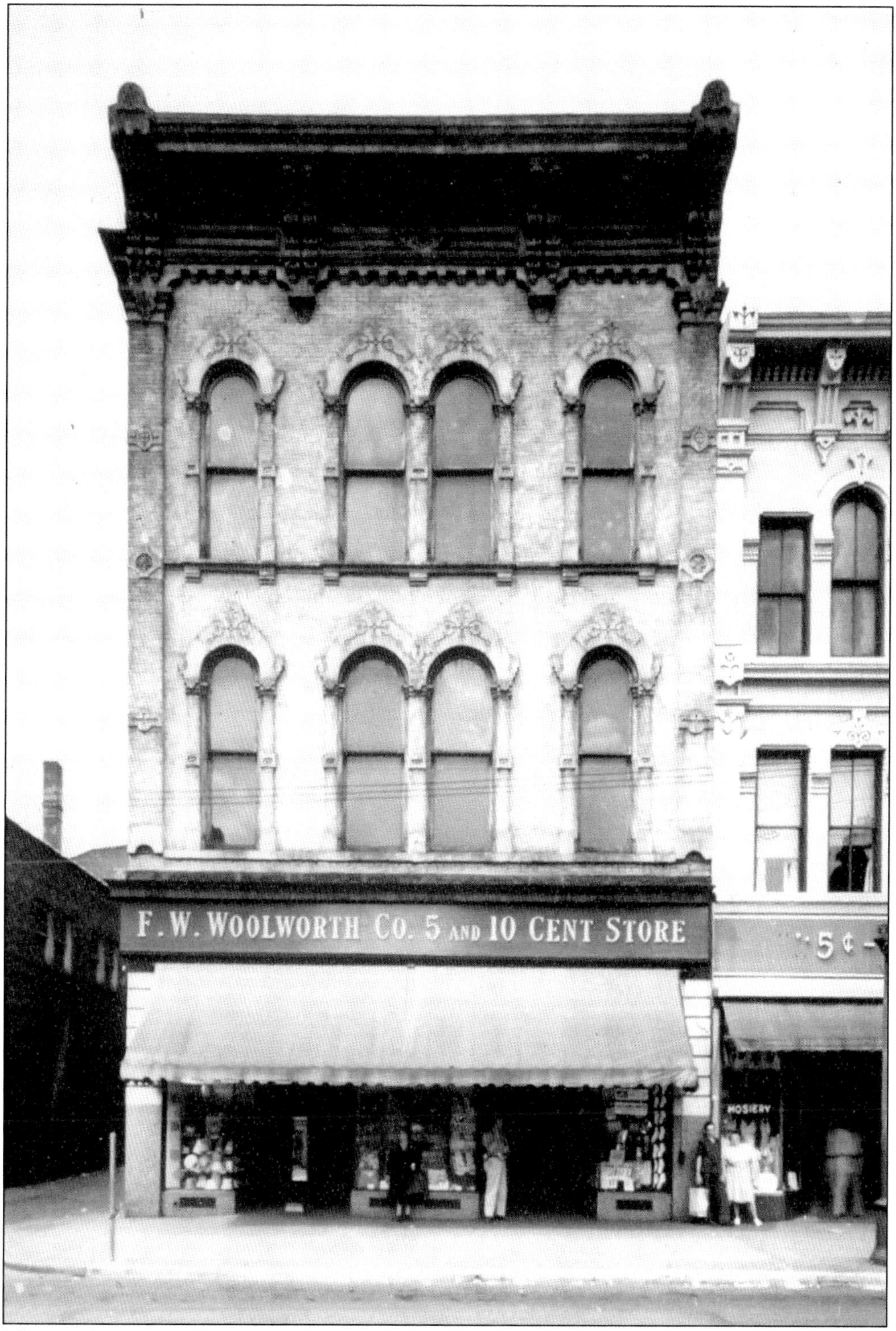

This is the F. W. Woolworth Company 5 and 10 Cent Store in the 1940s. (Courtesy of Wayne Estep.)

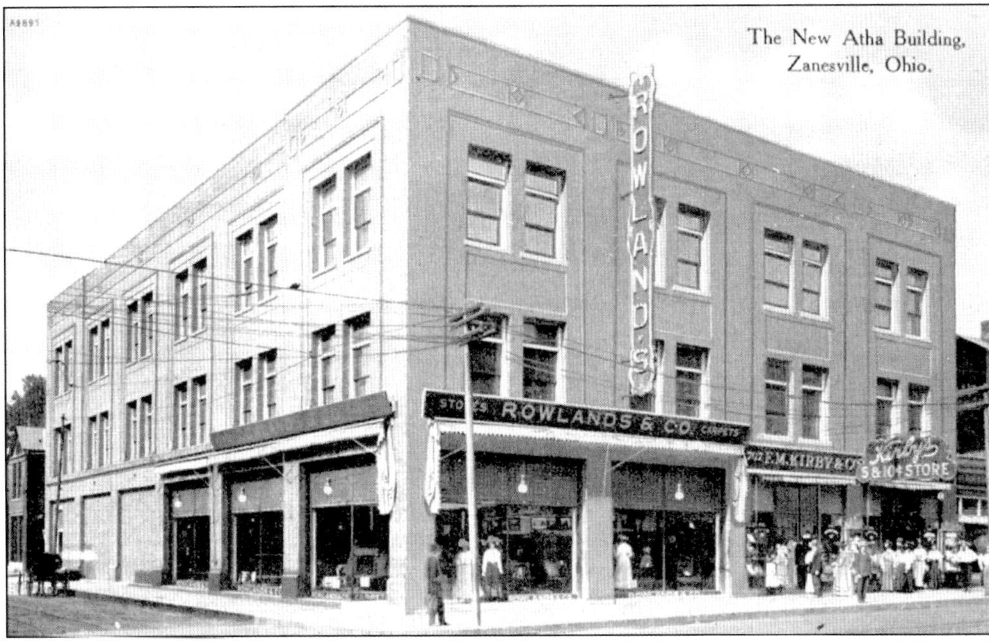

Rowlands and Company was located in the New Atha Building at the corner of Seventh and Main Streets. They sold stoves, carpets, and other household furnishings. (Courtesy of Chance Brockway.)

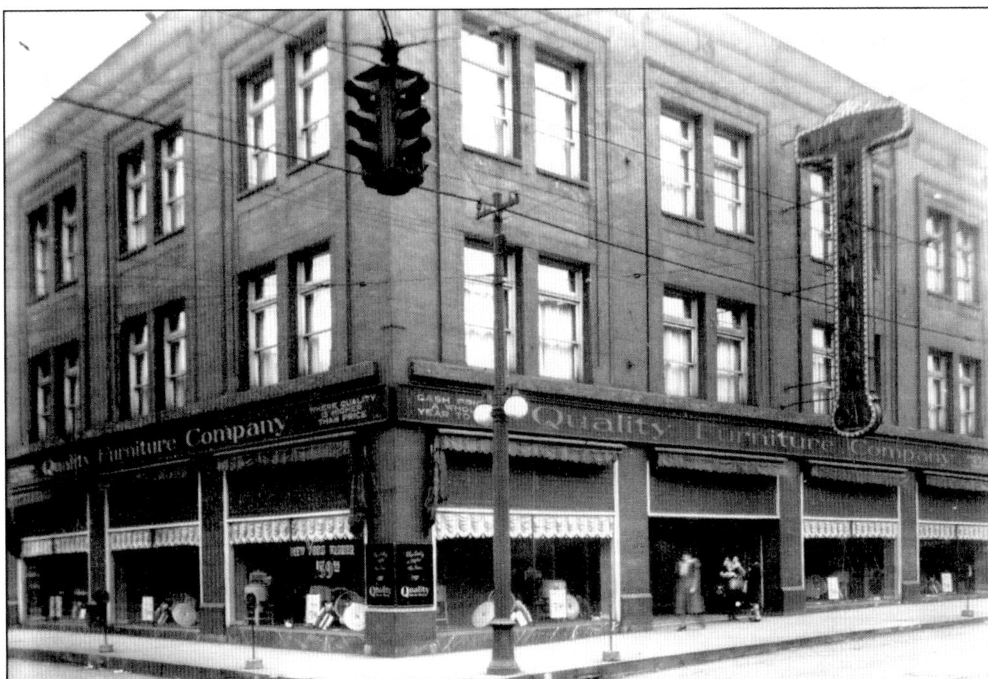

This is the Quality Furniture Company in the 1940s. It replaced Rowlands and Company at this location. (Courtesy of Wayne Estep.)

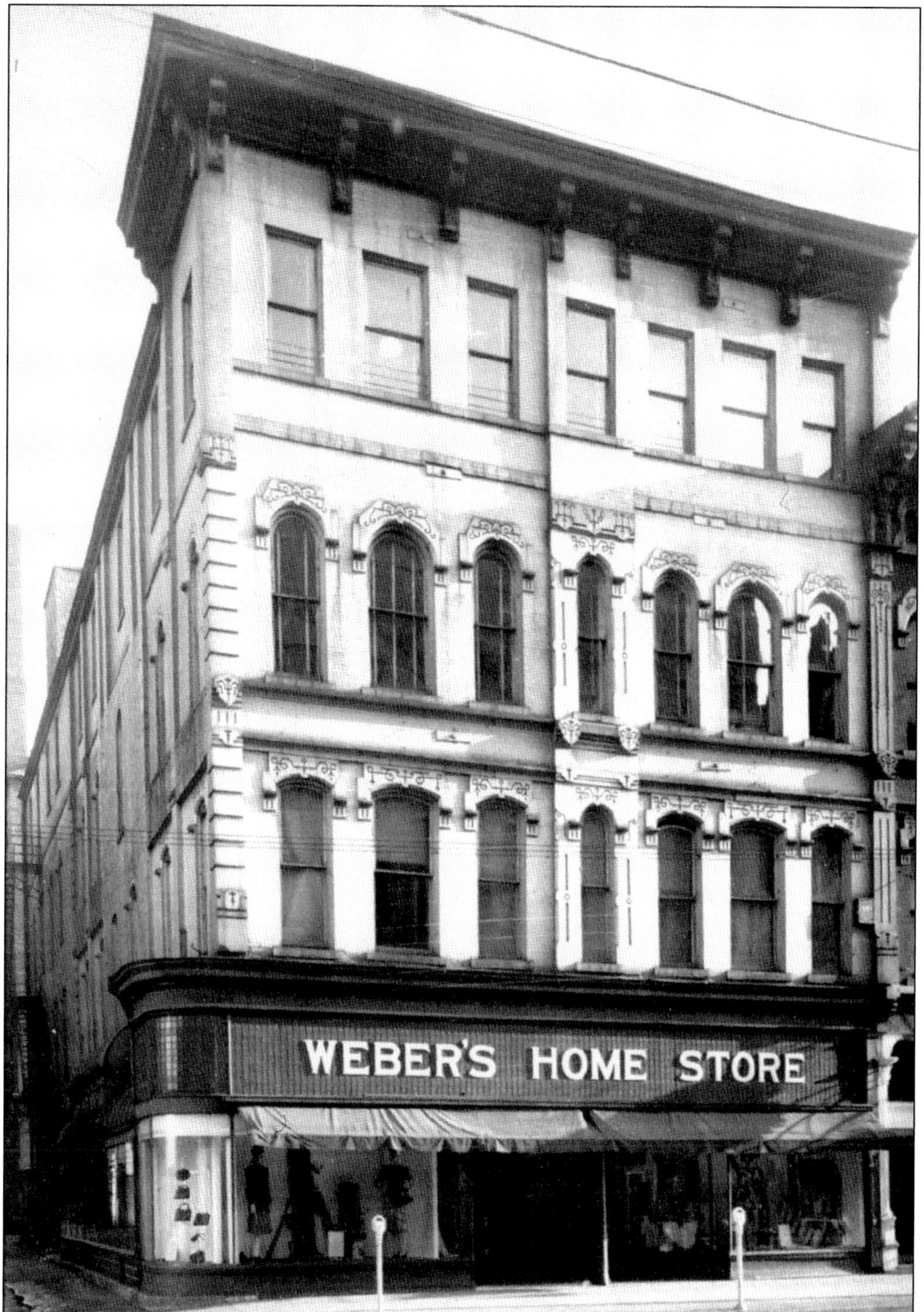

Weber's Home Store was located on Main Street just east of the Muskingum County Courthouse and conducted business from 1900 to 1967. The building was remodeled in 1969 to accommodate small retail space and offices. (Courtesy of Wayne Estep.)

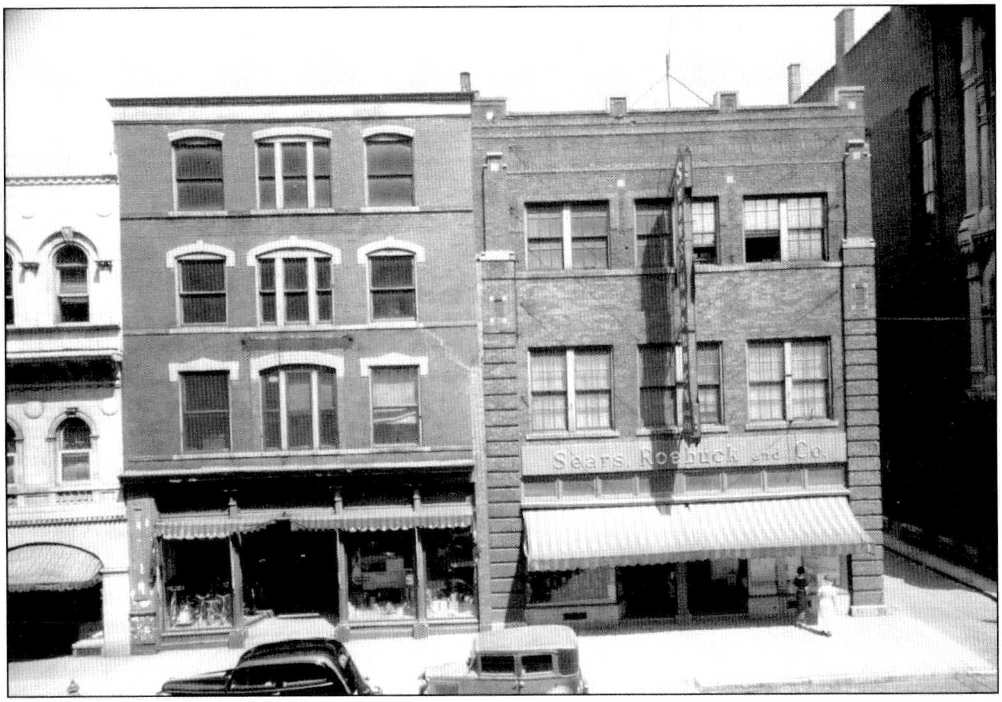

This is the Sears, Roebuck and Company in the 1930s. It was located on North Fifth Street. (Courtesy of Wayne Estep.)

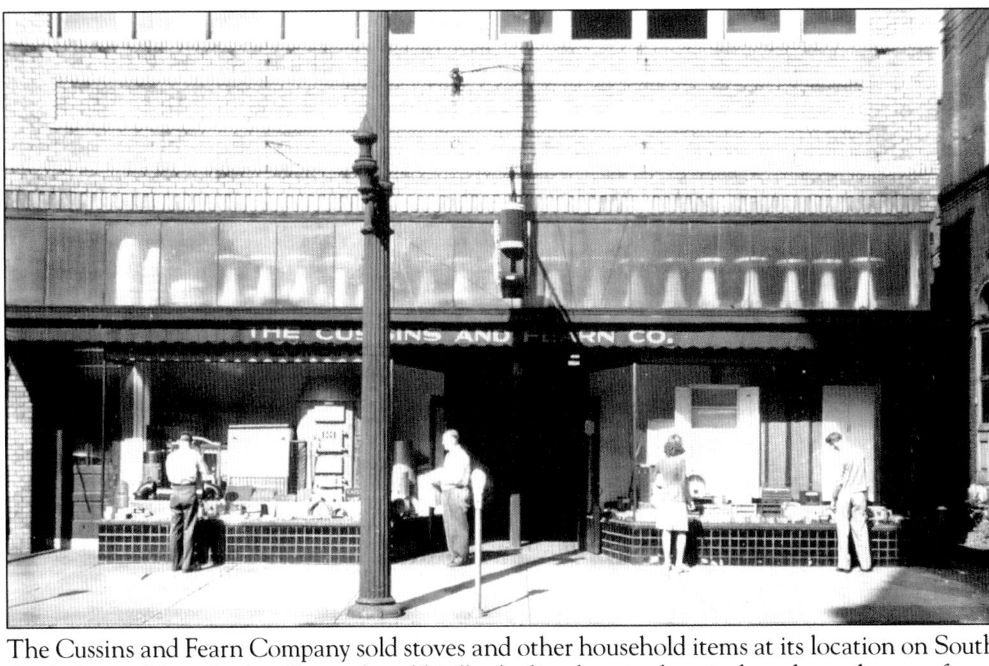

The Cussins and Fearn Company sold stoves and other household items at its location on South Sixth Street. Note the locally produced birdbaths lined up in the window above the storefront. (Courtesy of Wayne Estep.)

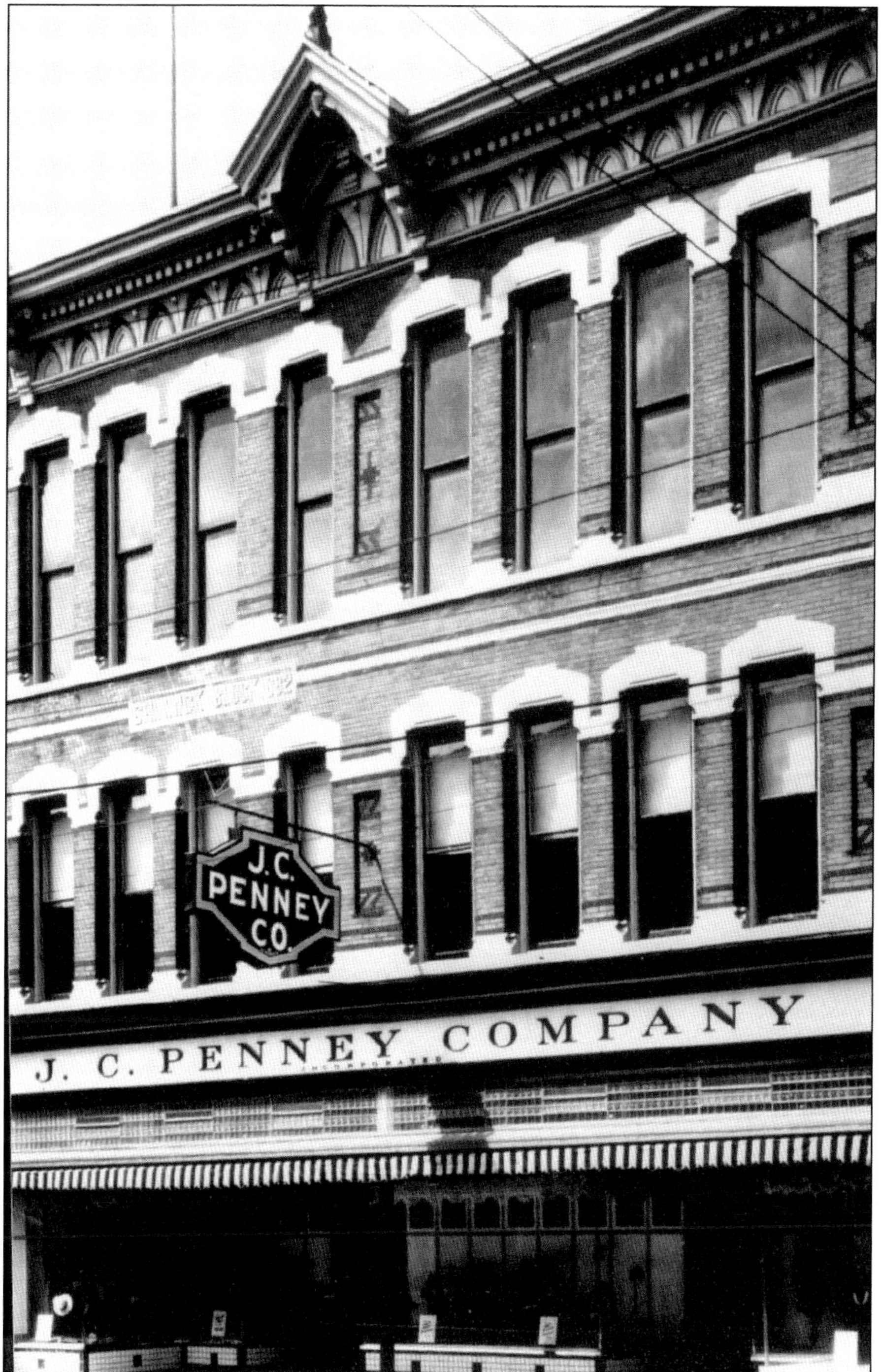

Zanesville's J. C. Penney Company store was originally located at 326 Main Street. In 1924, it moved to the building at 611–617 Main Street shown above. Note the locally produced tile adorning the exterior of the building. In 1954, the store relocated to a new building on North Fifth Street that replaced the old Schultz Opera House. (Courtesy of Wayne Estep.)

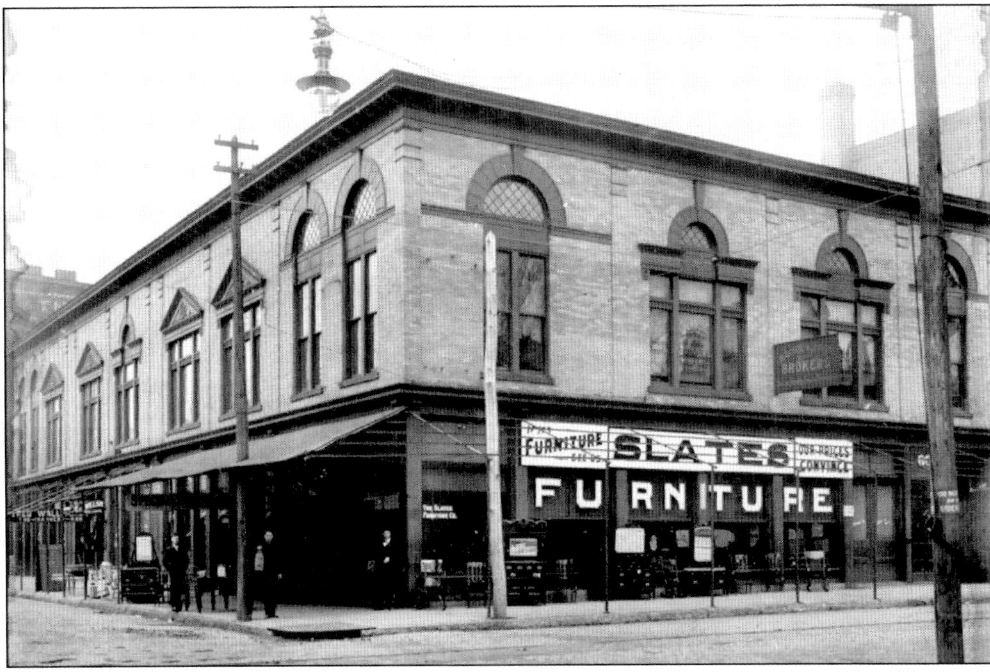

Slates Furniture was the first business to occupy this building, which was located at the corner of Fourth and Market Streets. The structure was erected in 1895 and demolished in 1965. (Courtesy of Mose Mesre.)

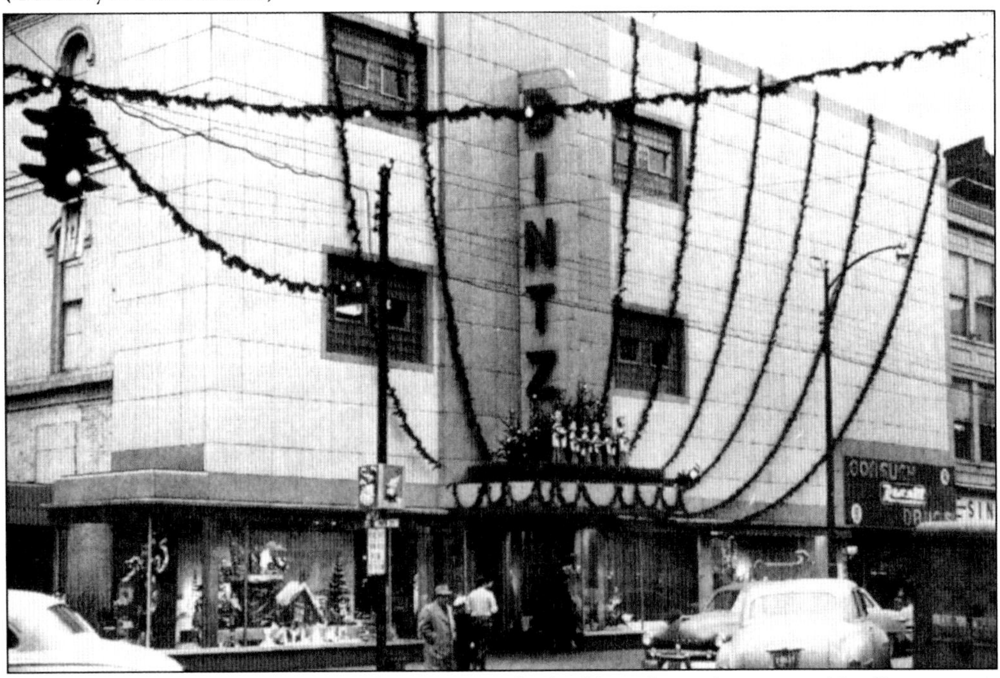

The Bintz department store opened in 1941 in the building formerly occupied by Sturtevant's at the corner of Third and Main Streets. This is the storefront in December 1954. Bintz's closed in 1972, and three years later the building was renovated to create office space. (Courtesy of Wayne Estep.)

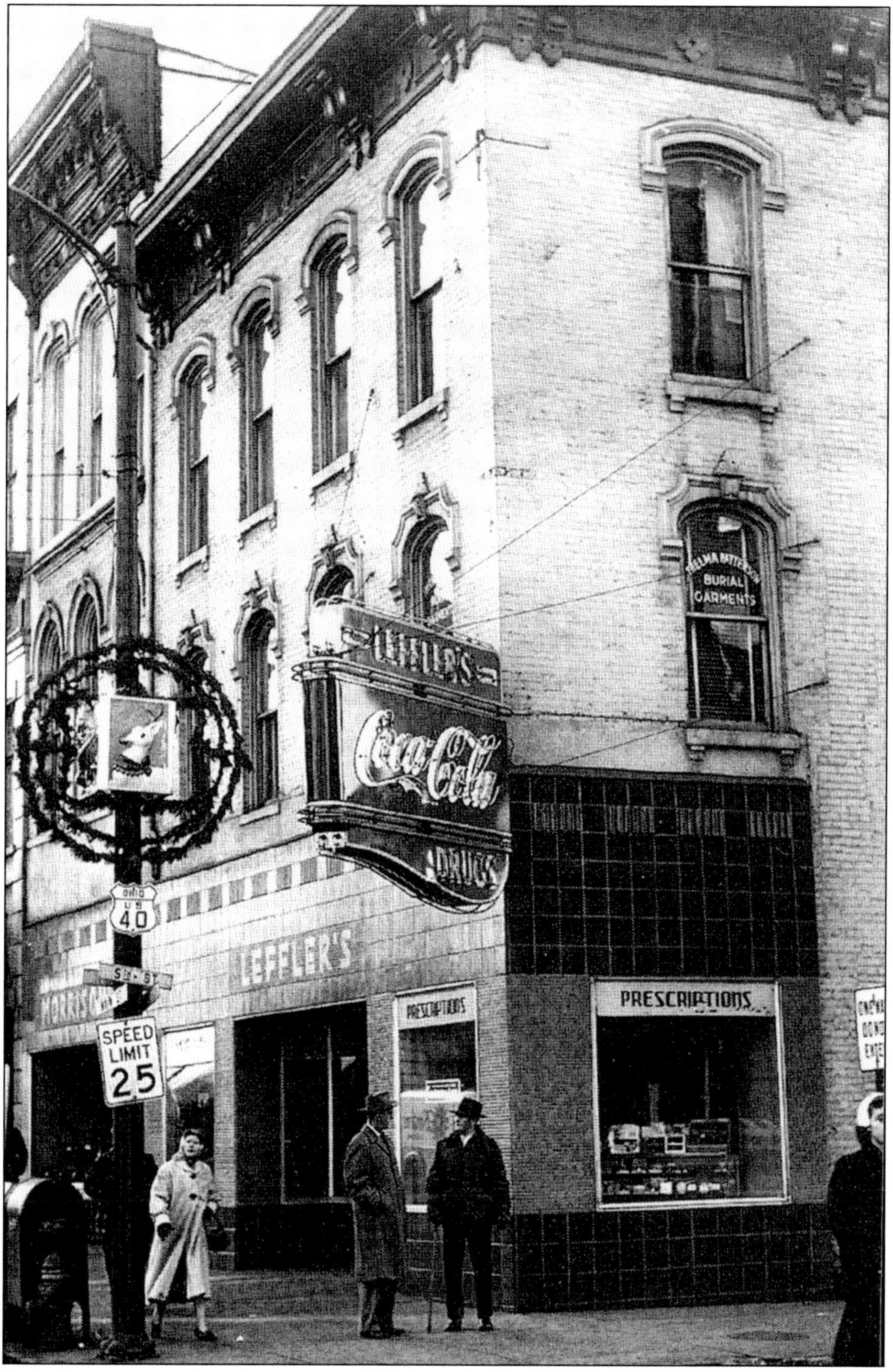

Leffler's Drug operated at the corner of Fifth and Main Streets from 1933 to 1964. People are seen walking in front of the drug store in December 1953. The building was erected in 1835 and was torn down in 1965. Note the locally produced tile that surrounds the exterior of the building. (Courtesy of the *Zanesville Times Recorder*.)

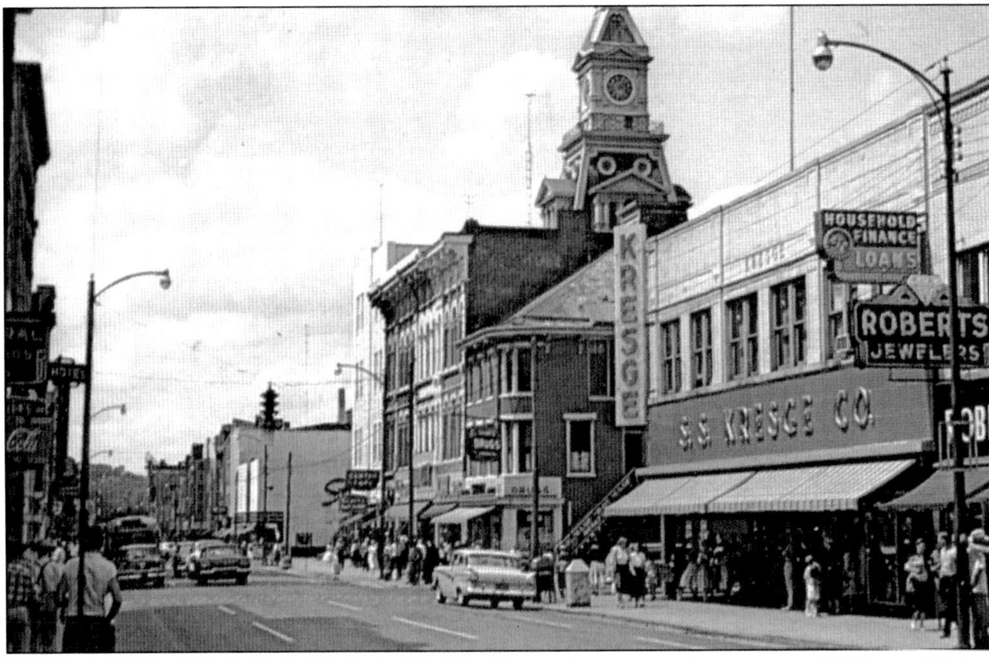

This is the S. S. Kresge Company and other businesses near the corner of Fifth and Main Streets on a summer day in the early 1960s.

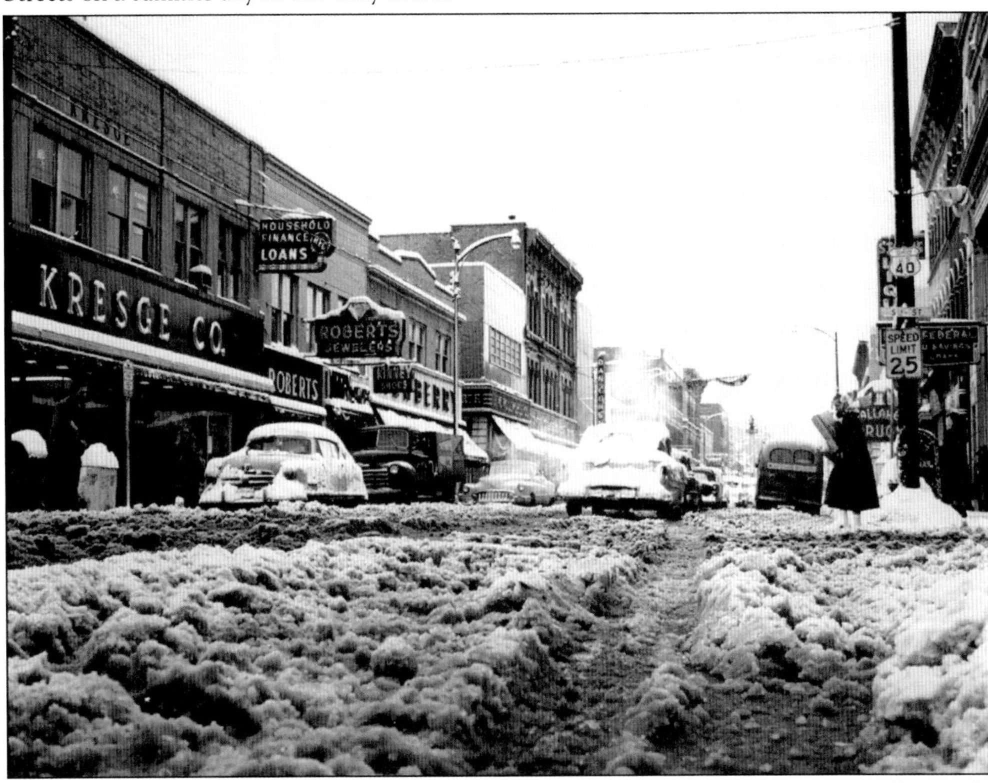

This is the S. S. Kresge Company and other businesses on Main Street on a winter day in the late 1940s. (Courtesy of Mose Mesre.)

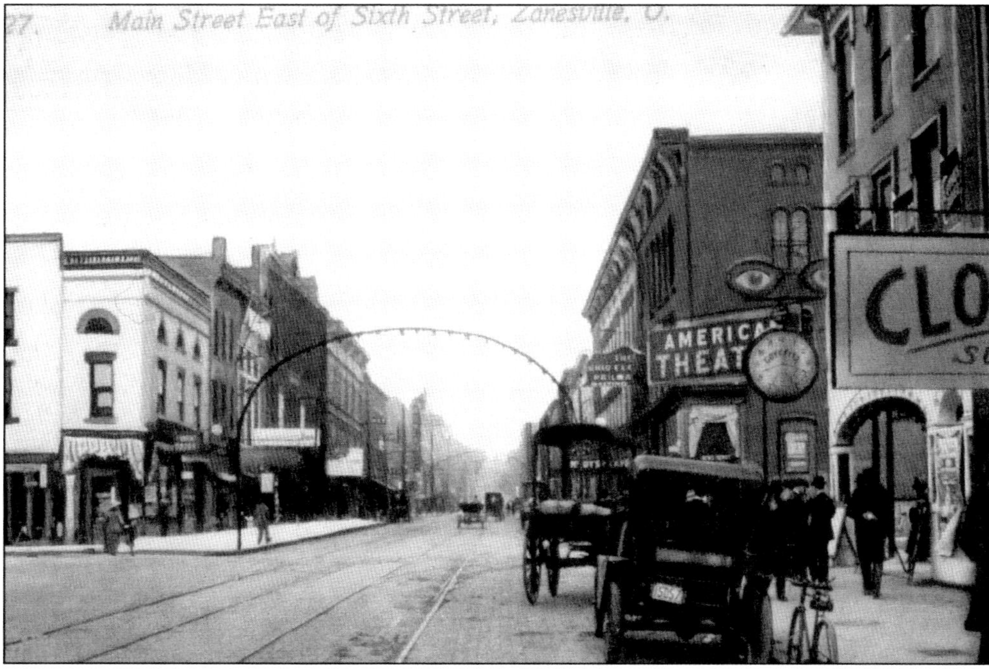

This is Main Street, just east of Sixth Street, looking west, in 1910. Note the marquee for the American Theatre. (Courtesy of Wayne Estep.)

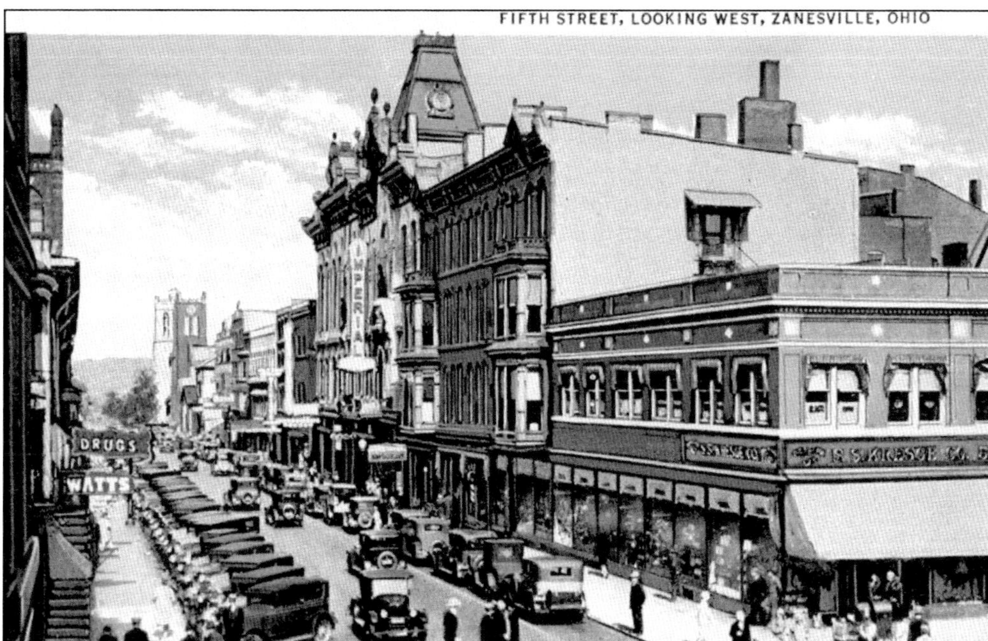

This is North Fifth Street, just above Main Street, in the 1930s. It is interesting to note that the cars were parked both parallel and head-in on the street. Unlike today, it was not a one-way street. (Courtesy of Chance Brockway.)

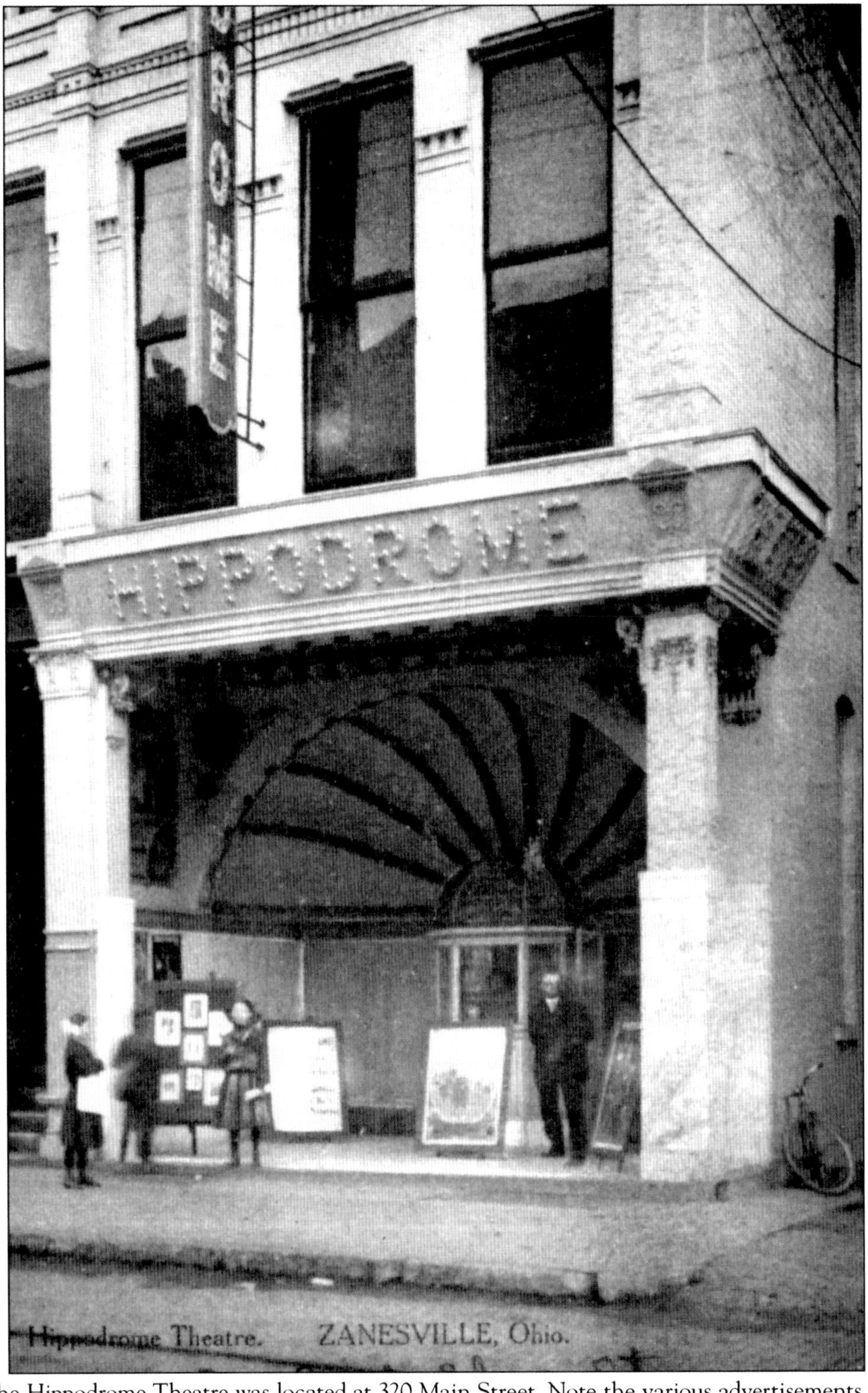

The Hippodrome Theatre was located at 320 Main Street. Note the various advertisements for high-class vaudeville acts. (Courtesy of Wayne Estep.)

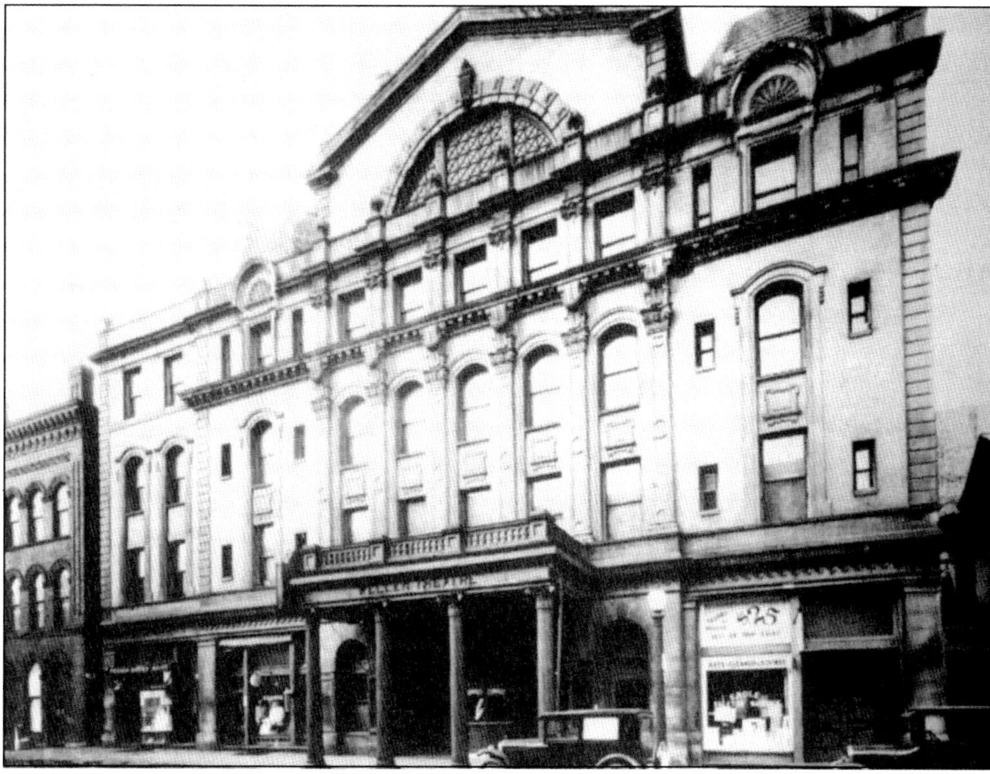

The Weller Theatre was located on the site of the Z. M. Clements residence on North Third Street. The theatre opened in 1903, and had a seating capacity of 1,300. The building was demolished in 1963. (Courtesy of Wayne Estep.)

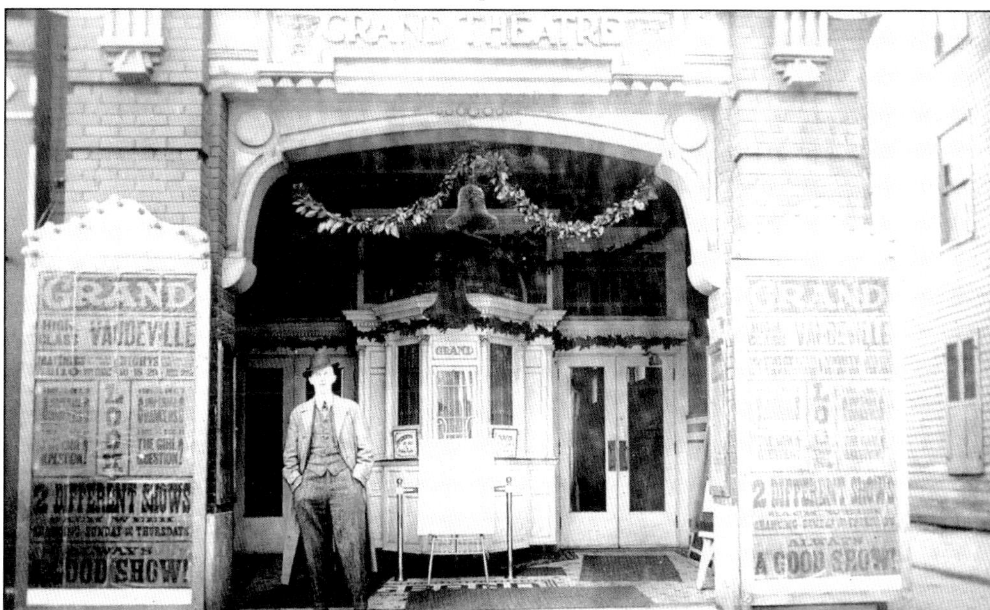

The Grand Theatre was located at 624 Main Street. Note the advertisements for high-class vaudeville acts on either side of the ticket booth. (Courtesy of Wayne Estep.)

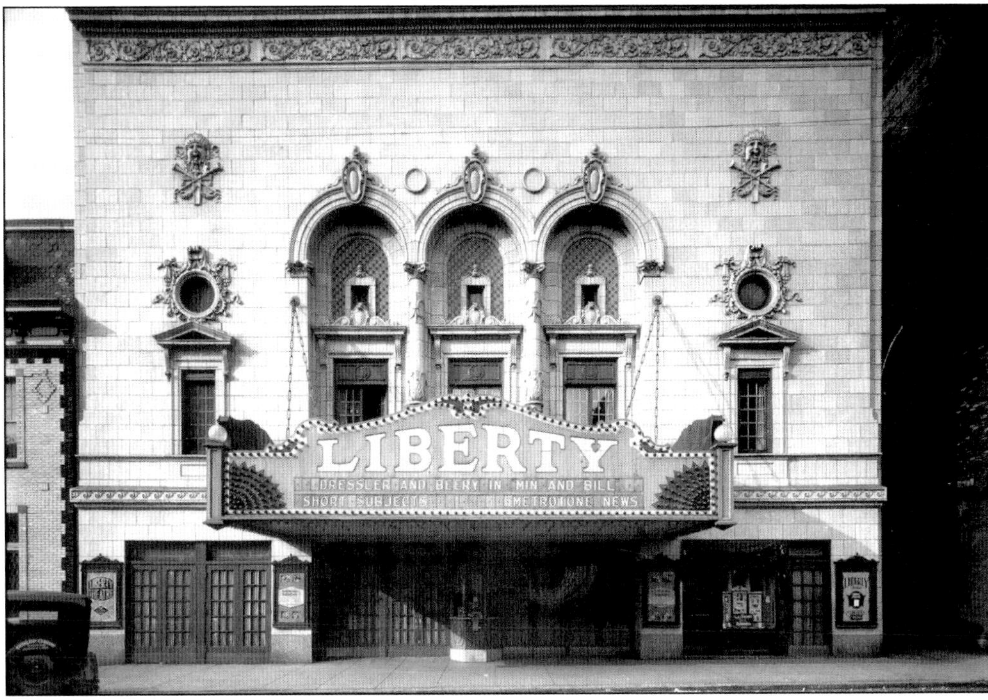

The Liberty Theatre was located at 13–15 South Fifth Street. It opened on October 13, 1927. (Courtesy of the *Zanesville Times Recorder.*)

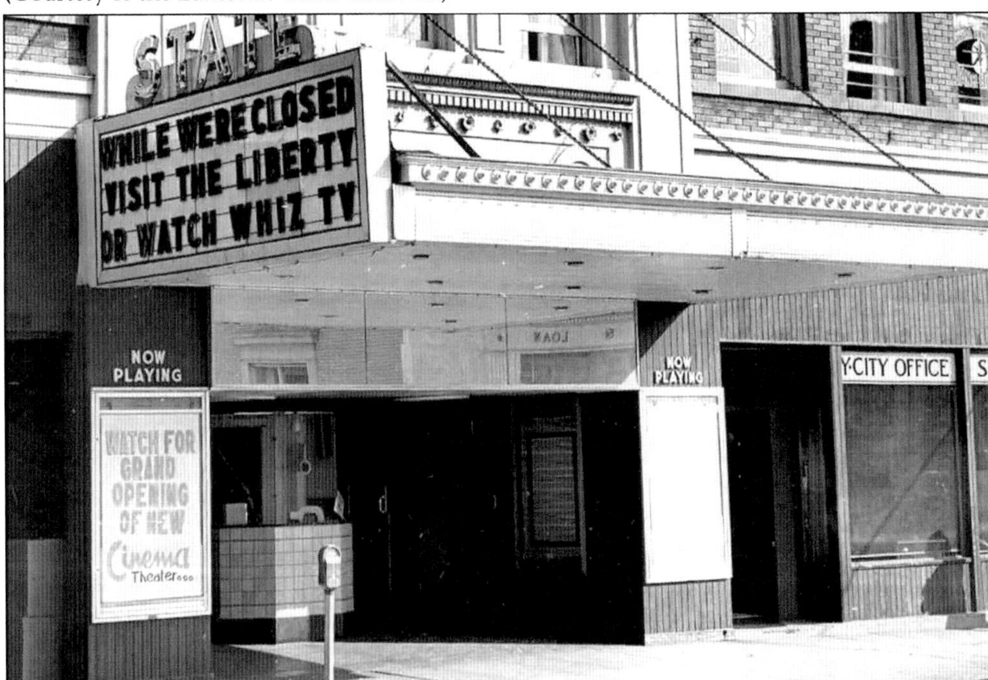

The State Theatre was located at 30 South Fifth Street. Note the marquee, advising for patrons to either visit the Liberty Theatre or to watch WHIZ TV while the theatre was closed. (Courtesy of MCCOGS.)

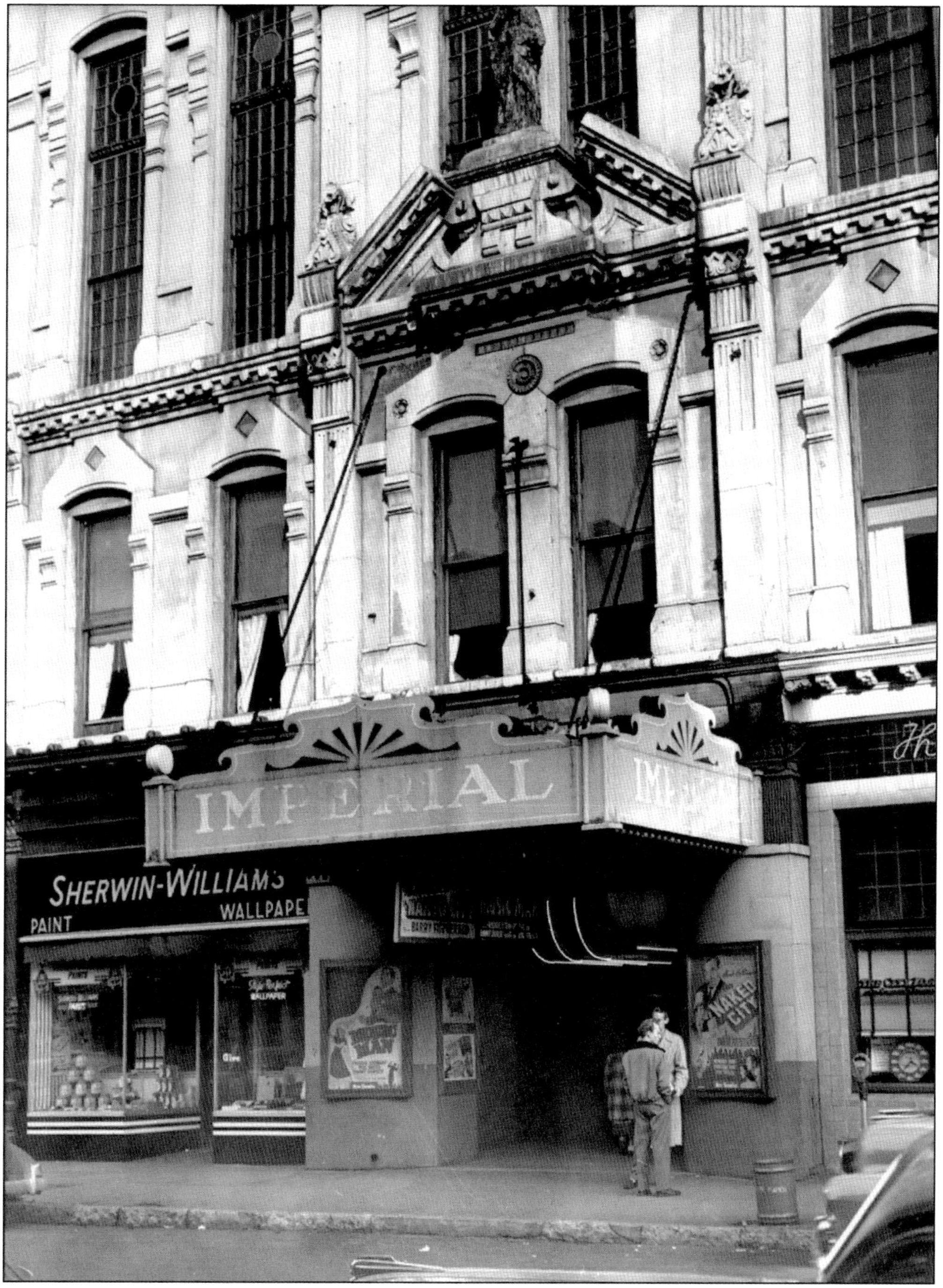

The Imperial Theatre occupied the building that once housed the Schultz Opera House on North Fifth Street. The Variety Theatre later occupied this location. (Courtesy of Mose Mesre.)

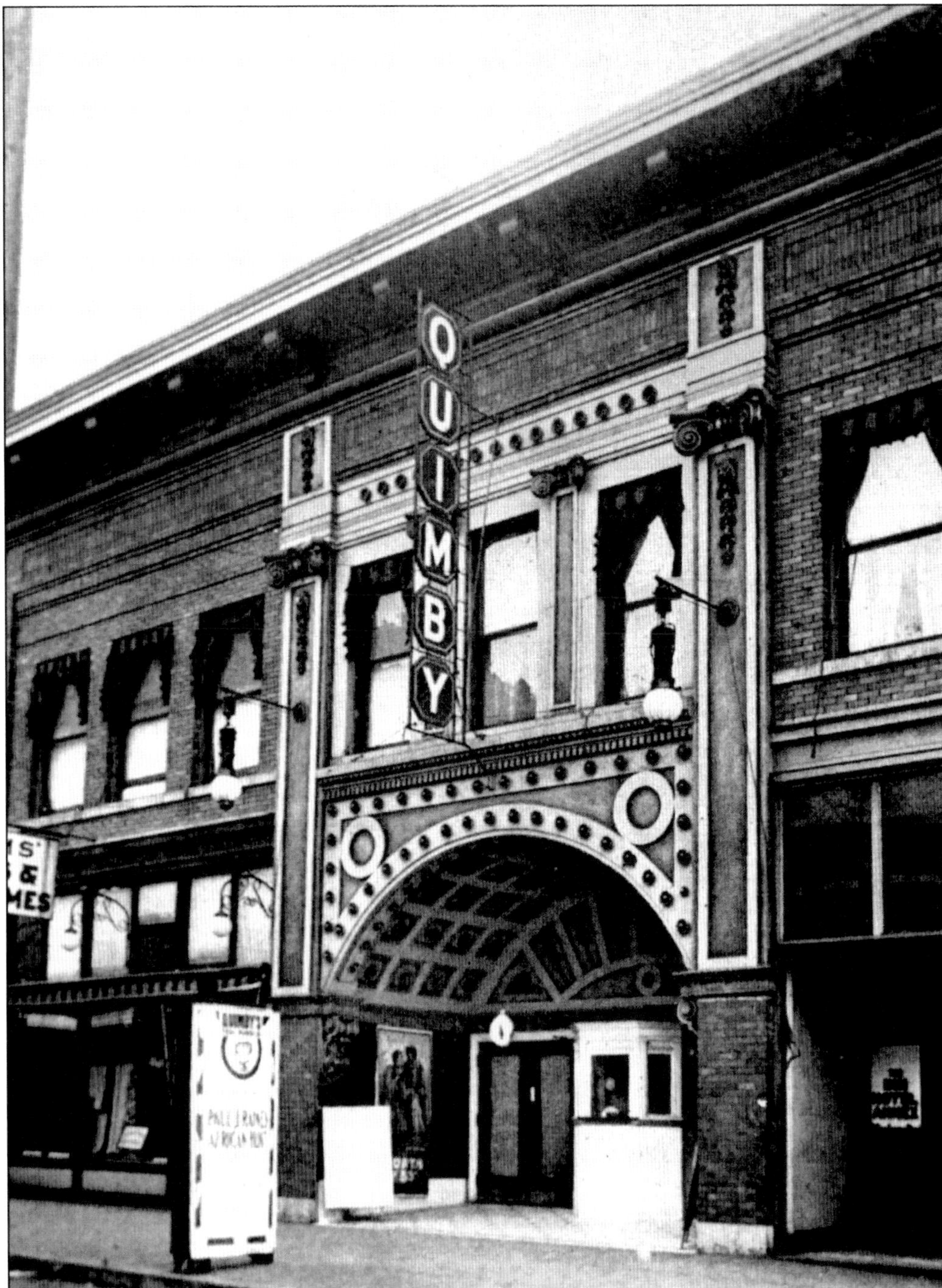

The Quimby Theatre opened in 1907 at 30 South Fifth Street. In 1924, A. C. White was the theatre manager. The theatre closed in 1953. The State Theatre later occupied this location. (Courtesy of the Theatre Historical Society of America.)

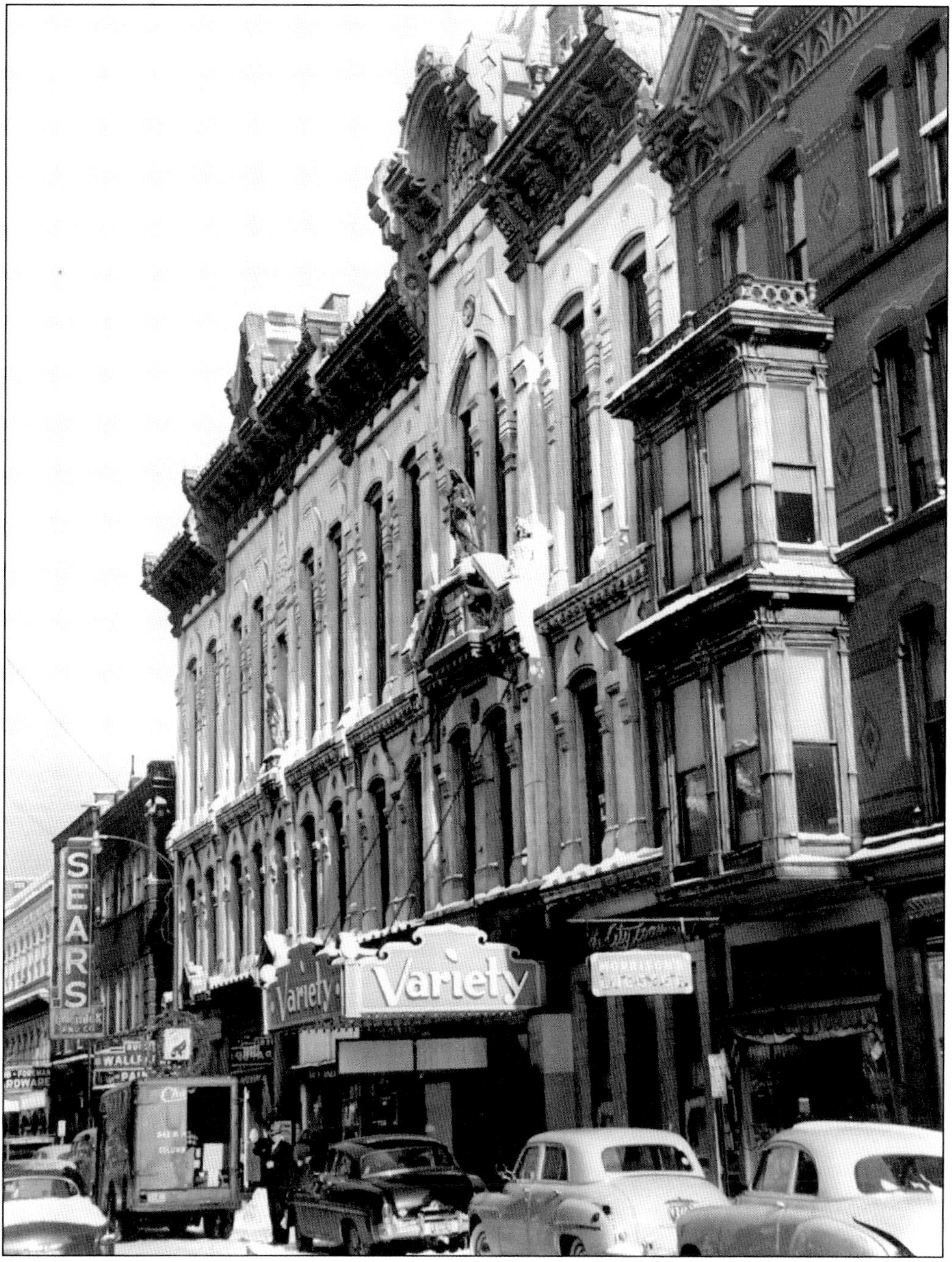

This is the Variety Theatre in the 1940s. It replaced the Imperial Theatre at this location on North Fifth Street. (Courtesy of Mose Mesre.)

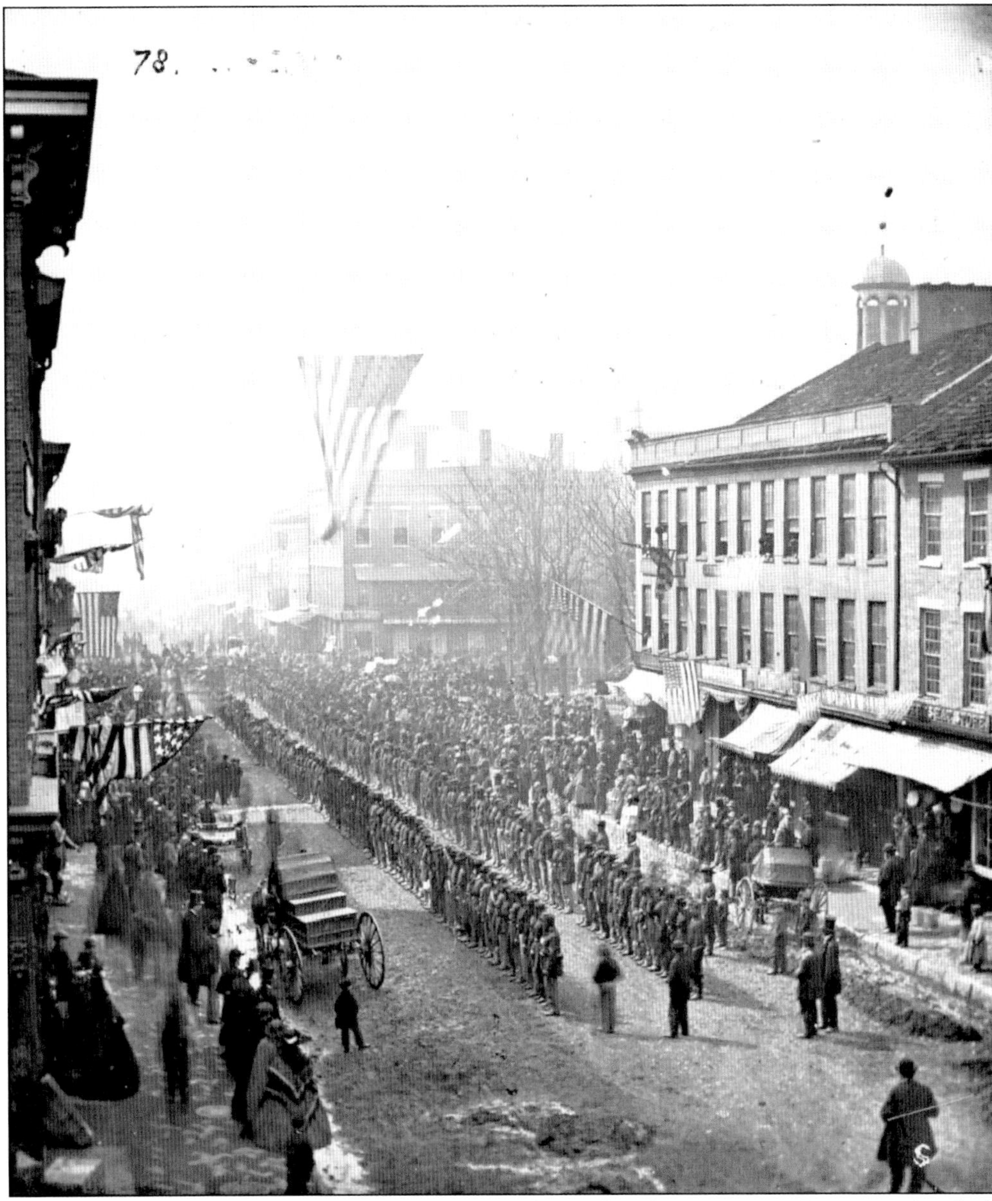

Soldiers from the 78th Ohio Valley Infantry are shown lined up on Main Street on April 12, 1864, when they returned to Zanesville for a 30-day furlough. (Private collection.)

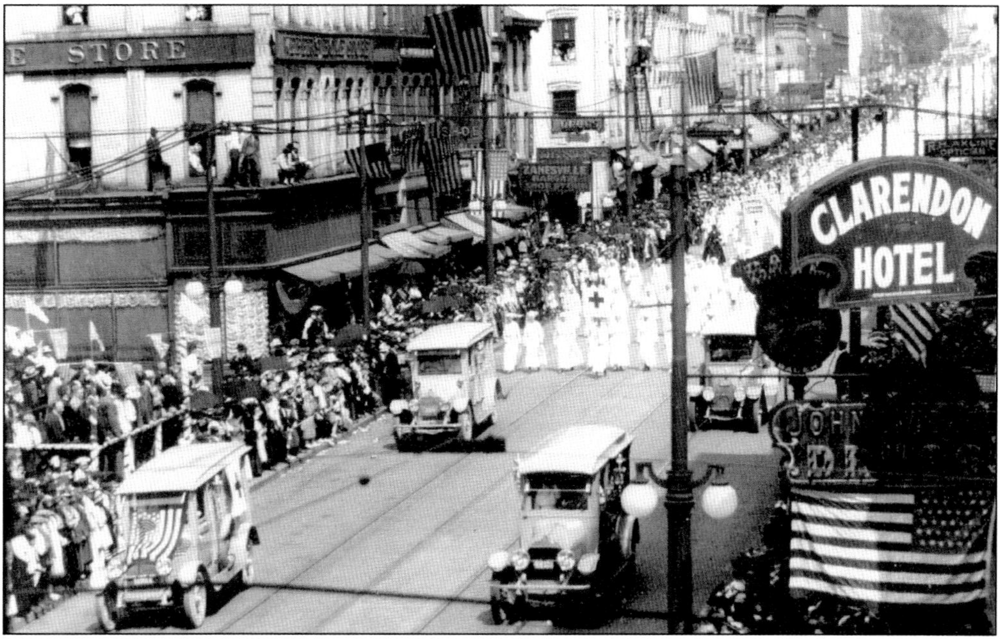

On May 18, 1918, known as Red Cross Saturday, more than 5,000 women from throughout the city and county, accompanied by several floats, five bands, and 150 automobiles, marched down Main Street in order to raise more than $64,000 in one of the city's largest fund-raising drives for the war. (Courtesy of Wayne Estep.)

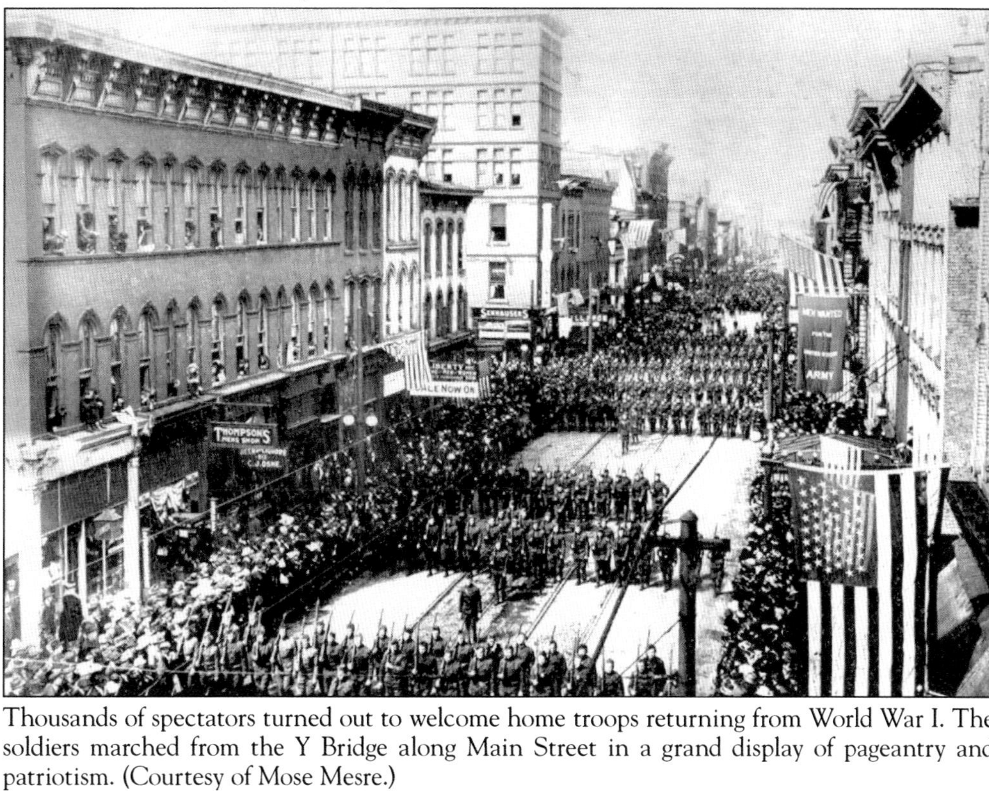

Thousands of spectators turned out to welcome home troops returning from World War I. The soldiers marched from the Y Bridge along Main Street in a grand display of pageantry and patriotism. (Courtesy of Mose Mesre.)

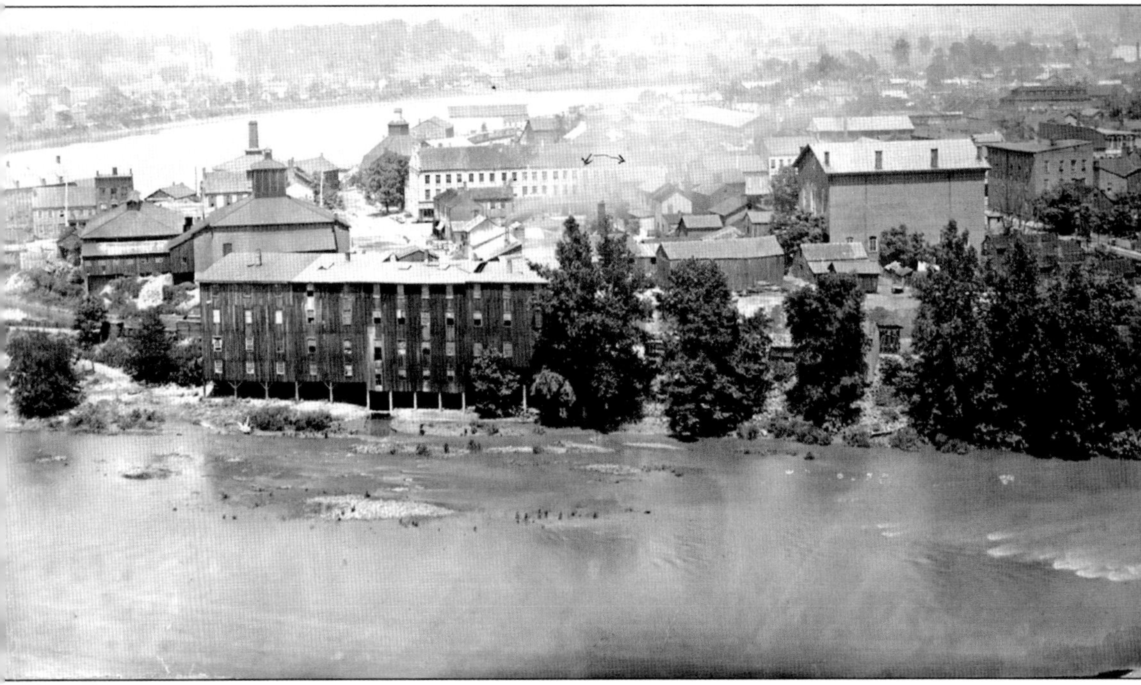

By 1865, the western end of the downtown area was rapidly becoming a manufacturing center. The four-story wooden building, shown at the river's edge, was the Gary Brother's and Silvey Furniture Factory. Behind the furniture factory, identifiable by their tall chimneys, were three different glass-producing buildings operated by the Kearns-Gorsuch Glass Company. Window glass was produced in the building directly behind the furniture factory, bottles were produced in the building directly behind the window-glass building, and flint glass was produced in the building to the right of the bottle-production building. The building along the river's edge, at left, was Edward Johnson's Pearl Barley and Feed Mill. (Courtesy of Wayne Estep.)

Five

MANUFACTURING, MINING, AND "CLAY CITY"

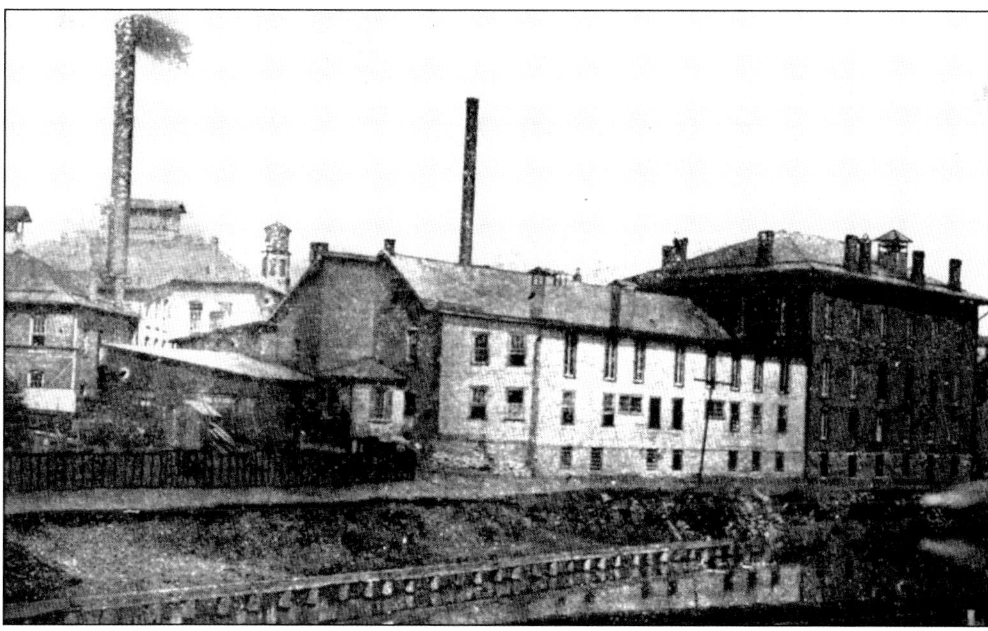

Robert Schultz went into the business of manufacturing soap and candles in 1853, when the rising popularity of railroad travel greatly reduced the demand for his stagecoaches. The Schultz and Company Soap Factory was located along Ohio Canal and Seventh Streets. Novel marketing strategies made his Star Soap a popular and nationally known brand. Proctor and Gamble bought the business in 1903 and moved the operation to Cincinnati. The vacant buildings were taken over by the Muskingum Laundry in 1906. (Courtesy of Wayne Estep.)

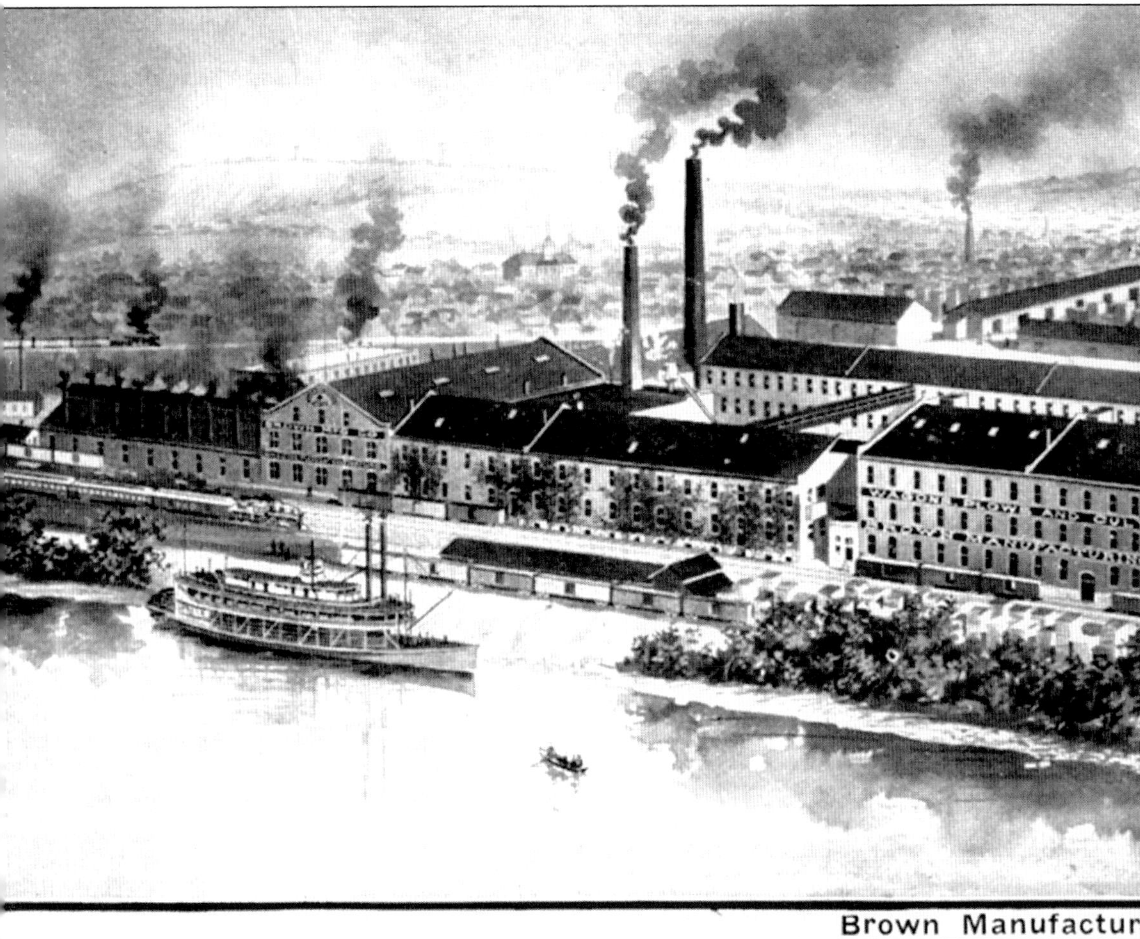

The Brown Manufacturing Company made farm and lumber wagons, cotton cultivators, and double-shovel plows at its facility at Seventh and Underwood Streets between 1874 and 1929. These items were sold to customers in the United States, Canada, Europe, and South America.

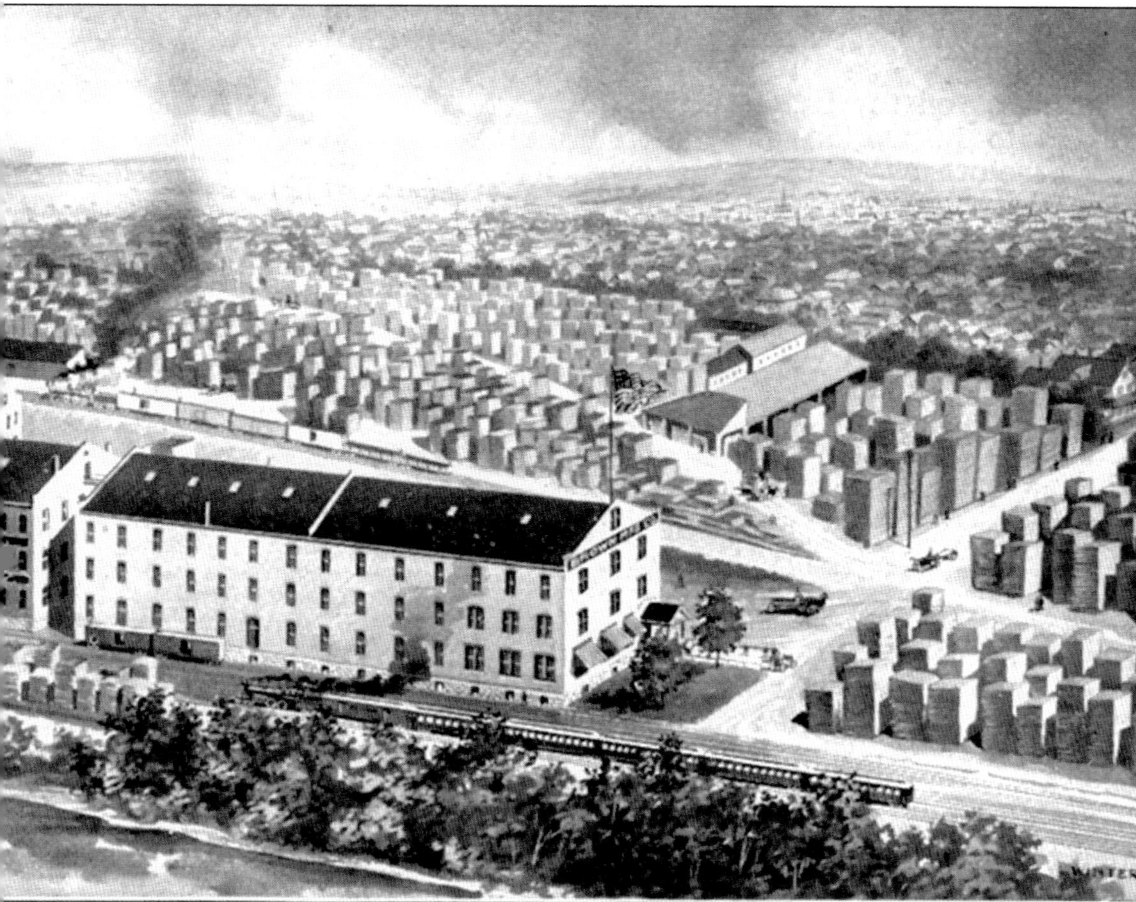

Zanesville, Ohio.

James Herdman was Brown's president in 1895, and D. S. Brown was the superintendent. The company was forced to close when automobiles and trucks replaced wagons as the primary means of transportation.

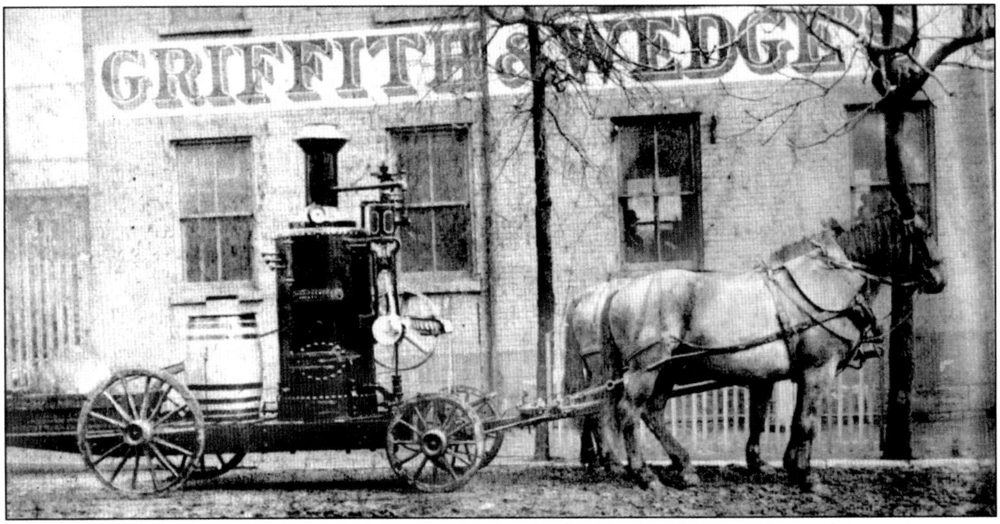

In 1856, Thomas Griffith and Francis Wedge assumed control of a foundry and manufacturing operation established along the Ohio Canal at 93 South Fifth Street. Elias Ebert and Mark Lowden had started the business in 1840. Griffith and Wedge manufactured steam engines, boilers, and various kinds of machinery, castings, and forgings. Their rock-crushing machines and portable sawmills were in strong demand from mining companies and lumbermen. The company was in operation until 1917, when it was sold to the Mark Manufacturing Company. (Courtesy of Wayne Estep.)

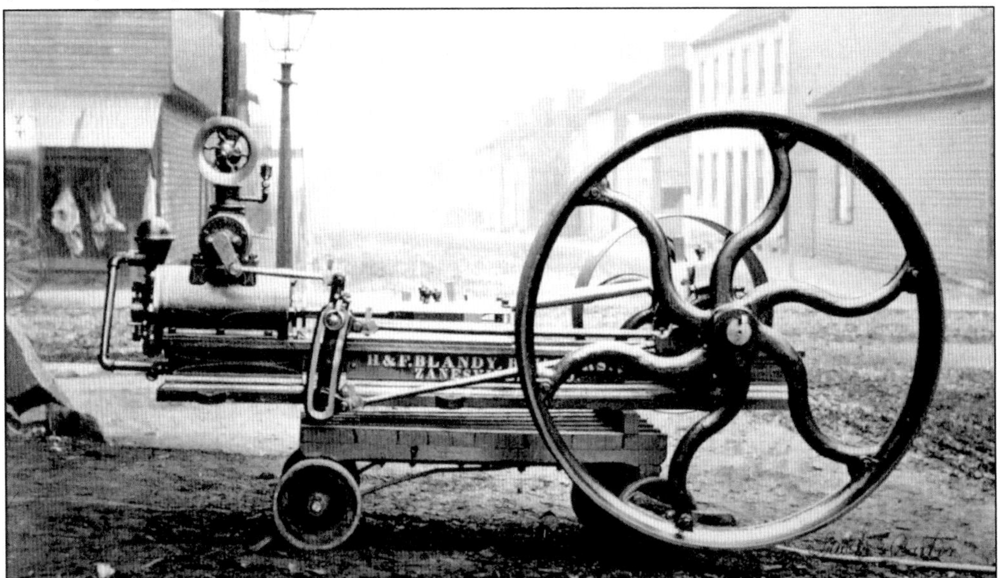

This small steam engine was made by the Blandy Foundry and Machine Company in the 1880s. Brothers Fred and Henry Blandy began making locomotives, engines, boilers, forgings, castings, and stoves in 1840 at their facility located at the corner of Underwood and Elm Streets. In 1854, they began manufacturing portable steam engines so their customers could "take the engine to the work instead of taking the work to the engine." The Union Machine Company succeeded the business in 1898 and operated the foundry and machine shop until 1901. The buildings were later used as garages for the city's streetcars. (Courtesy of Wayne Estep.)

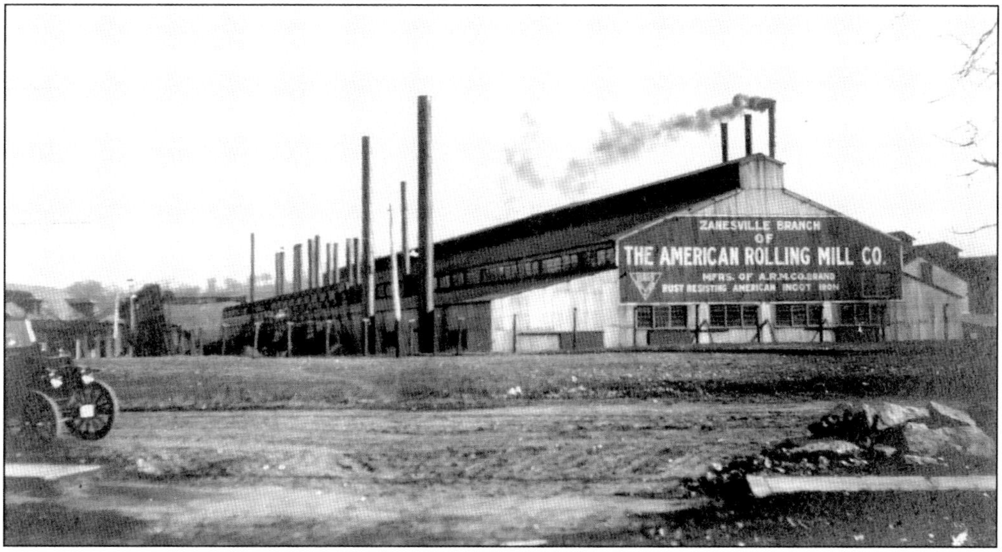

The American Rolling Mill Company, more commonly known by its acronym ARMCO, began operating at its Linden Avenue location in 1905. The Curtis Sheet Steel Company had built the mill in 1901. ARMCO enlarged their facilities and made the mill the center of its research and production of electrical steel. (Courtesy of Tom Brown.)

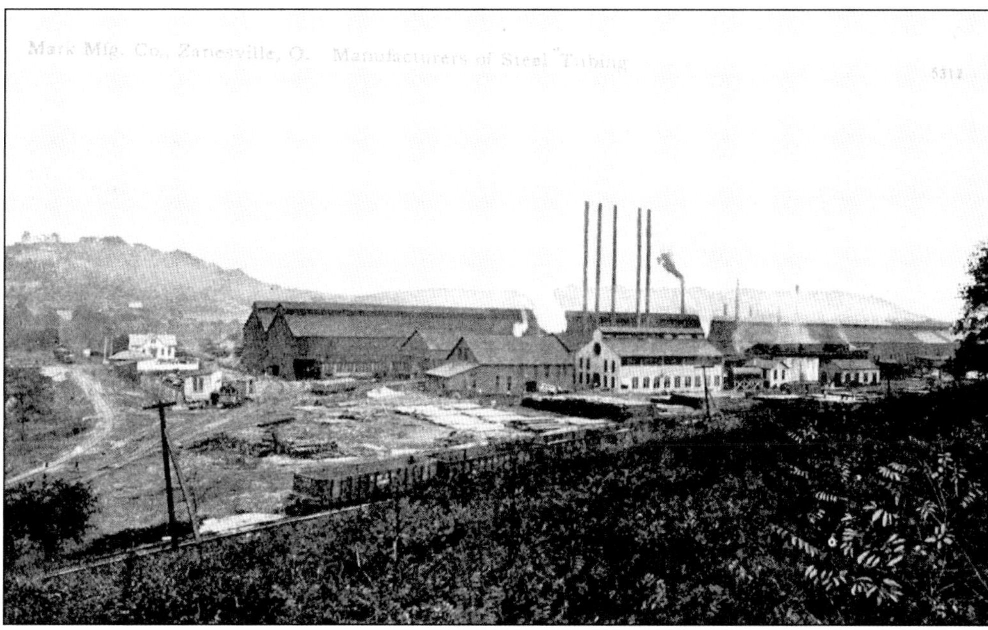

The Mark Manufacturing Company, also known as the "Tube Mill," produced seamless steel pipes between 1901 and 1930. The company was located on Cleveland Street at the south end of Moxahala Avenue. The building was razed in 1938, and the city's sewage treatment plant now occupies a portion of the old Tube Mill site. (Courtesy of Chance Brockway.)

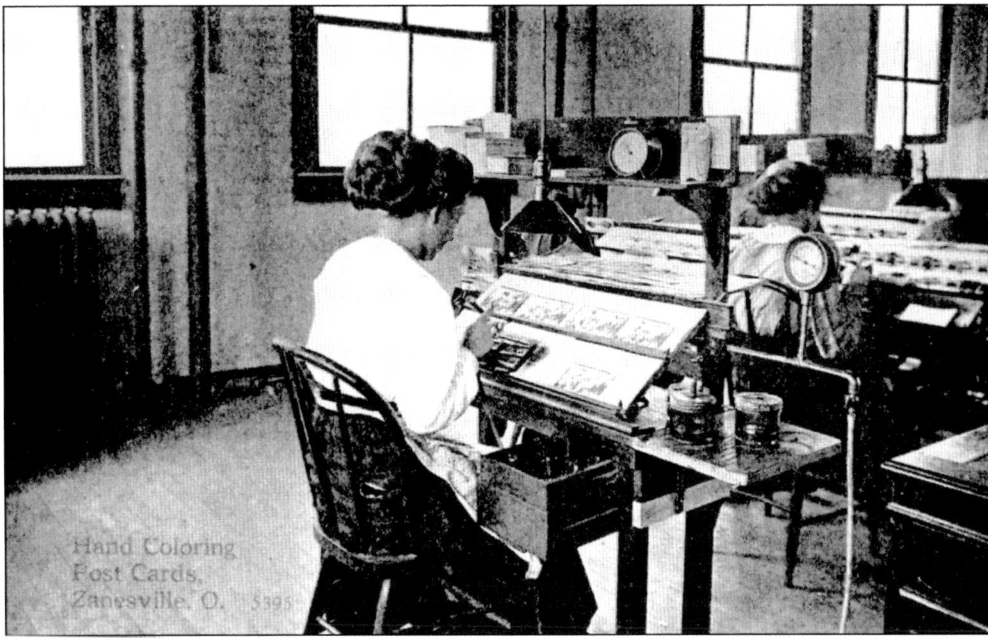

The Art Manufacturing Company was located at the corner of Lincoln and Muskingum Avenues. They produced postcards and calendars between 1910 and 1912. Employees of the art department are shown using airbrushes to hand-color postcards. (Courtesy of Chance Brockway.)

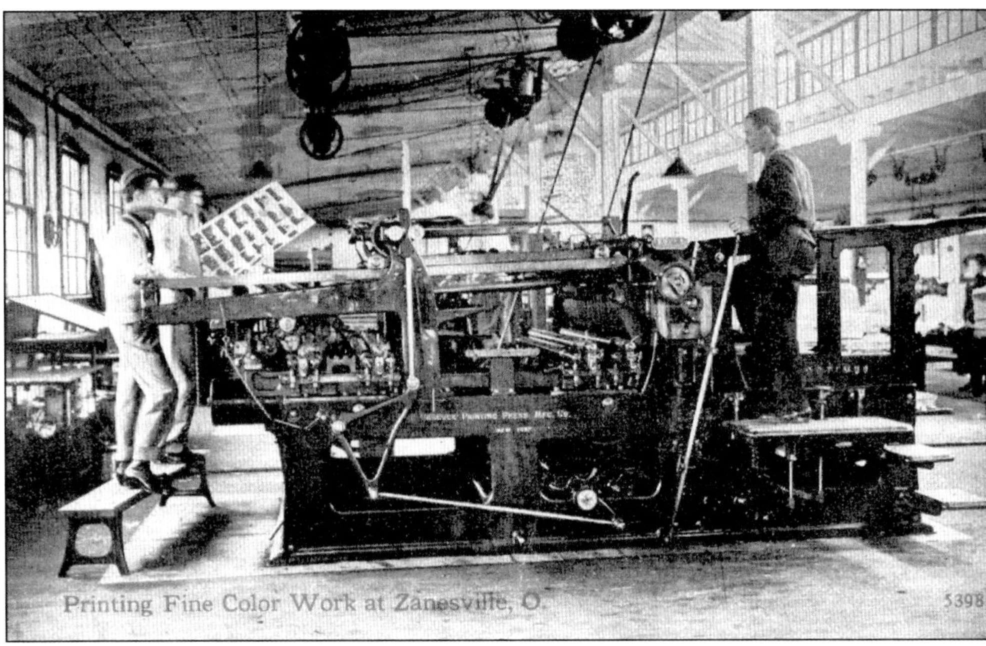

Printers at the Art Manufacturing Company are shown hard at work on the printing presses that turned out thousands of postcards each day. (Courtesy of Tom Brown.)

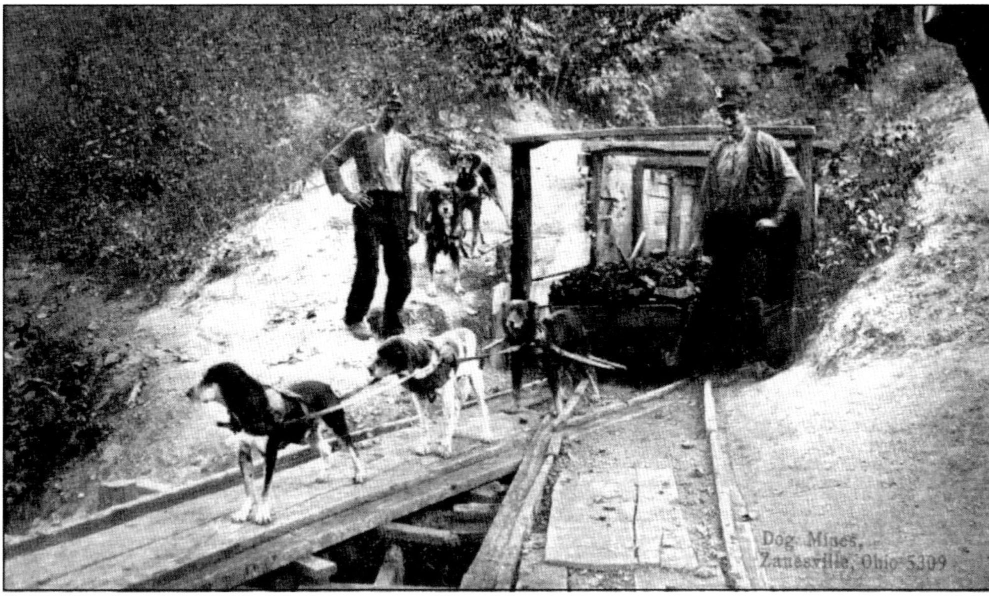

Coal mines once abounded within the city limits. There were as many as 50 mines in 1869 and at least half that many in the 1920s. Most of the mines were small one- or two-man operations. Dog teams were often used to pull loaded cars out of the mines. (Courtesy of Tom Brown.)

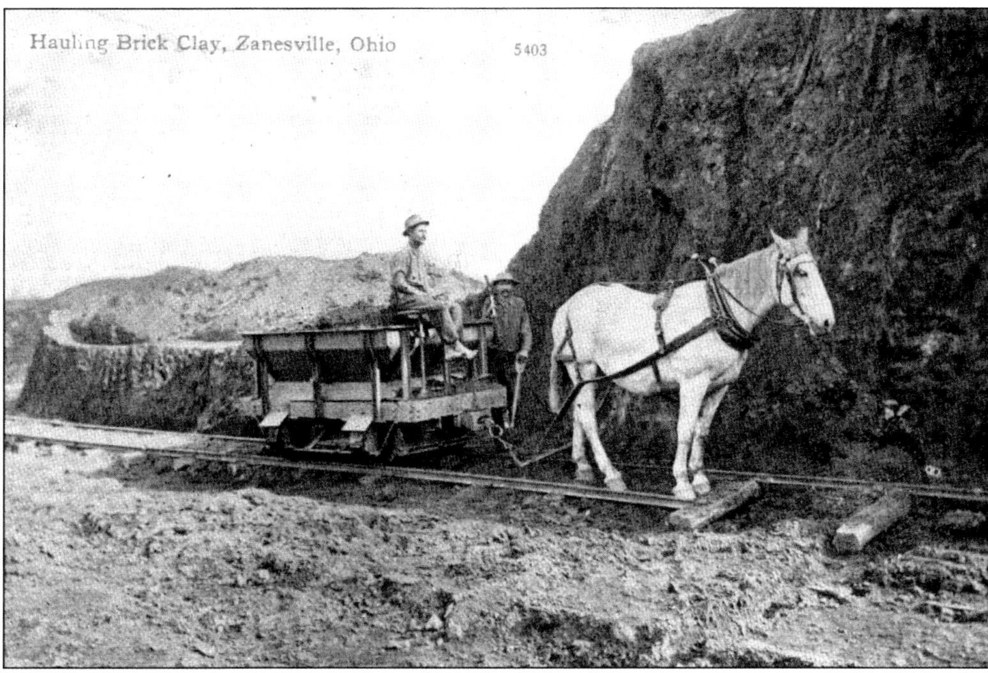

Vast sections of Pioneer Hill were mined for their rich deposits of clay and shale. Many former residents who returned to Zanesville were surprised when they saw how much of the top of the hill had disappeared. A horse-drawn wagon is seen hauling a load of clay to a nearby brick works in the early 1900s.

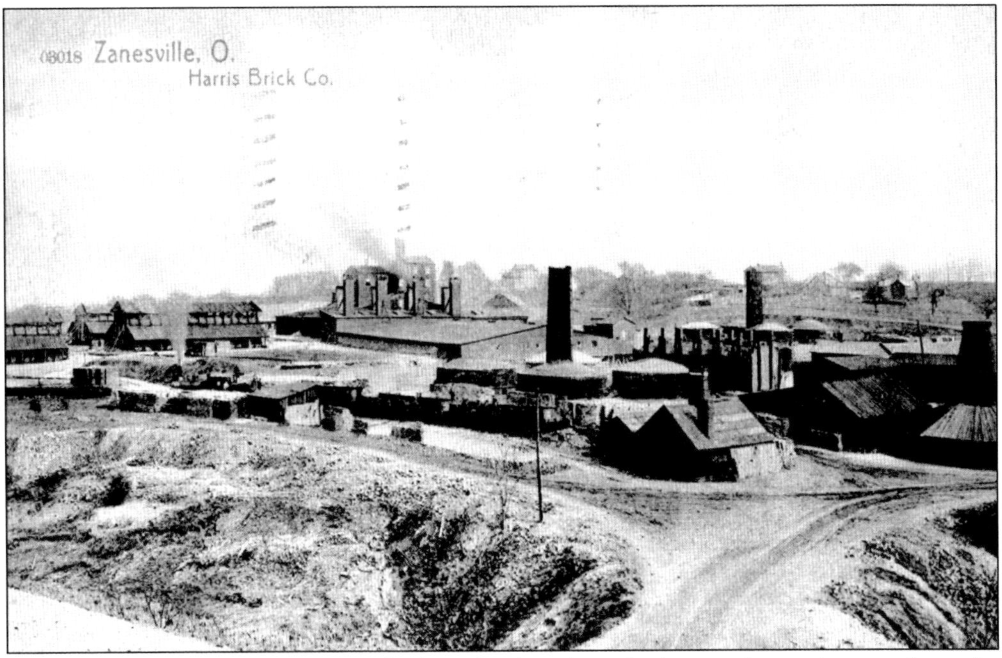

The Harris Brick Company operated a large brick-making facility on the city's east side in the 19th and 20th centuries. The Harris brothers began making bricks in 1860 and within a few years became very successful with the introduction of the vitrified street paver as the demand for brick-paved streets grew throughout the country. (Courtesy of Chance Brockway.)

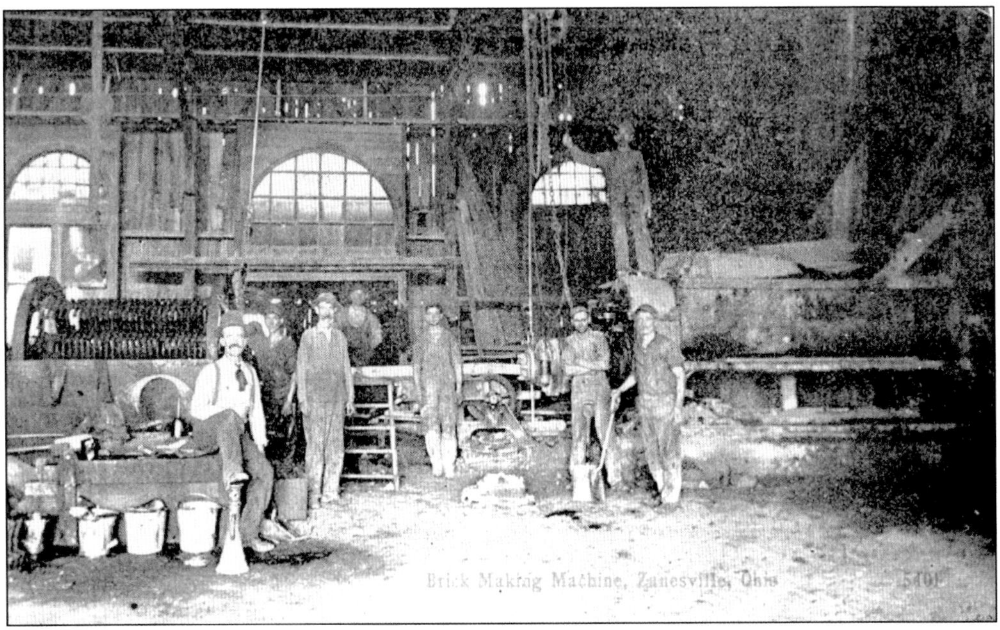

An early 1900s brick-making machine is shown here in operation. A ribbon of clay came from the pug mill, on the right, and was then cut into individual bricks by the apparatus shown on the left. (Courtesy of Chance Brockway.)

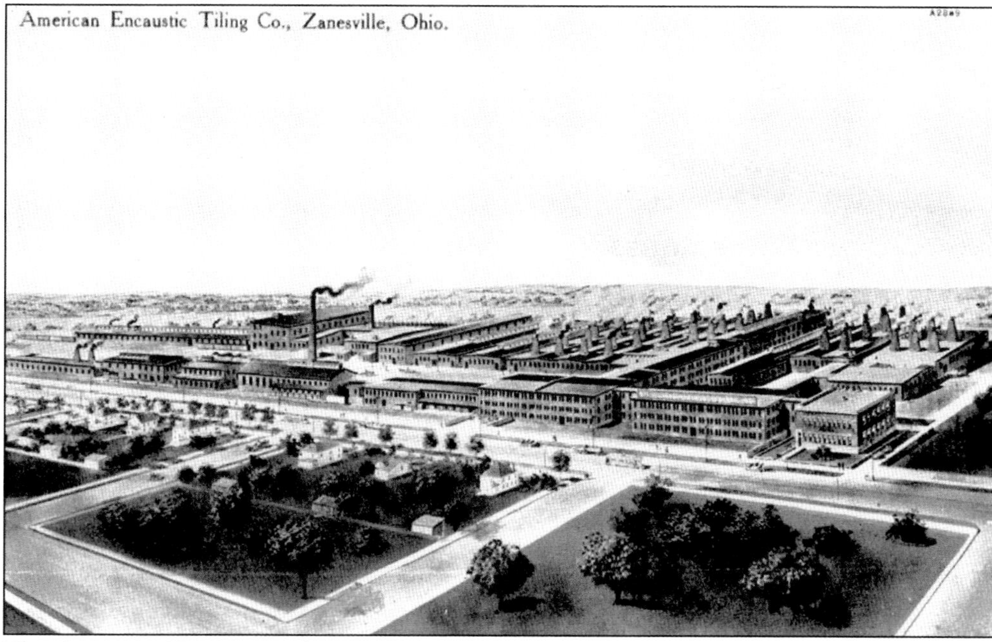

The American Encaustic Tile Company was organized in 1875 and, by 1888, employed more than 172 people. When orders out stripped the plants production capacity, the company built this tile-making facility on Linden Avenue in 1892. The tile company closed in 1935. (Courtesy of Chance Brockway.)

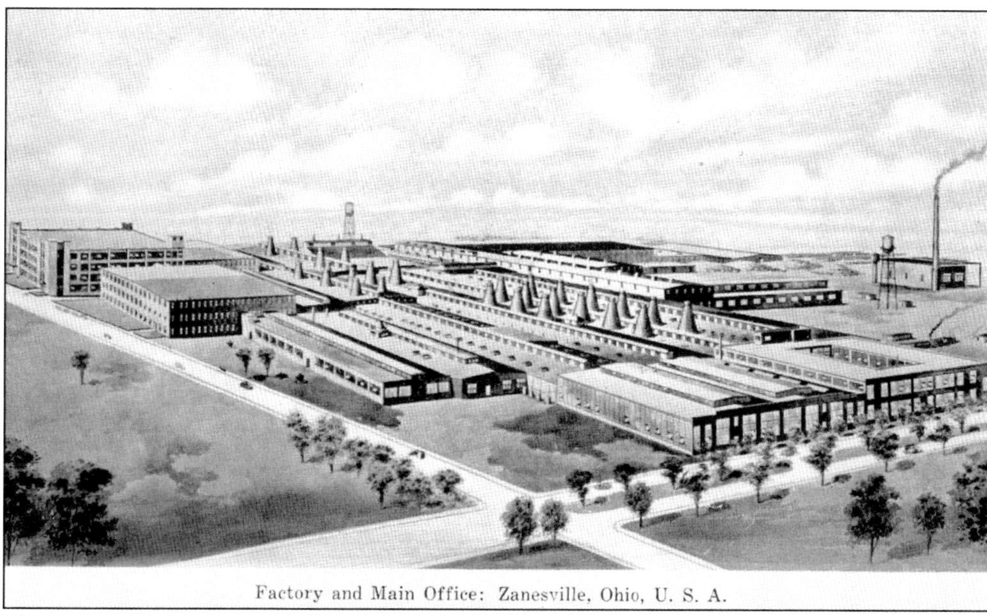

The Mosaic Tile Company began operations on Pershing Road in 1894. Former American Encaustic Tile employees Karl Langenbeck and Herman Mueller started the company with one kiln and 30 employees. At the height of its production history, the Mosaic Tile Company was the largest tile producer in the world. The company ceased operating in 1967. (Courtesy of Betty Ward.)

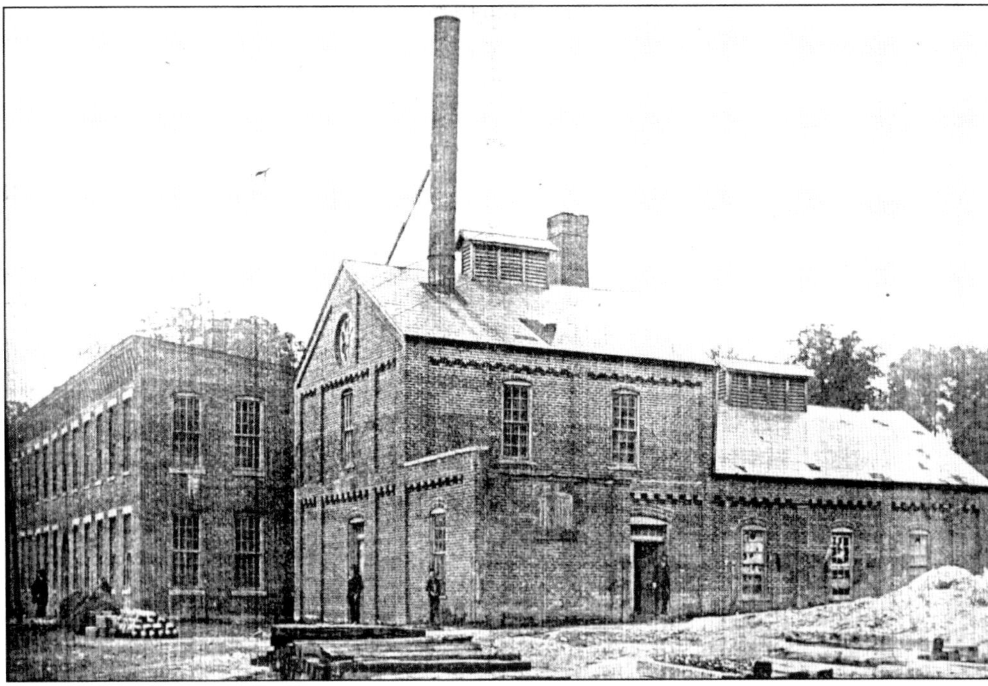

The Ohio Encaustic Tile Company was established in 1883 by a group of local businessmen as a speculative venture. It was located at the corner of Woodlawn Avenue and Pershing Road. The business failed in 1886. The idle buildings were sold at a sheriff's sale in 1887 and briefly became the E. G. Bowen Company. Bowen's stoneware manufacturing venture was reorganized in 1899 as the Zanesville Stoneware Company. (Courtesy of M. H. Linn III.)

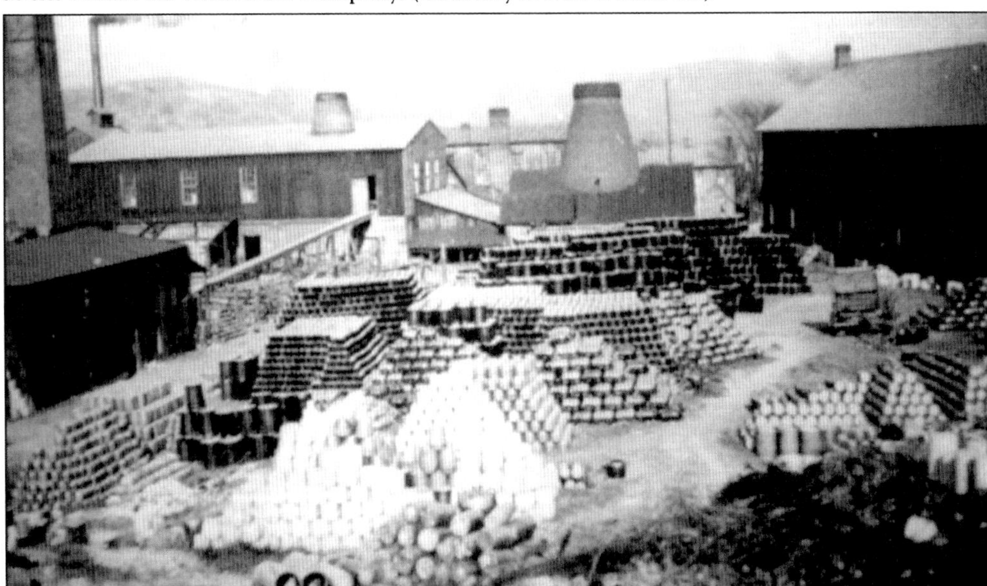

The Zanesville Stoneware Company was in full operation in this image from 1895. The stoneware company was one of the leading producers of utilitarian stoneware during the early part of the 20th century. A fire destroyed the building and many photographs of the company in 1990. (Courtesy of M. H. Linn III.)

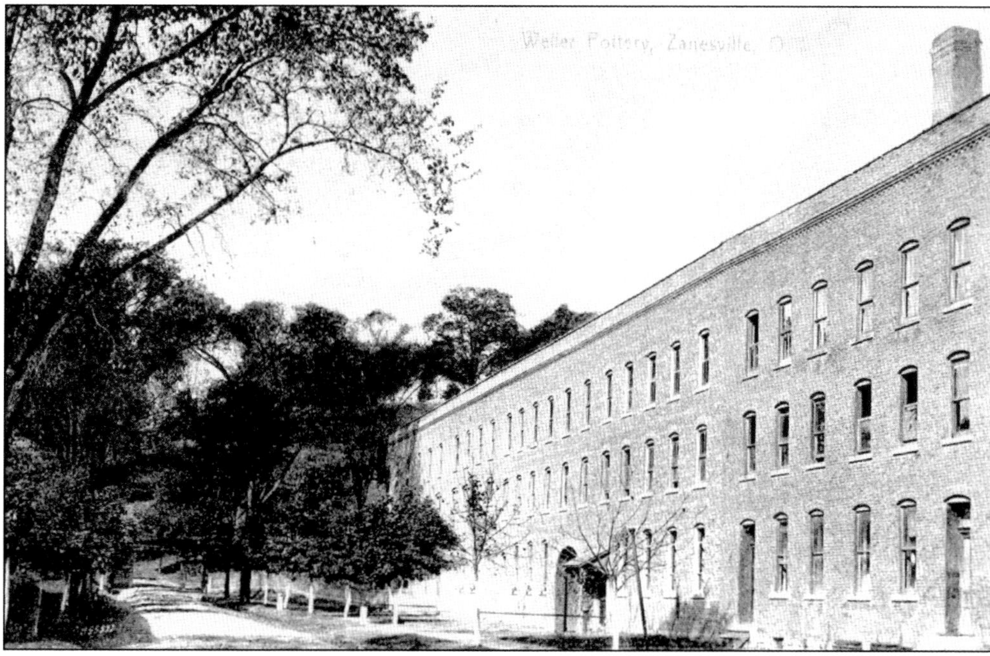

Samuel Weller moved his pottery operations to this building on Pierce Street in 1890. Weller's Pottery, the Roseville Pottery, and the J. B. Owens Pottery were known as the "big three" in Zanesville for art pottery production. (Courtesy of Chance Brockway.)

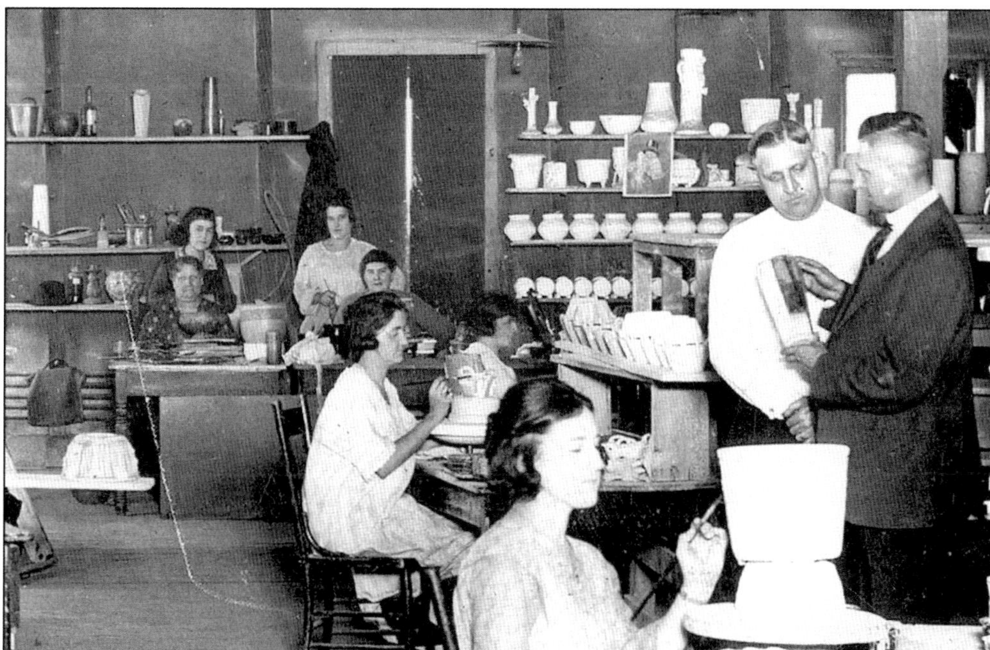

Weller Pottery employed many talented artists like the ones shown above in the 1920s. Note the two men standing to the right: Walter Gitter is on the left and Ed Pickens is on the right. (Courtesy of Wayne Estep.)

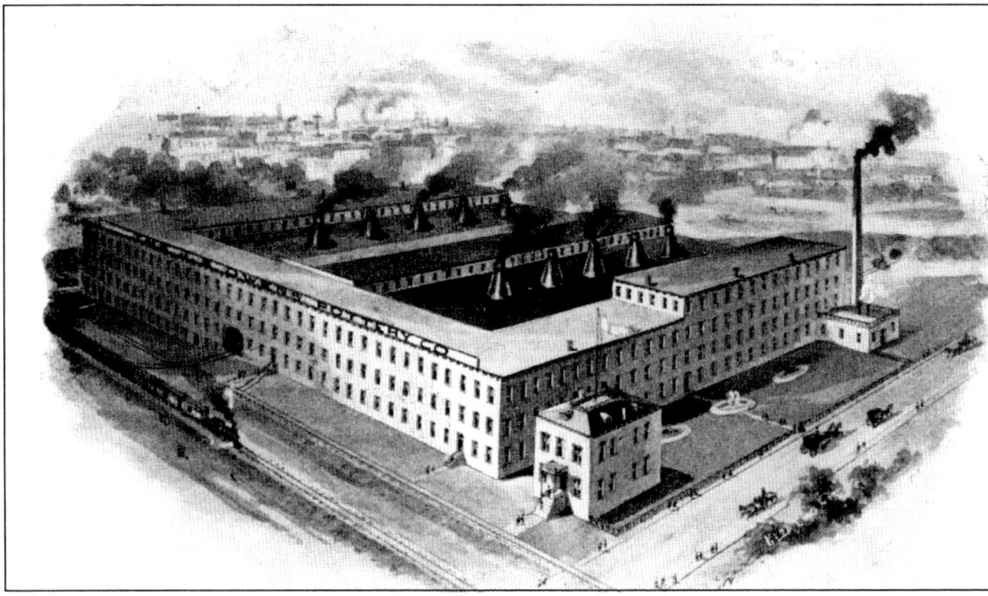

The J. B. Owens Pottery began operations in Roseville in 1885. With the offer of free land and greater access to the railroad to transport daily carloads of pottery, the company relocated in 1892 to Dearborn Street in the newly established Brighton subdivision. In 1906, the company went into receivership and later reemerged as the Zanesville Tile Company.

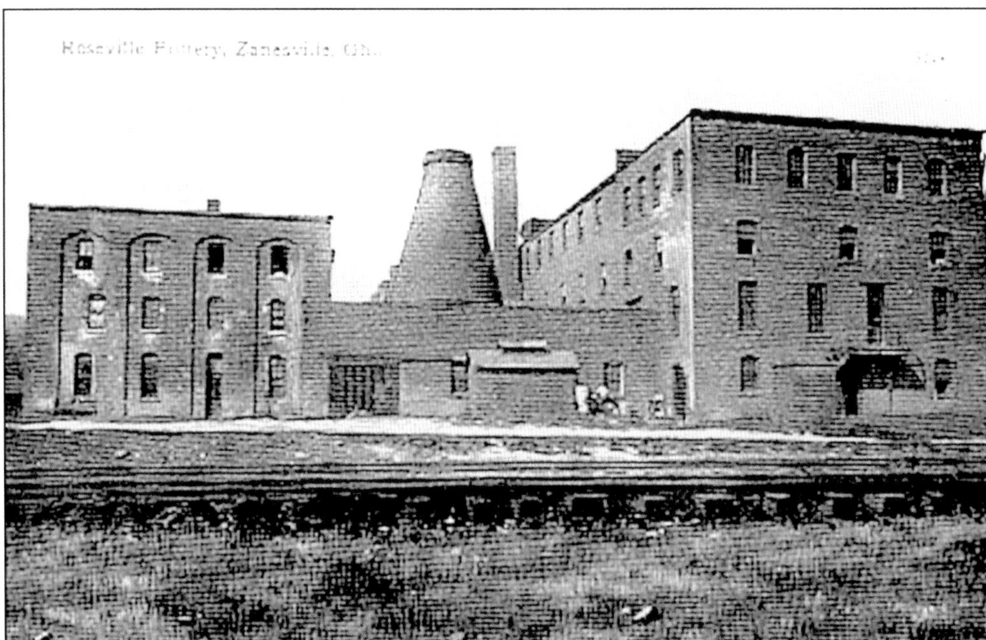

The Roseville Pottery began operations in Roseville in 1890. By 1898, the pottery had relocated to the buildings of the former Clark Stoneware Company on Linden Avenue. The pottery ceased operation in 1954.

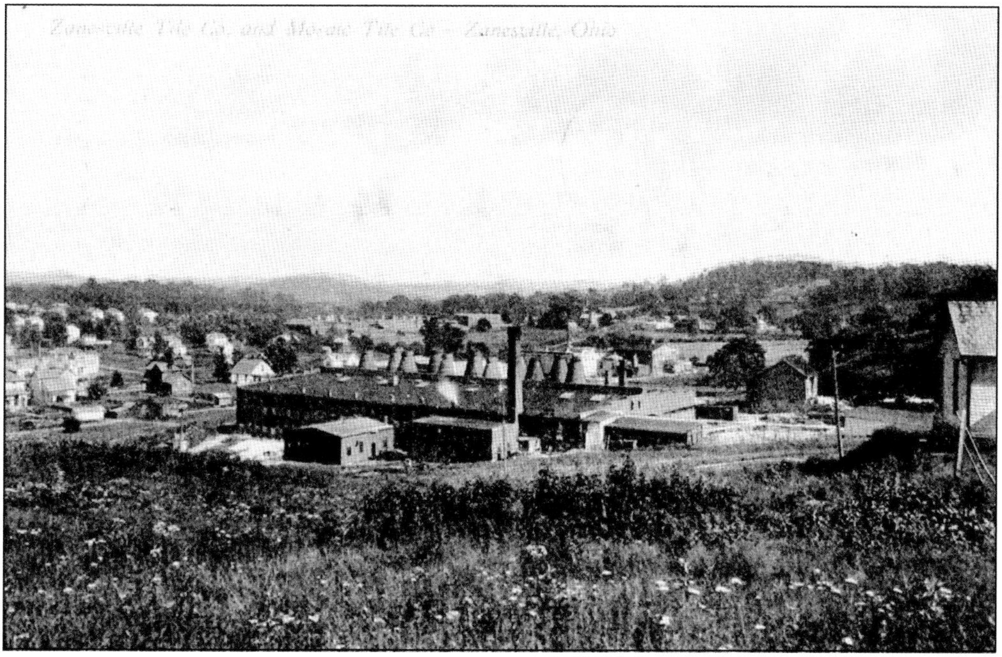

J. B. Owens established the Zanesville Tile Company, visible in the foreground, in 1906. The business failed and was twice reorganized, first as the J. B. Owens Floor and Wall Tile Company and then as the Empire Floor and Wall Tile Company. Fire destroyed the facility in 1928, but it was rebuilt in 1929. Because of the onset of the Great Depression, the facility never reopened. (Courtesy of Chance Brockway.)

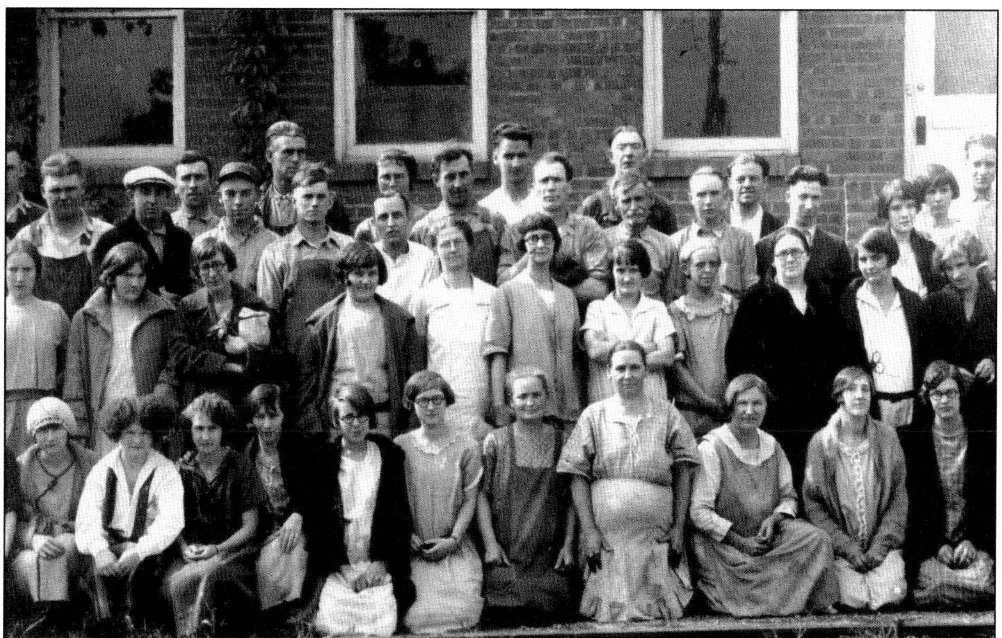

Employees of the Empire Floor and Wall Tile Company gathered for a company photograph in 1925. (Private collection.)

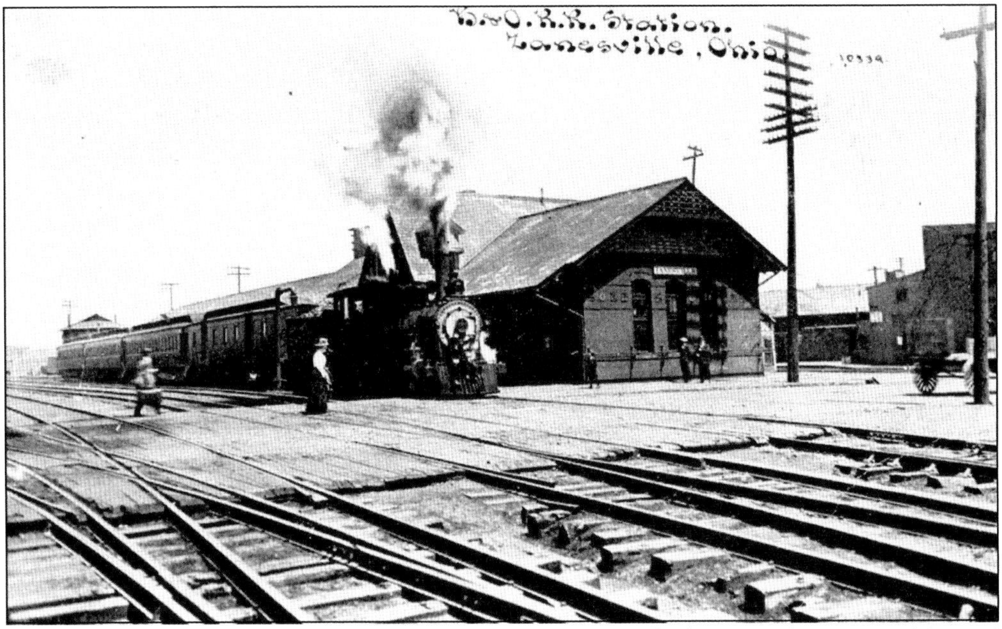

A Baltimore and Ohio train boards passengers at the Zanesville depot, at the corner of Second and Market Streets in the early 1900s. (Courtesy of Chance Brockway.)

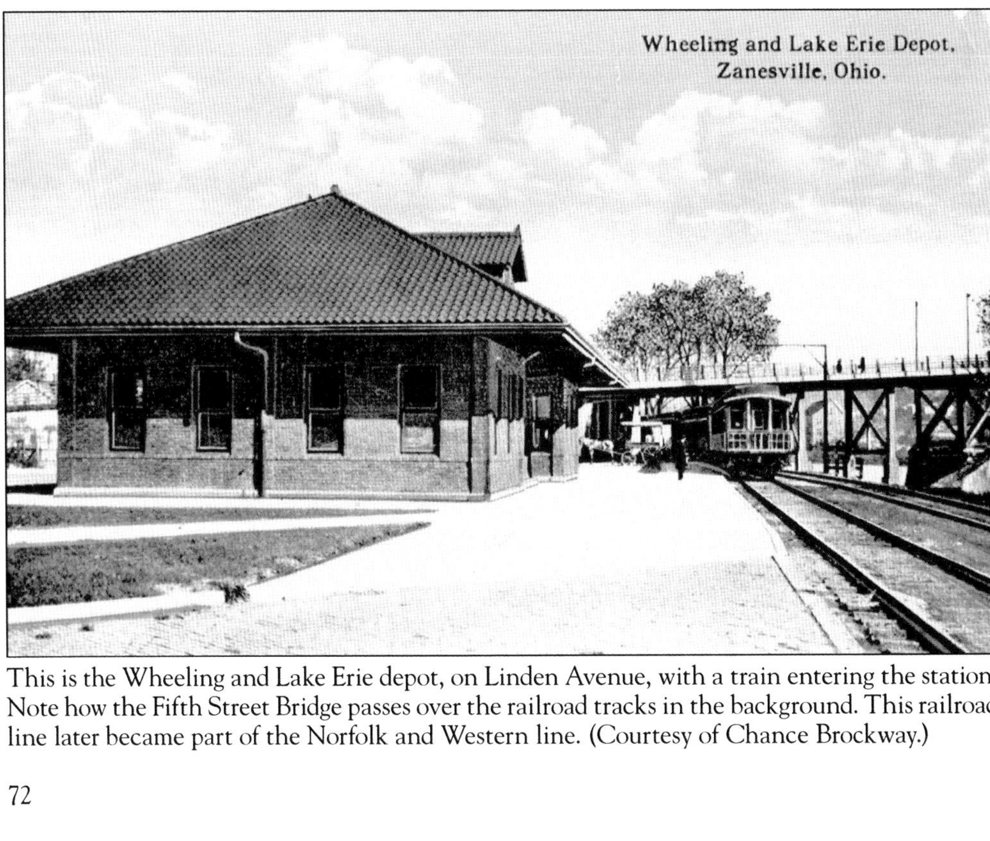

This is the Wheeling and Lake Erie depot, on Linden Avenue, with a train entering the station. Note how the Fifth Street Bridge passes over the railroad tracks in the background. This railroad line later became part of the Norfolk and Western line. (Courtesy of Chance Brockway.)

Six

TRAINS, TROLLEYS, AUTOMOBILES, AND AN AIRPLANE

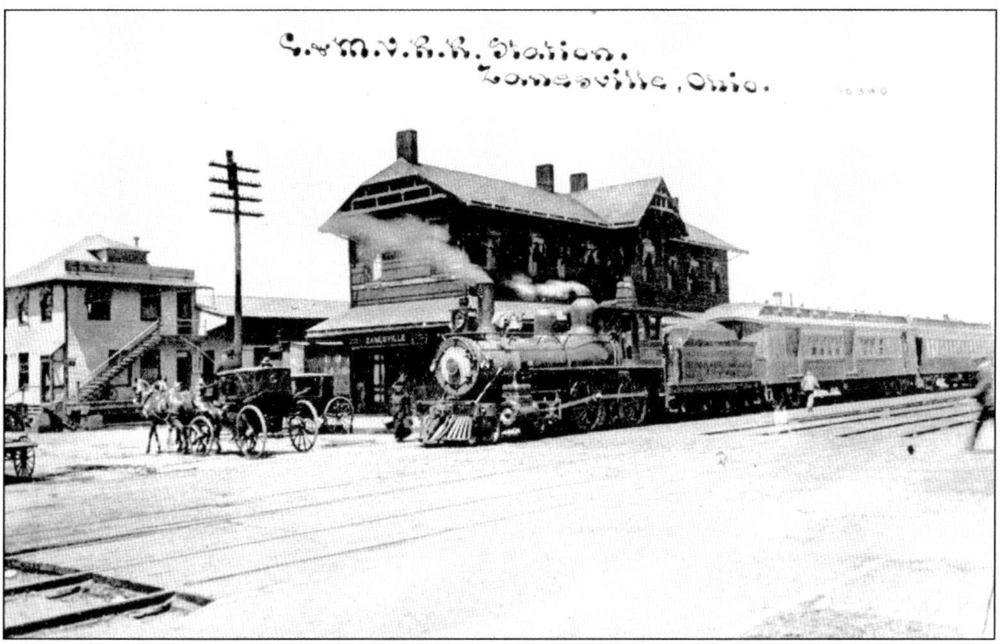

A passenger train, pulled by a 4-4-0 engine, is shown stopped beside the Zanesville depot of the Cincinnati and Muskingum Valley Railroad, located at the corner of First and Market Streets. Tracks for the Cincinnati and Muskingum Valley Railroad were laid down in Zanesville in 1854, and the line eventually became part of the Pennsylvania Railroad. (Courtesy of Chance Brockway.)

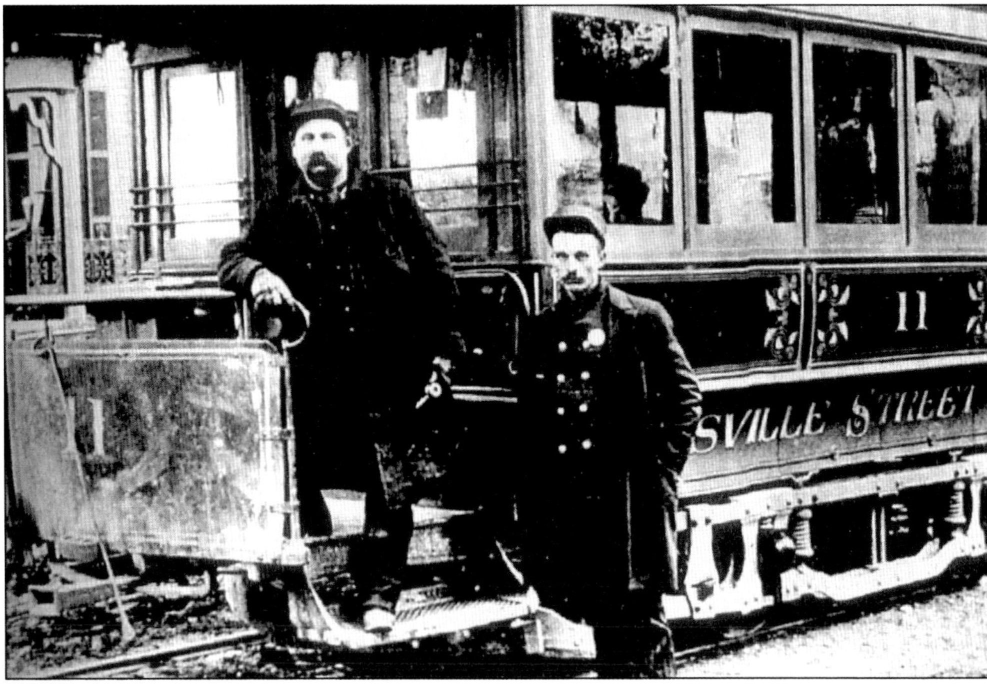

Mule- and Horse-drawn trolleys were a popular means of public transportation within the city between 1875 and 1890. (Courtesy of Wayne Estep.)

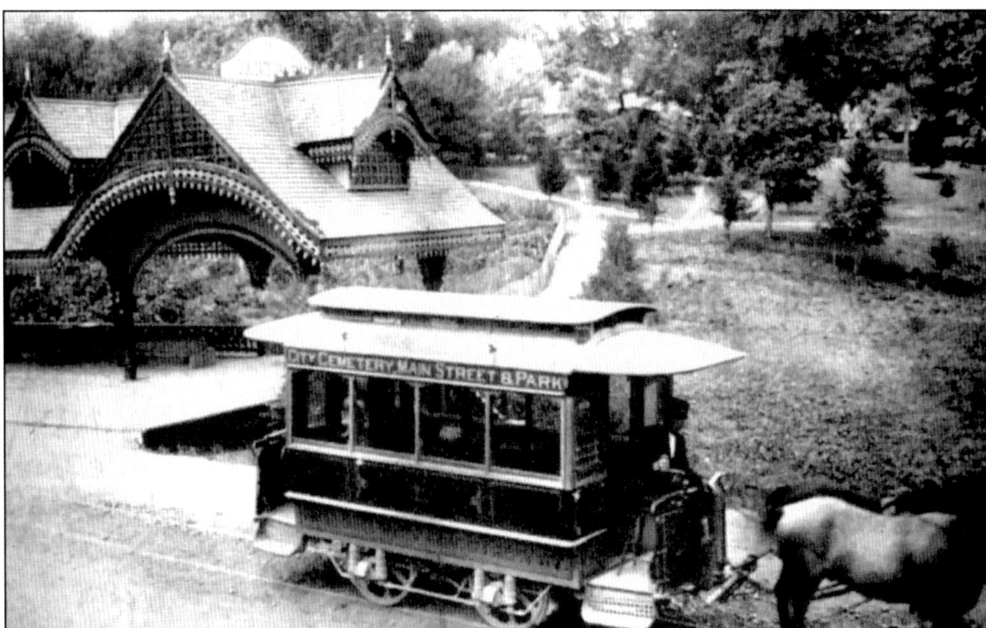

A horse-drawn trolley that traveled between the City Cemetery, Main Street, and Grant Park is shown leaving the park in the late 1880s.

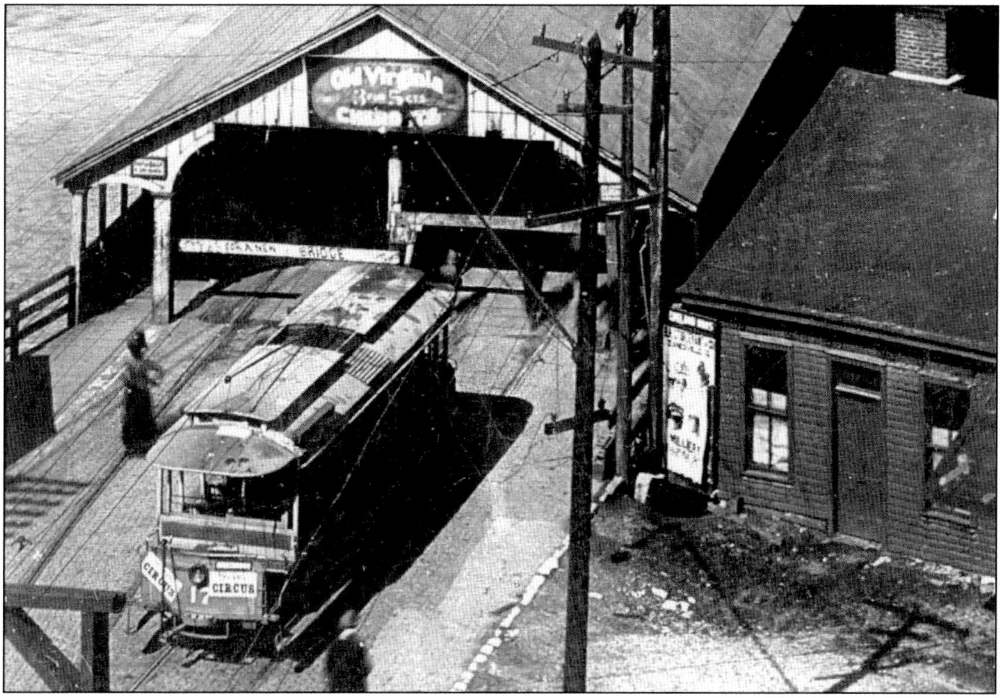

By 1890, electric streetcars became the preferred method of getting around town. A streetcar is shown coming off the Main Street end of the Y Bridge in 1900. Note the sign near the roof of the covered bridge, asking people to "Say Yes for a New Bridge." A campaign to gain public support for the construction of a new Y Bridge was in progress at this time. (Courtesy of Wayne Estep.)

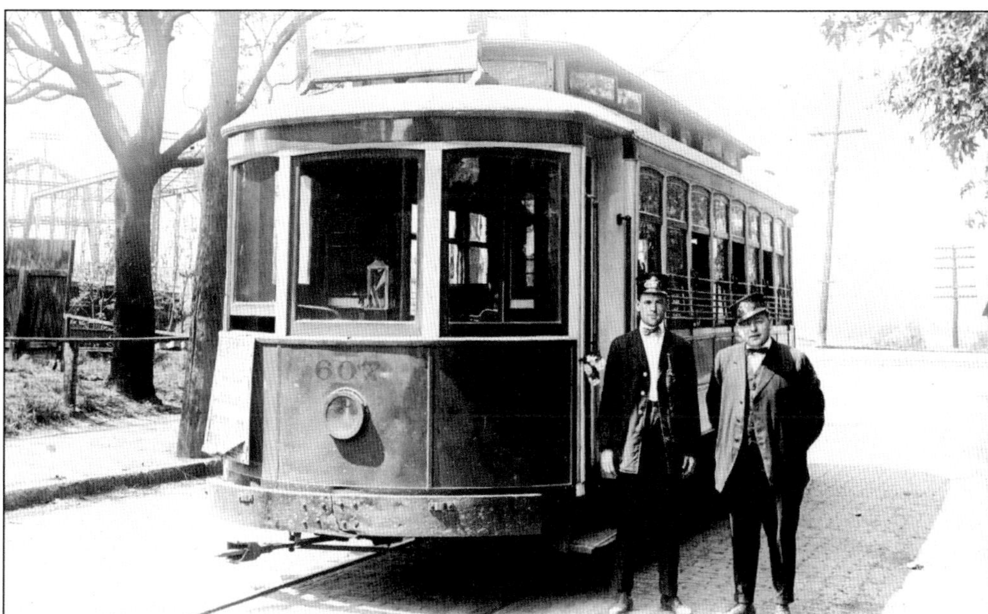

Streetcar No. 607 is shown near the Monroe Street Bridge in the late 1920s. Note the paper advertisement on the front of the streetcar. It reads "Liberty-Elsie Ferguson-Hearts of the Wild-Tues-Wed-Thurs- May 27-28-29." (Courtesy of Tom Brown.)

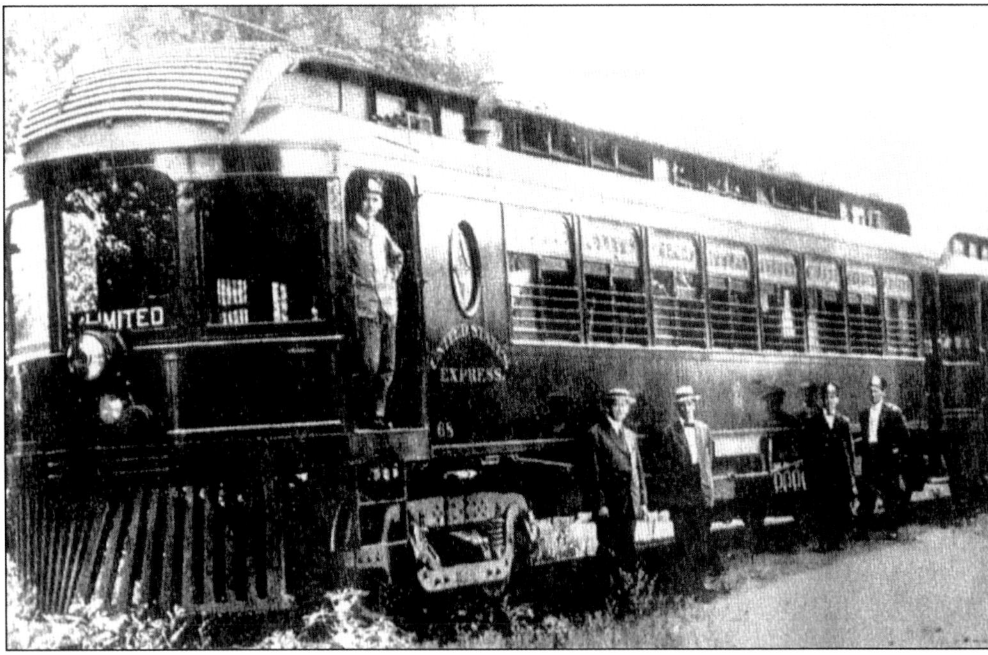

Electric-powered streetcars like interurbans provided an alternative to regular railroad service. Their popularity grew during the first two decades of the 20th century. The Columbus, Newark, and Zanesville Railroad opened a line between these three cities in 1904. The Southeastern Ohio Railway, Light, and Power Company built a line to South Zanesville in 1905 and eventually extended the tracks to Crooksville. (Courtesy of Wayne Estep.)

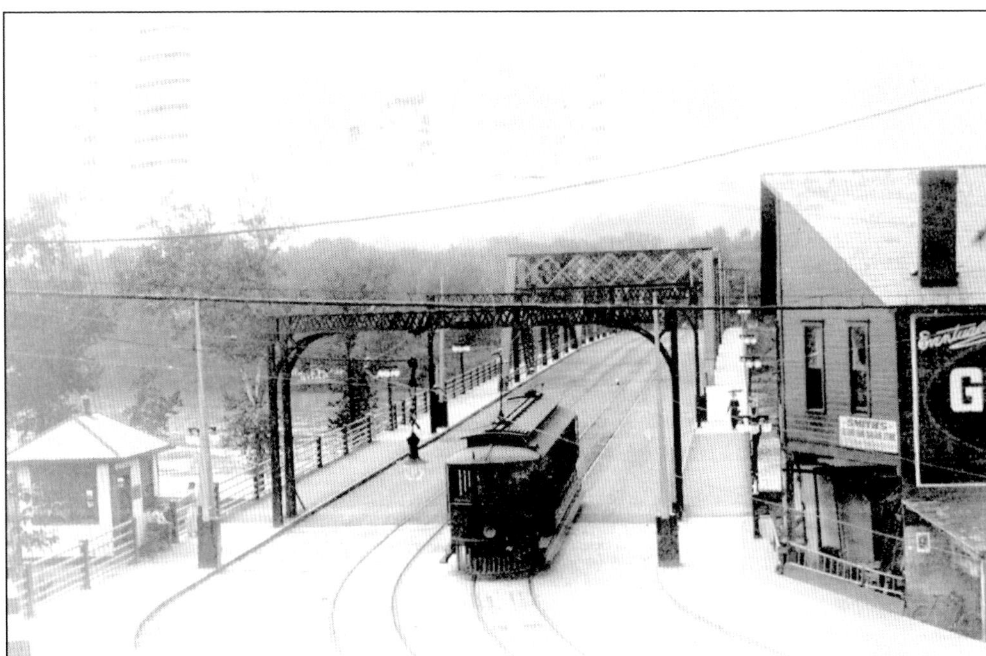

An interurban is shown coming off the downtown end of the Sixth Street Bridge in 1918. (Courtesy of Chance Brockway.)

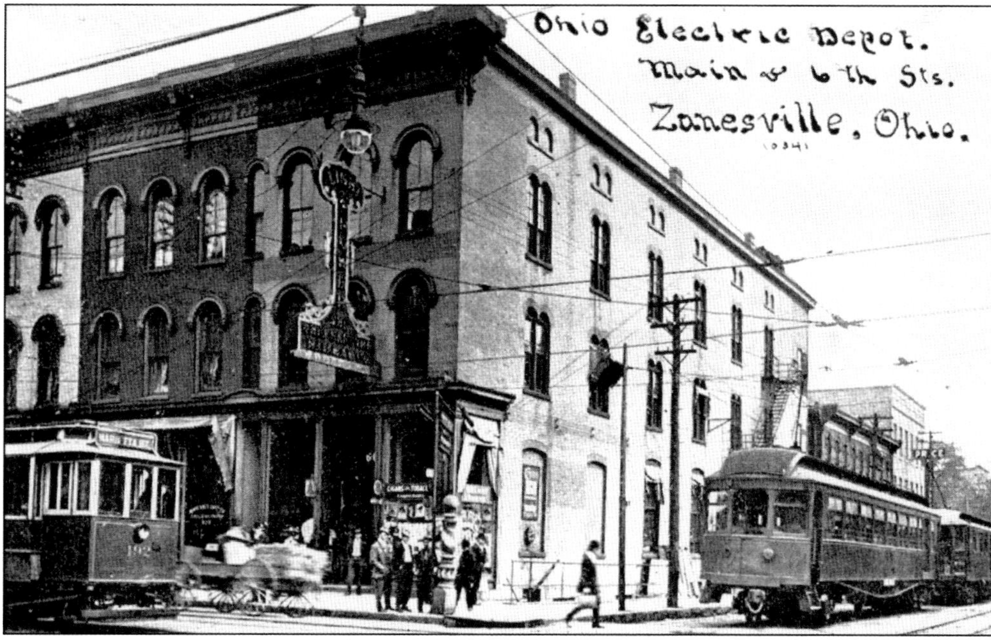

Interurban cars from the Columbus, Newark, and Zanesville line departed every hour from the company's depot at the corner of Sixth and Main Streets. Upon arriving in Newark, passengers could change cars to transfer to lines traveling to either Buckeye Lake or Columbus. (Courtesy of Chance Brockway.)

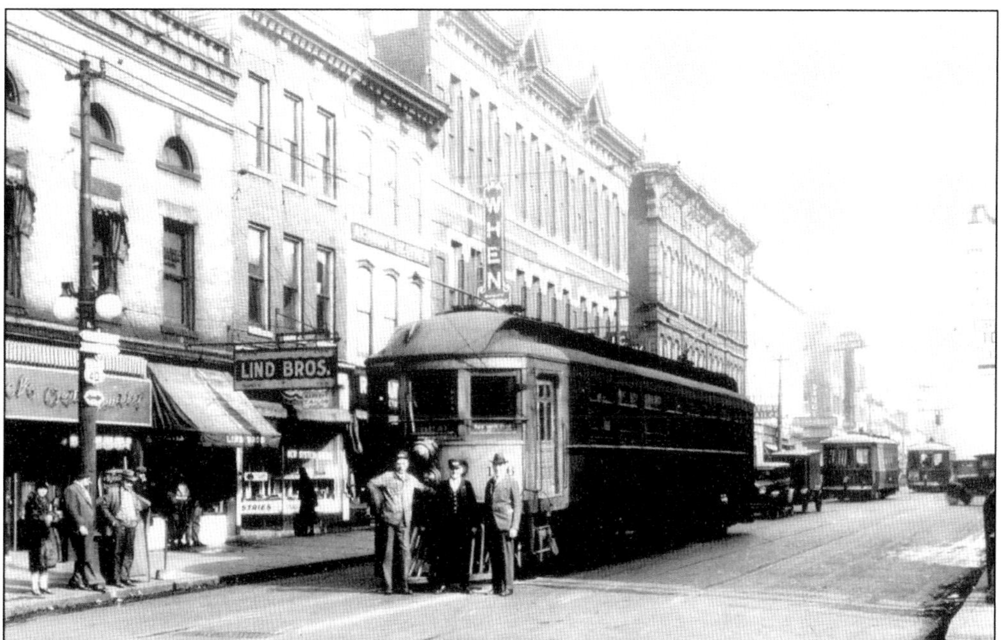

The Columbus, Newark, and Zanesville interurban is shown shortly before it departs on its final run between Zanesville and Newark on February 15, 1929. (Courtesy of Wayne Estep.)

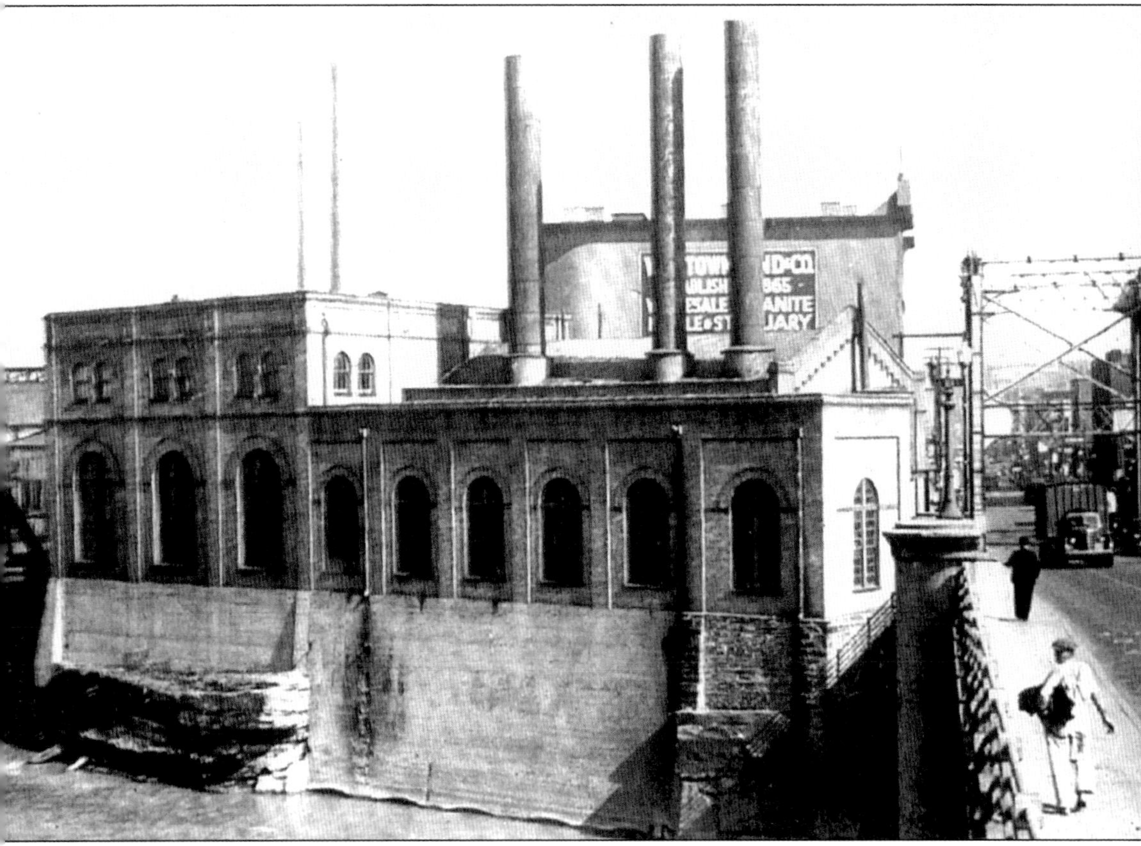

The Southeastern Ohio Railway, Light, and Power Company built this hydraulic power plant in 1903 to provide its interurbans with electricity. The Southeastern Ohio Railway interurbans ceased operation in 1924. The power plant is shown in this image shortly before it was razed in 1945. (Courtesy of Wayne Estep.)

Charles Fritz is shown at the lever of his Locomobile Steamer in 1901. In 1905, he was arrested for driving in excess of six miles an hour. Fritz, along with his brother J. S. took their passion for cars and turned it into a profitable business.

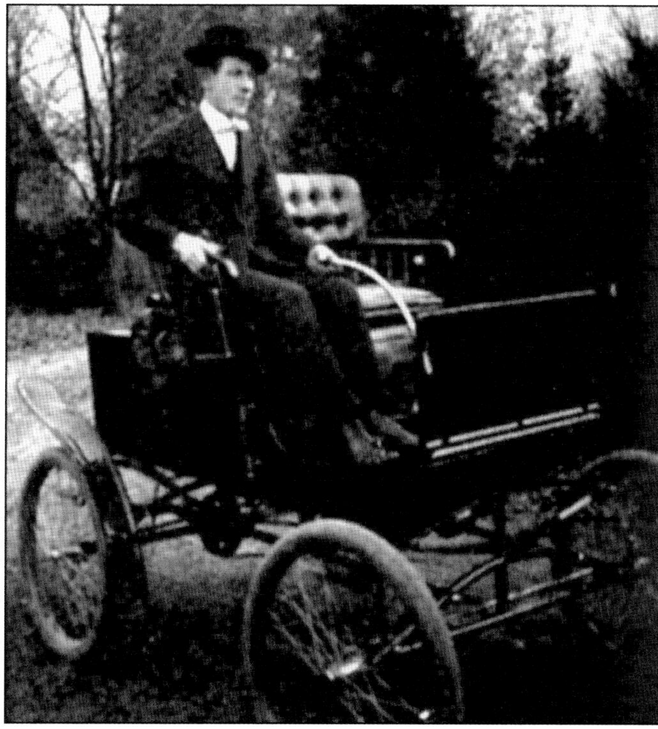

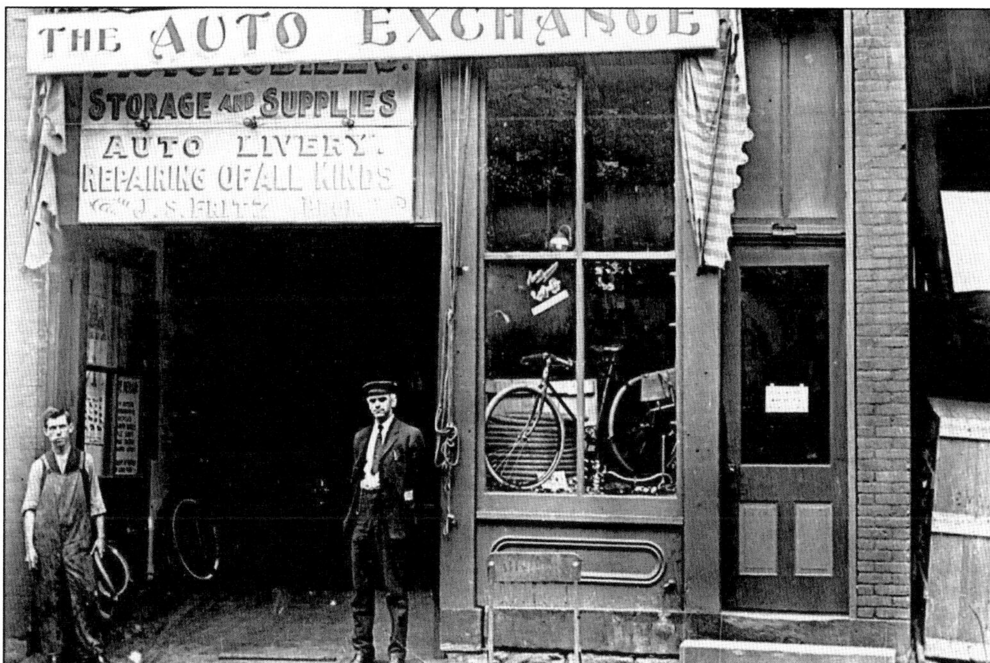

This is the Auto Exchange in 1902. It started out as the Bicycle Shop at 19 North Sixth Street. As the automobile became commercially available and local citizens began to take an interest in owning automobiles, J. S. Fritz turned his bicycle shop into the first automobile dealership in Zanesville. (Courtesy of Chance Brockway.)

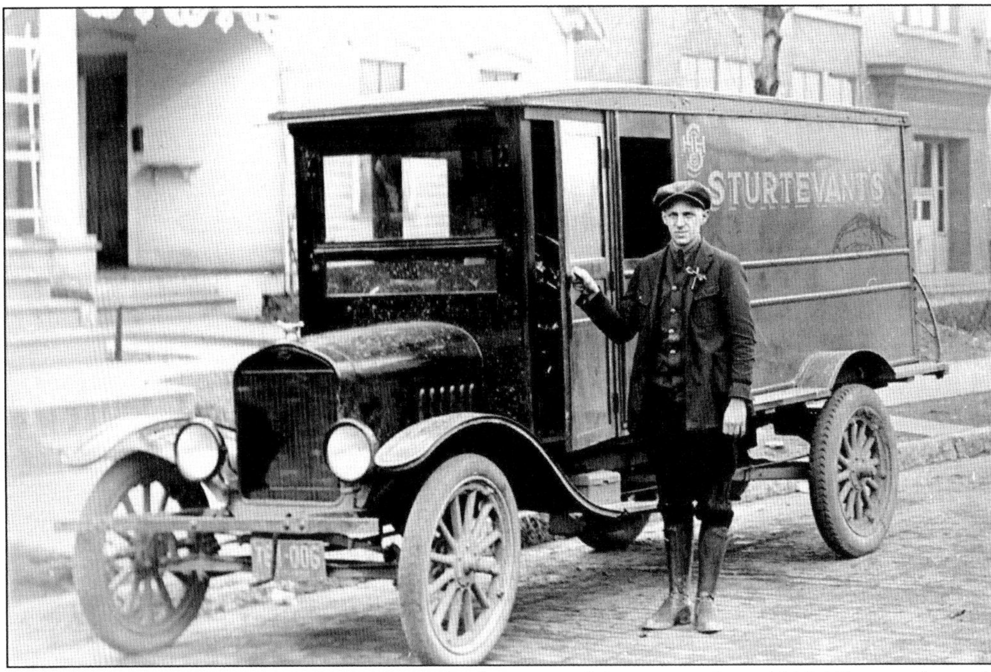

The H. H. Sturtevant Department Store had its own delivery truck in 1915. The truck made deliveries all over town from the store's location at the corner of Third and Main Streets. (Courtesy of Mose Mesre.)

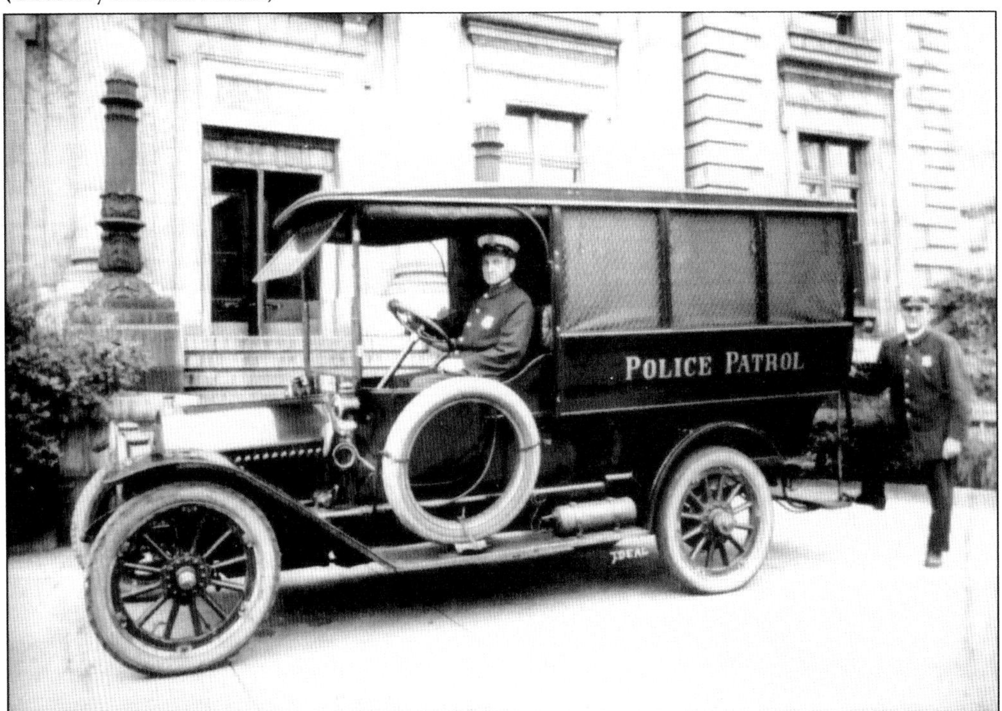

A police patrol car is shown parked beside the post office, at the corner of Fifth and South Streets, in 1913. (Courtesy of MCCOGS.)

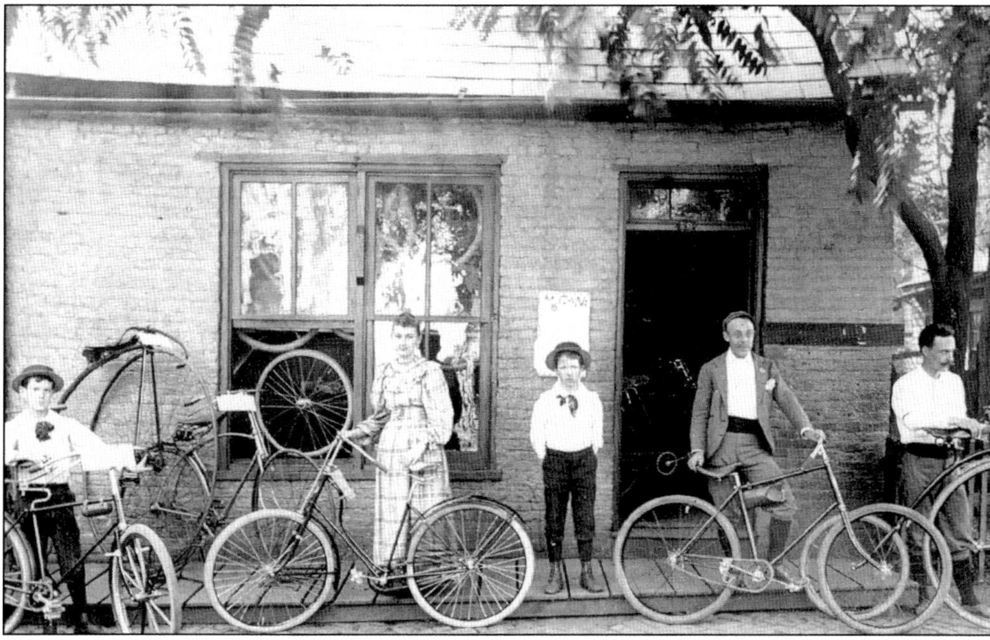

This is the Perry Gath Bicycle Shop in 1892. It operated at the corner of Sixth and Main Streets. Gath, shown standing at the far right, later became the manager of the Wedge Garage Company. (Courtesy of Wayne Estep.)

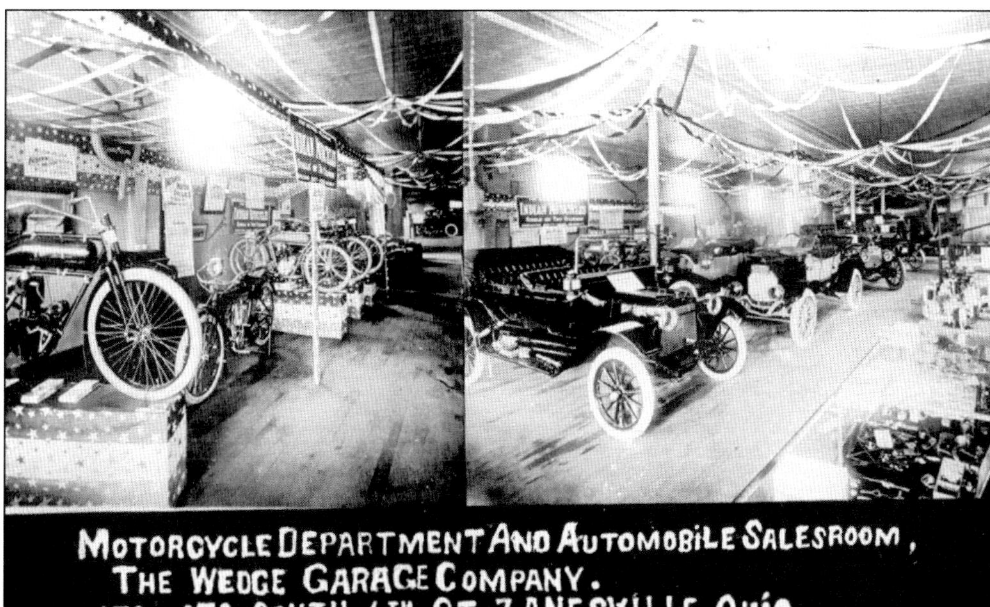

The Wedge Garage Company was located at 170–172 South Sixth Street and sold Hupmobiles, Maxwells, RCEs, and Lozier automobiles as well as Indian motorcycles. A 1912 newspaper article stated that the Wedge Garage Company had sold 21 vehicles that year. (Courtesy of Chance Brockway.)

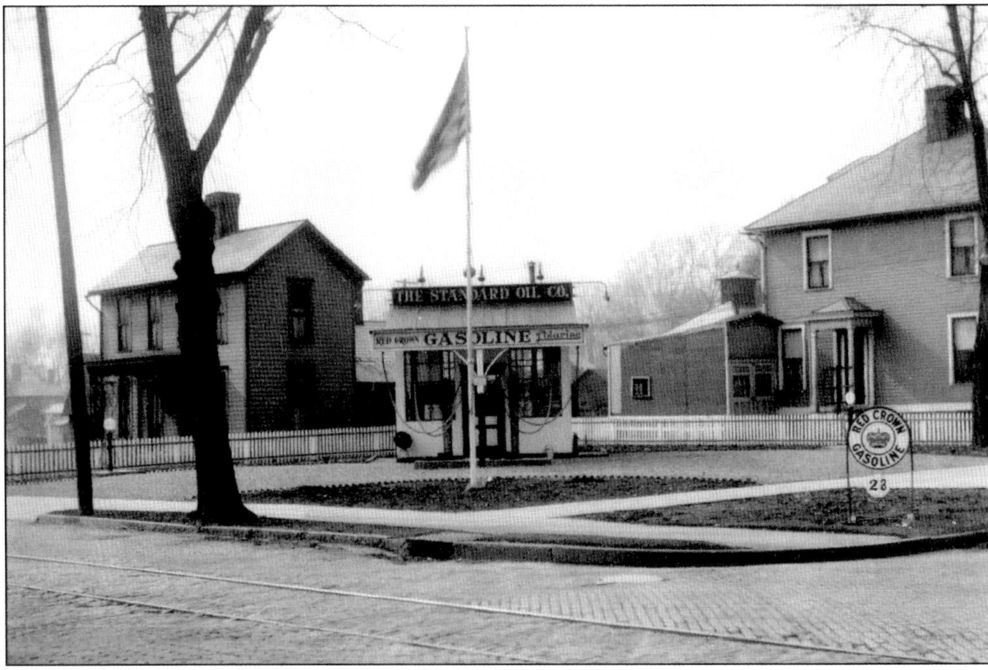

This Standard Oil filling station was one of five the company operated in Zanesville in the 1920s. Its surroundings suggest that the station may have been the one located on Linden Avenue. Other Standard Oil filling stations were located on Main, Market, and Sixth Streets and on Cooper Mill (now Pershing) Road. (Courtesy of Wayne Estep.)

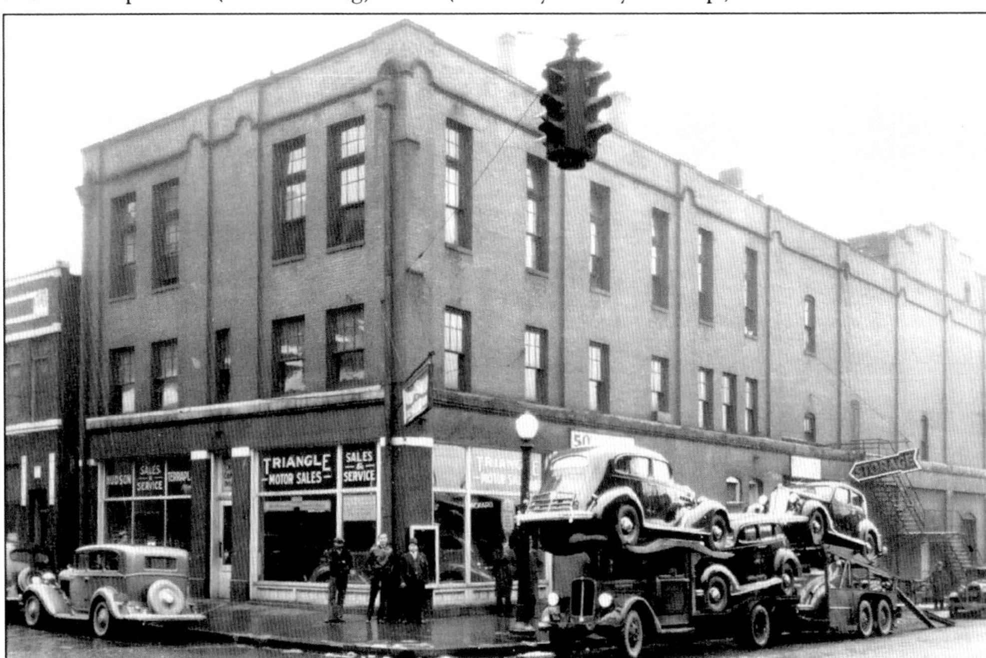

This is the Triangle Motors car dealership in 1936. They sold Hudsons, Packards, and Terraplanes from their Fourth and Market Streets location. Note that four new Packards had just been delivered. (Courtesy of Wayne Estep.)

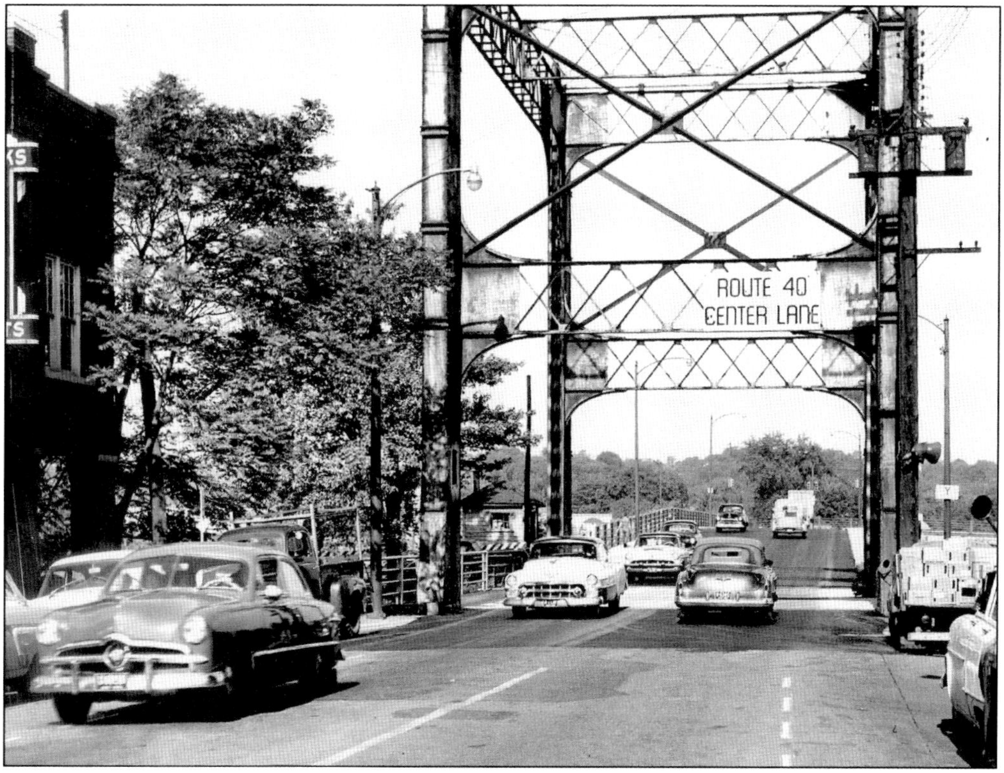

Cars are shown coming off the Y Bridge into the downtown area in the early 1950s. (Courtesy of the *Zanesville Times Recorder.*)

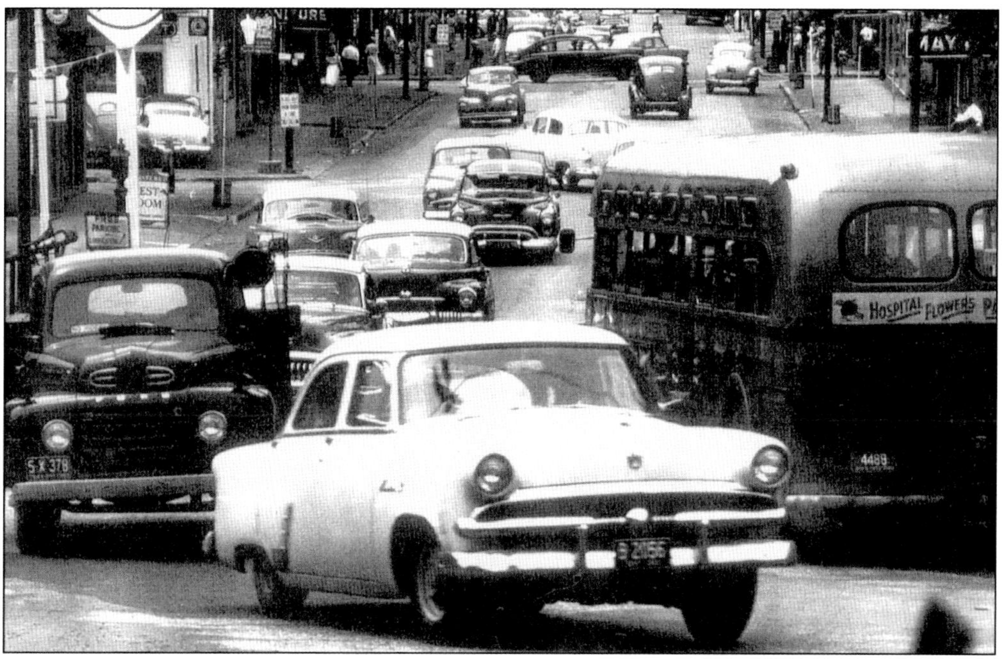

Cars and trucks make the turn from Main Street onto Underwood Street in the 1950s. (Courtesy of Wayne Estep.)

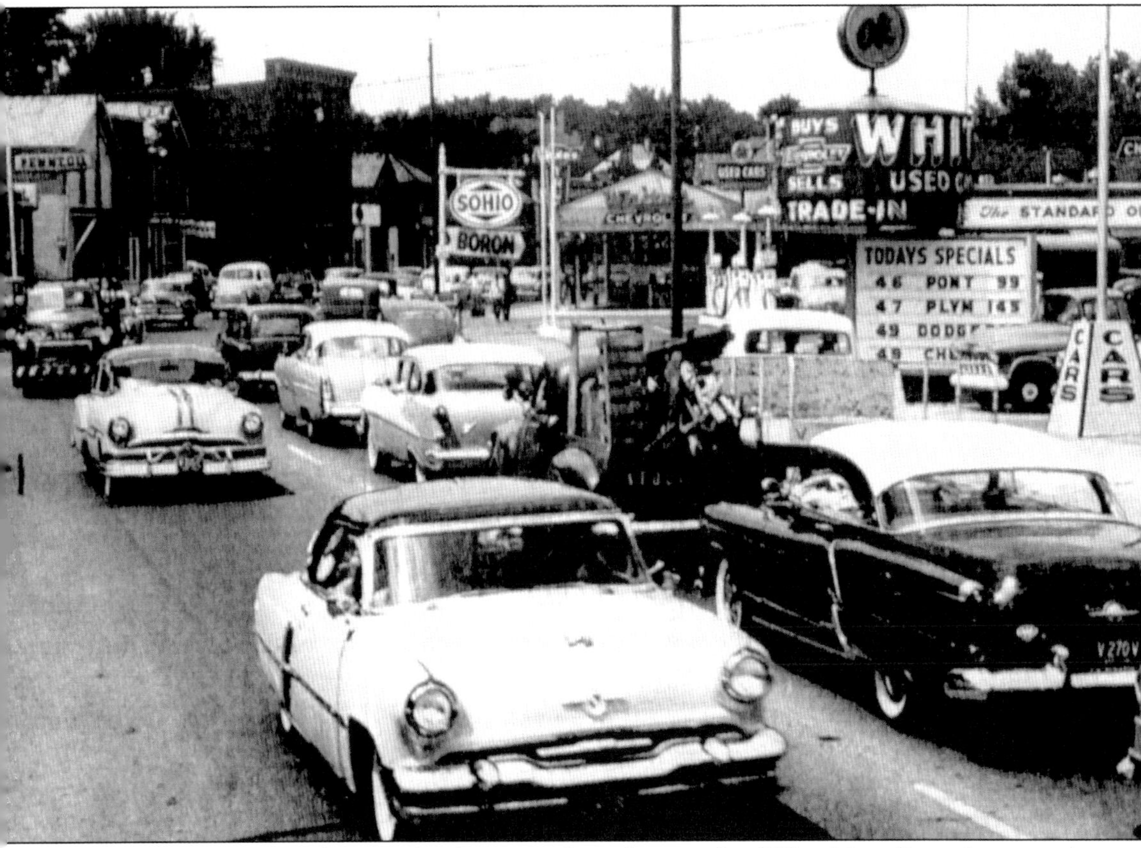

A steady of stream of cars make their way along the stretch of West Main Street between the end of the Y Bridge and Pine Street in the 1950s. Note the sign for one of the Standard Oil filling stations on the right. (Courtesy of Wayne Estep.)

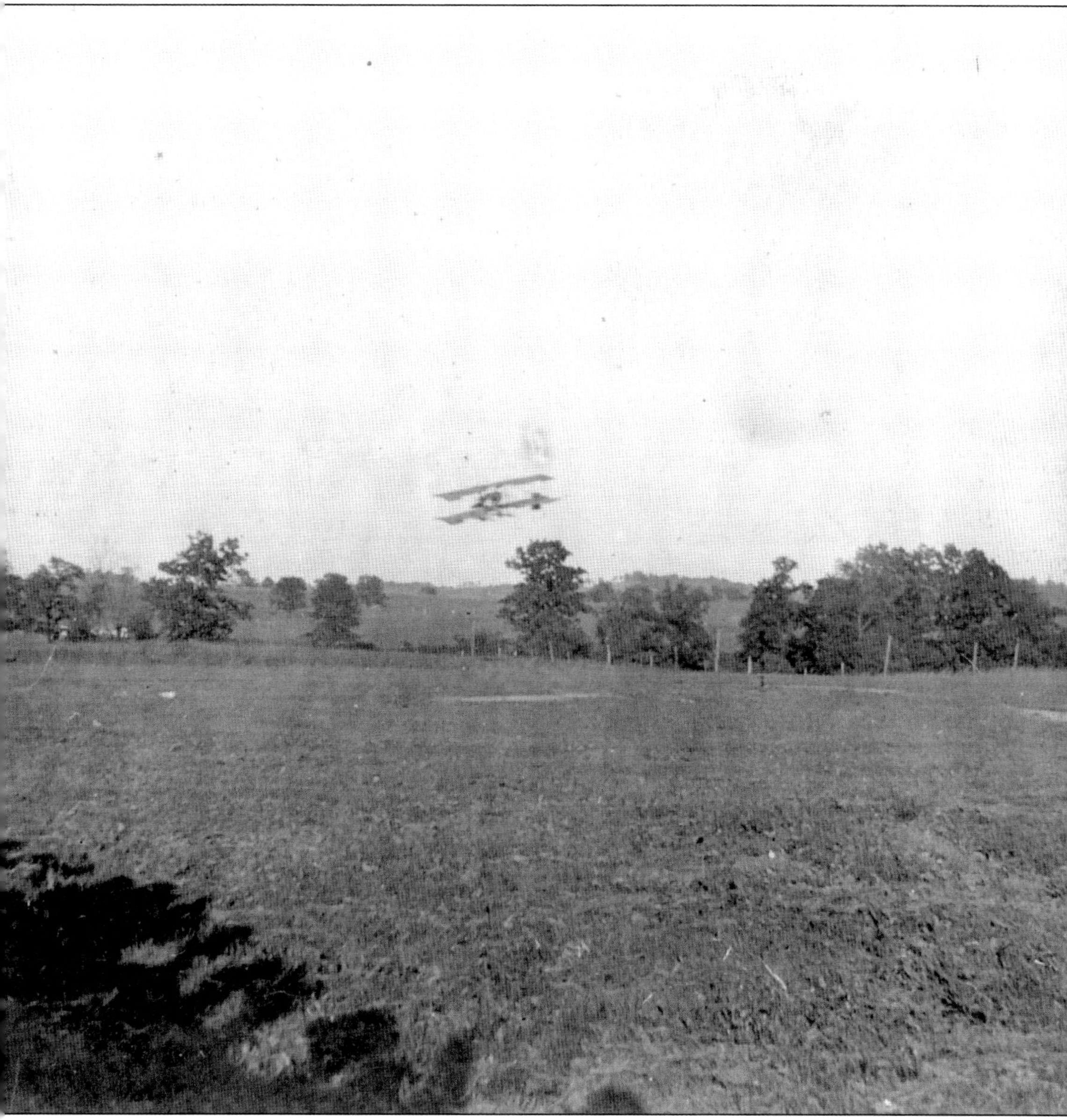

In 1911, Lincoln Beechy used a flat area at the fairgrounds as a landing strip when he made what were probably the first airplane flights over the city. (Courtesy of Wayne Estep.)

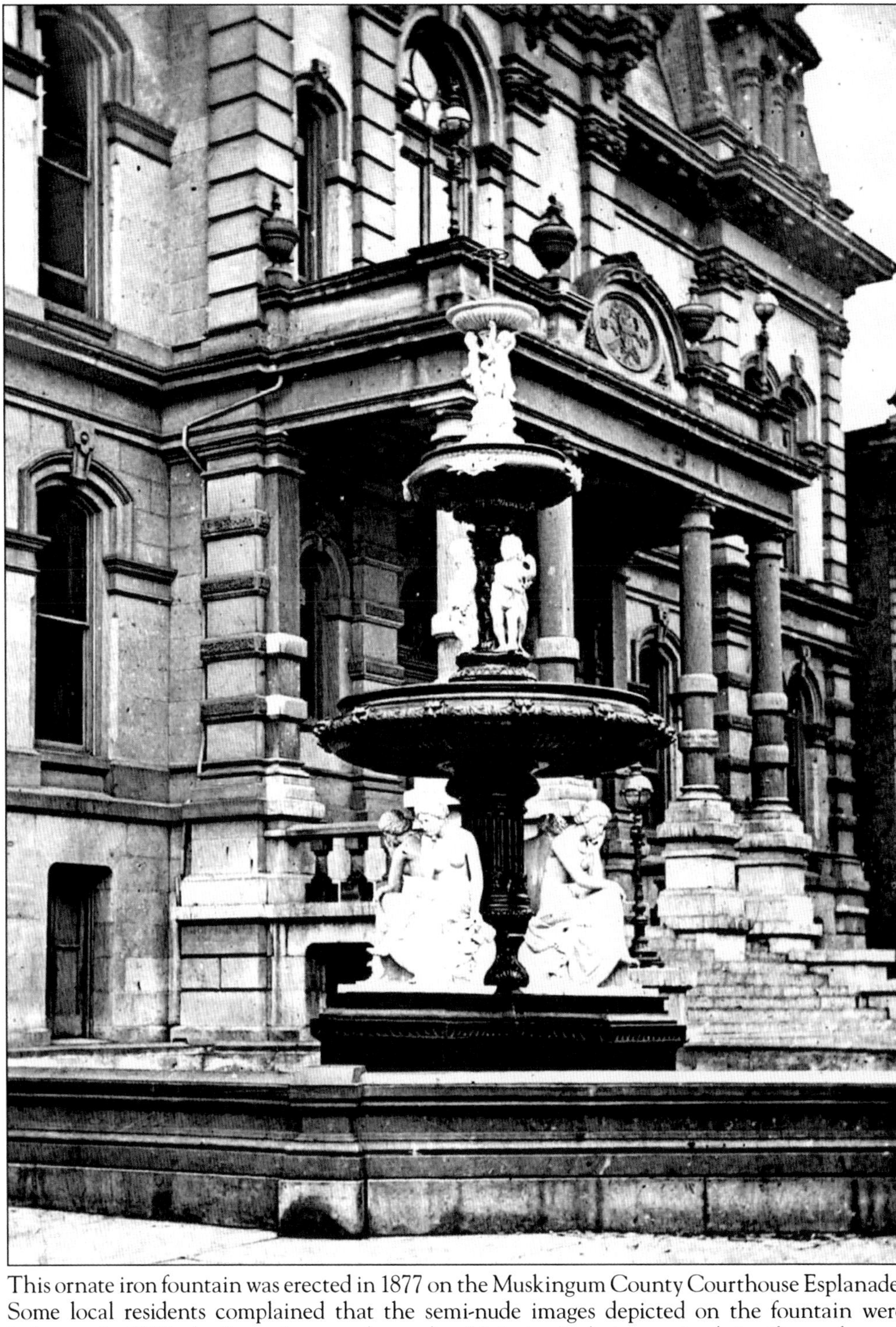

This ornate iron fountain was erected in 1877 on the Muskingum County Courthouse Esplanade. Some local residents complained that the semi-nude images depicted on the fountain were indecent. In 1900, the fountain was relocated to McIntire Park. It sustained significant damage during the Flood of 1913 and was ultimately sold for scrap. (Private collection.)

Seven

Local, State, and Federal Landmarks

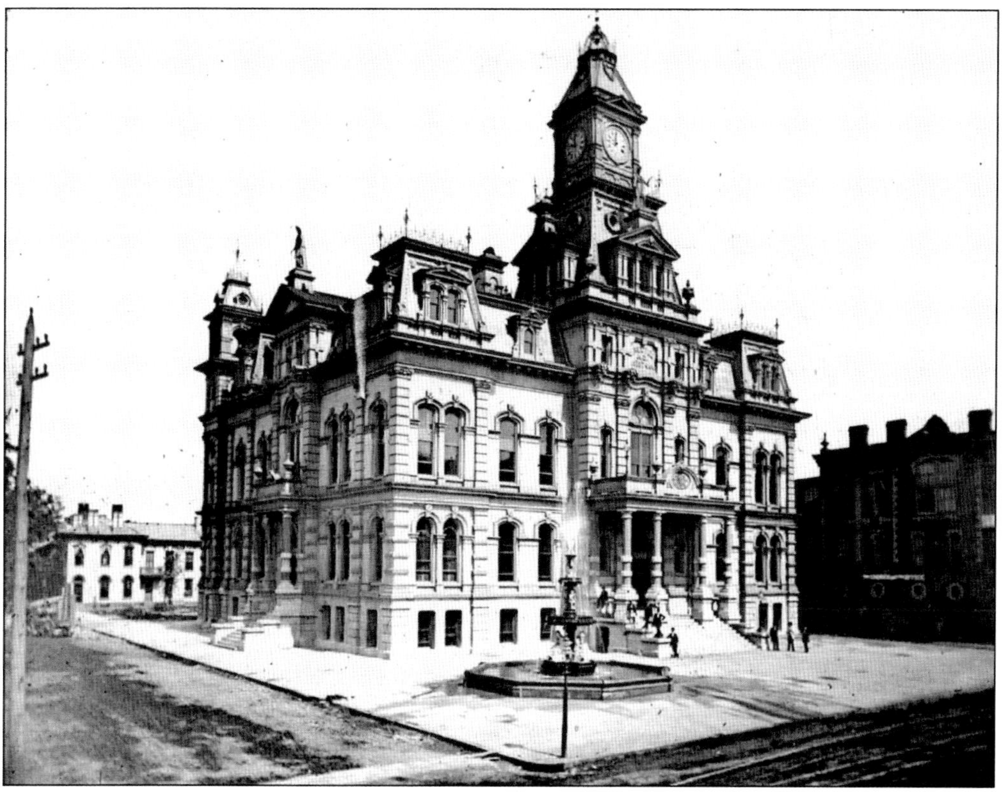

The current Muskingum County Courthouse was constructed between 1874 and 1877 on the site of Old 1809. The Second Empire/Eclectic architectural style attributed to this building makes it one of the city's most distinguishable landmarks. Its tile floors, which were manufactured in Zanesville, are the oldest surviving American-made tile installation in the nation. (Private collection.)

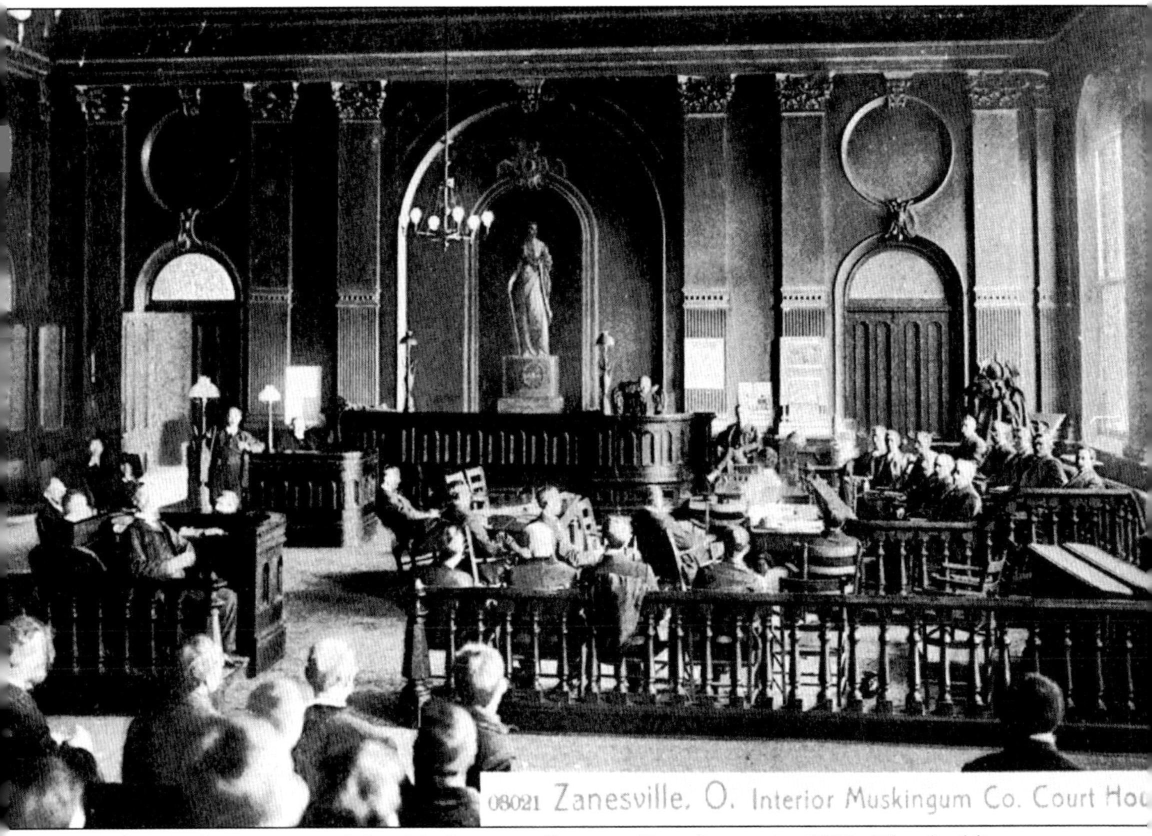

This is the interior of the Muskingum County Courthouse in 1900. The building was as ornately beautiful on the inside as it was on the outside. There appears to be some sort of legal proceedings taking place as the gentlemen look on. Note that there are no women present in the courtroom. (Courtesy of Chance Brockway.)

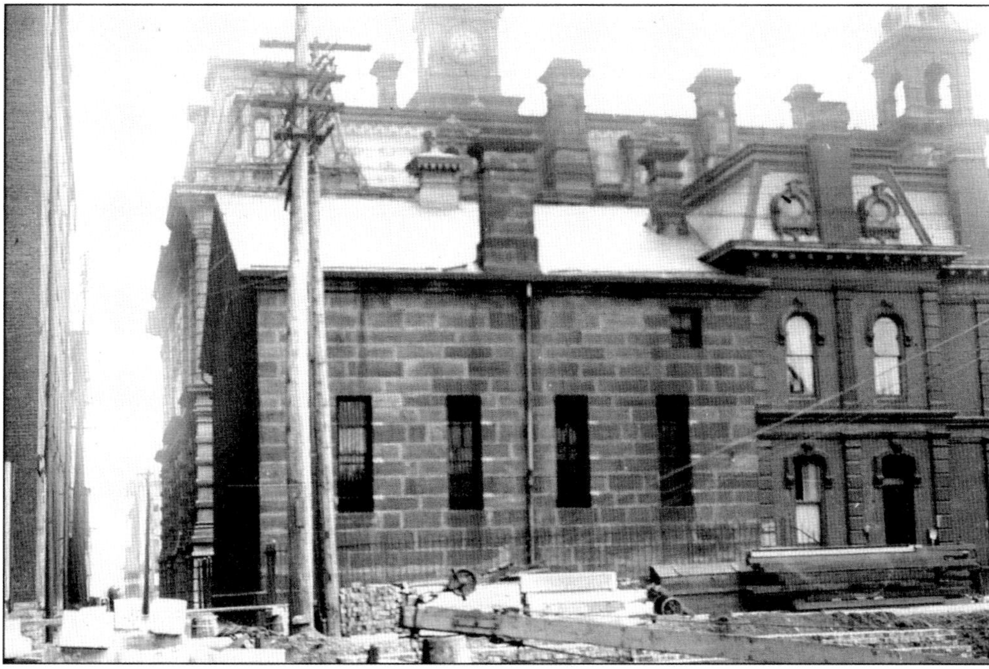

This is the north side of the Muskingum County Jail in 1902. The jail was built on this site in 1874 and torn down in 1975 to make way for a new jail building. Note the courthouse clock tower dominating the skyline. (Courtesy of Wayne Estep.)

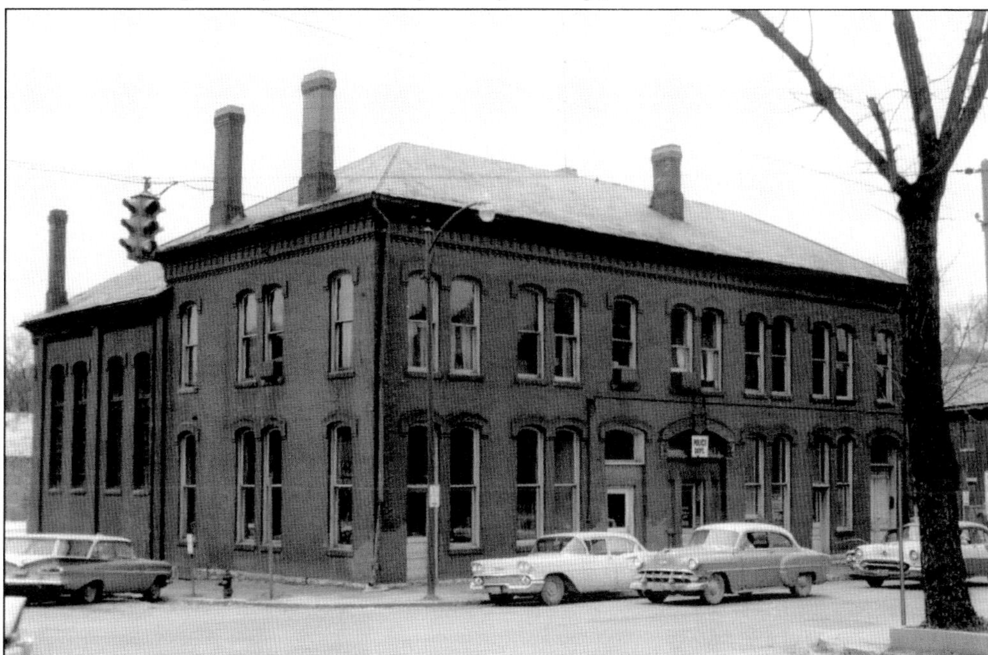

This is the Workhouse as it appeared in the 1960s. It was erected at the southwest corner of Fourth and South Streets in 1886. The inmates confined to the Workhouse came from various counties throughout the state. The male prisoners cracked stones, and the female prisoners made brooms. The building was later used as a police station. (Courtesy of MCCOGS.)

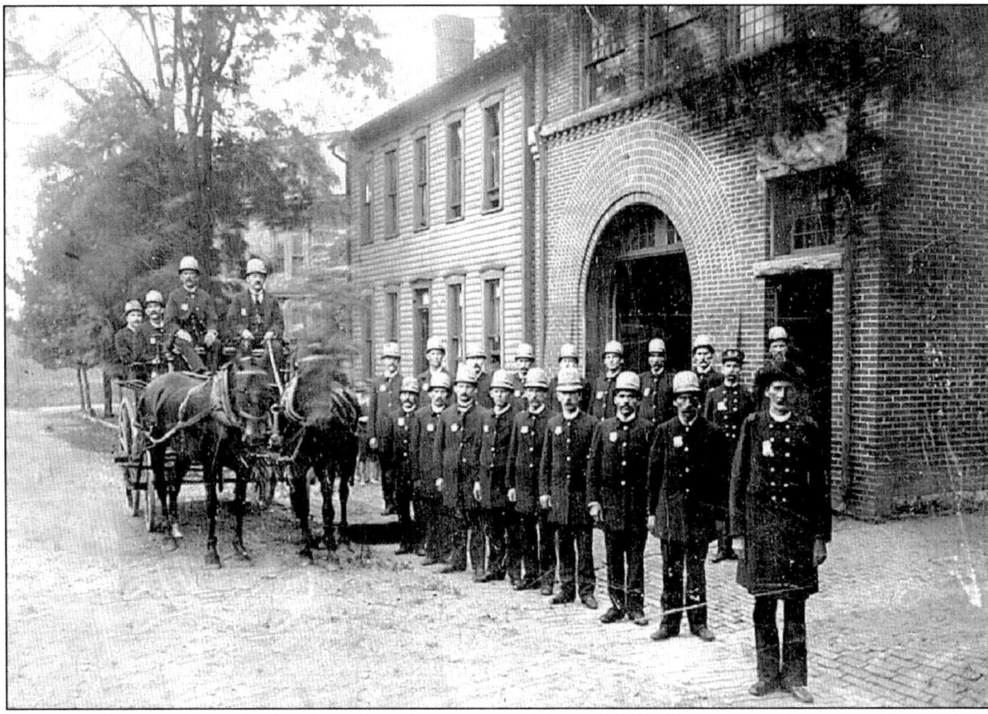

Members of the Zanesville Police Department gathered for this group photograph in 1899. (Courtesy of the *Zanesville Times Recorder.*)

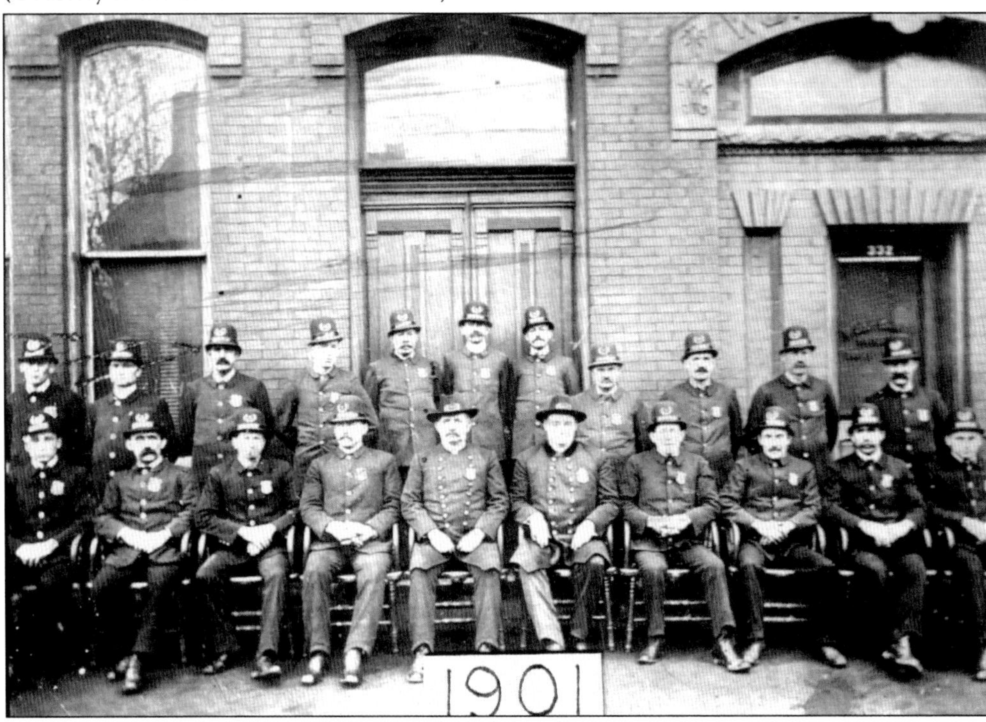

A group of Zanesville police officers gathered for this group photograph in 1901. (Courtesy of MCCOGS.)

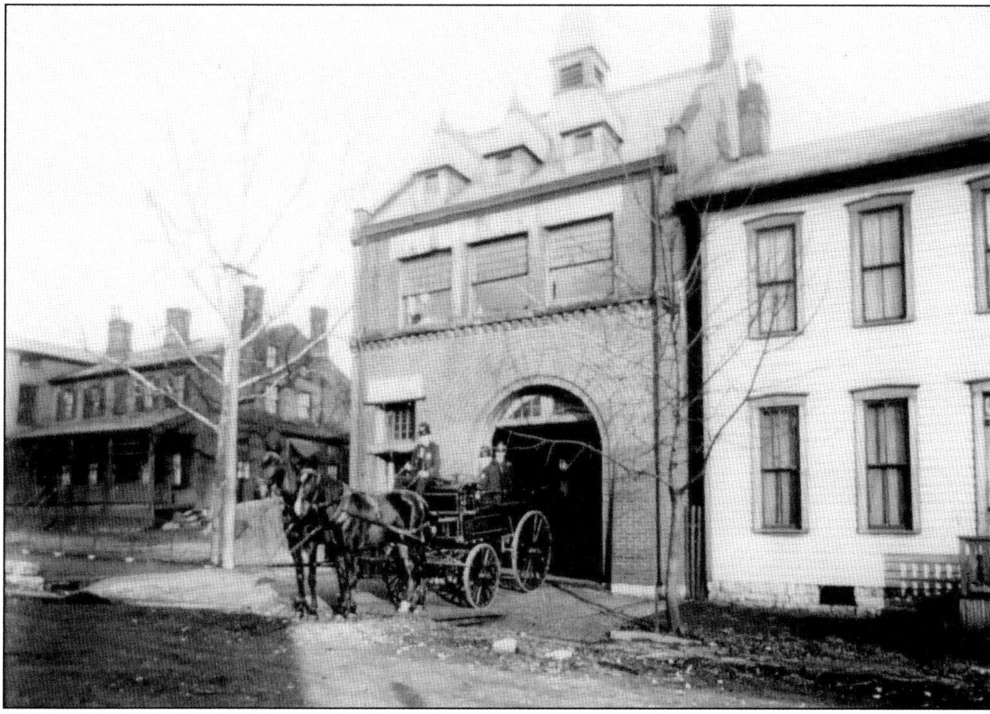

This is the South Fourth Street Police Station in the early 1900s. (Courtesy of MCCOGS.)

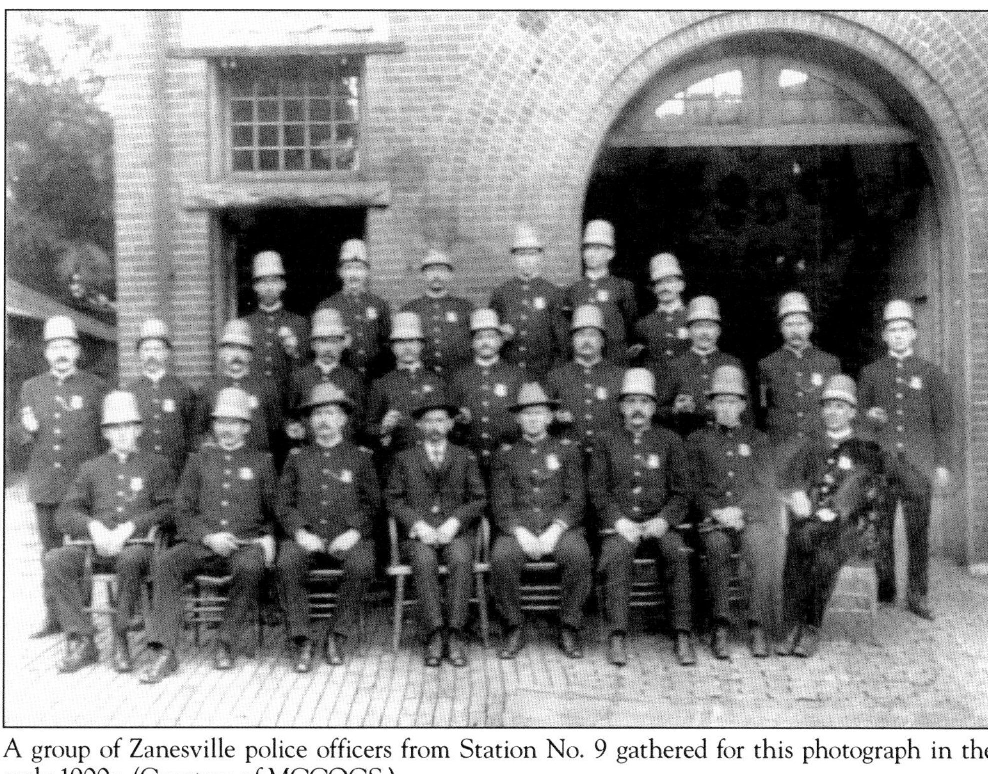

A group of Zanesville police officers from Station No. 9 gathered for this photograph in the early 1900s. (Courtesy of MCCOGS.)

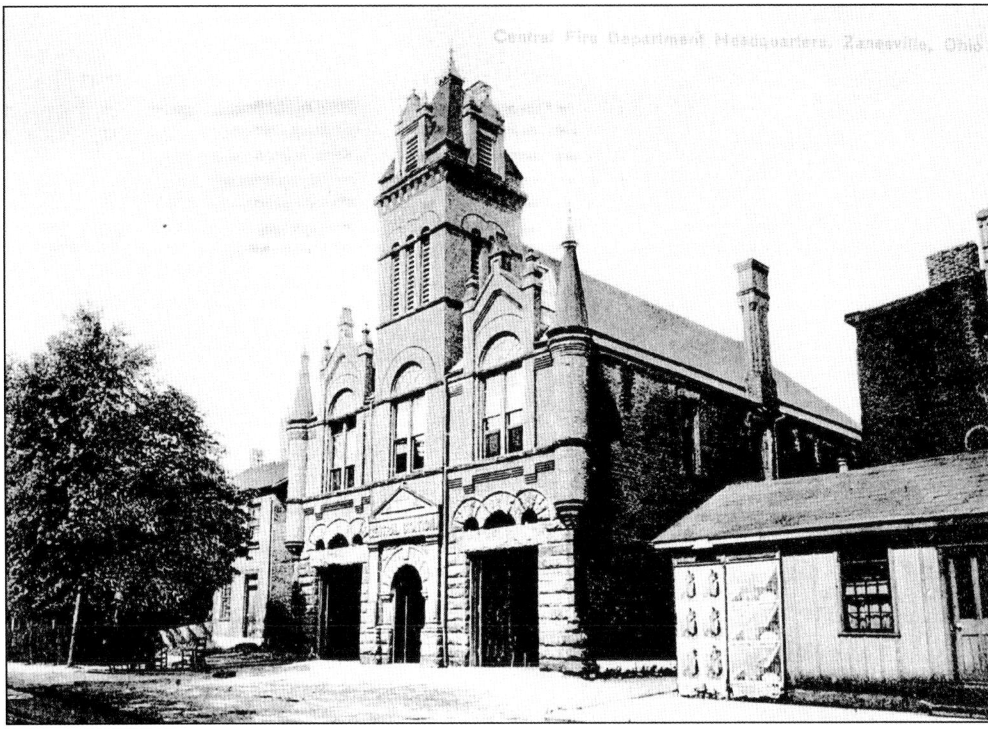

The Central Fire Station served as the headquarters of the fire department from this location on North Sixth Street. (Courtesy of Chance Brockway.)

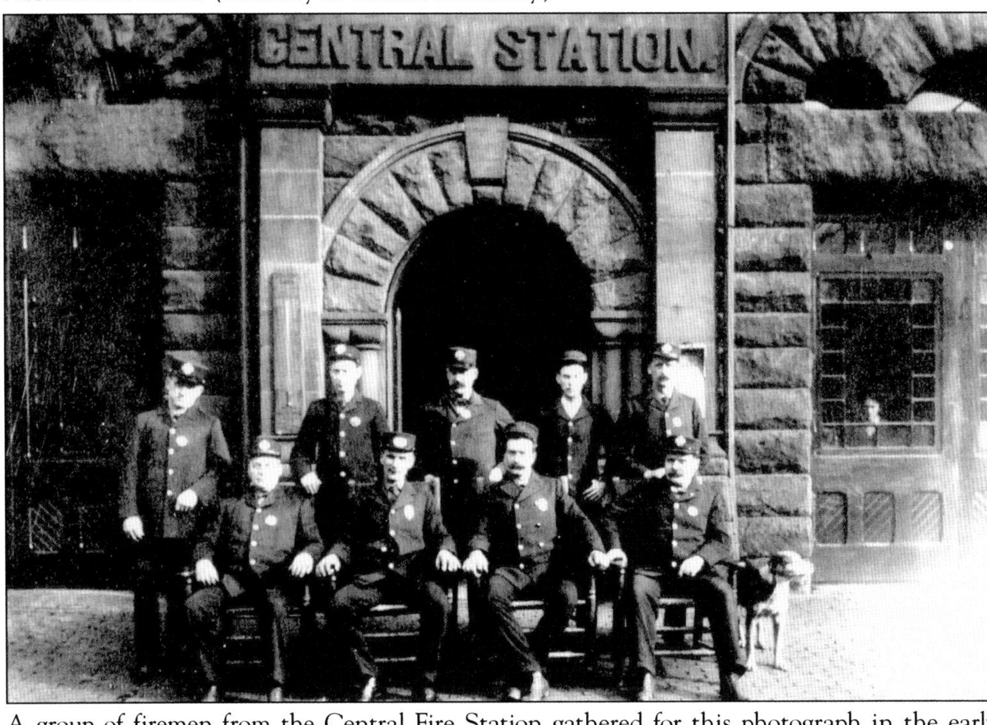

A group of firemen from the Central Fire Station gathered for this photograph in the early 1900s. (Courtesy of Wayne Estep.)

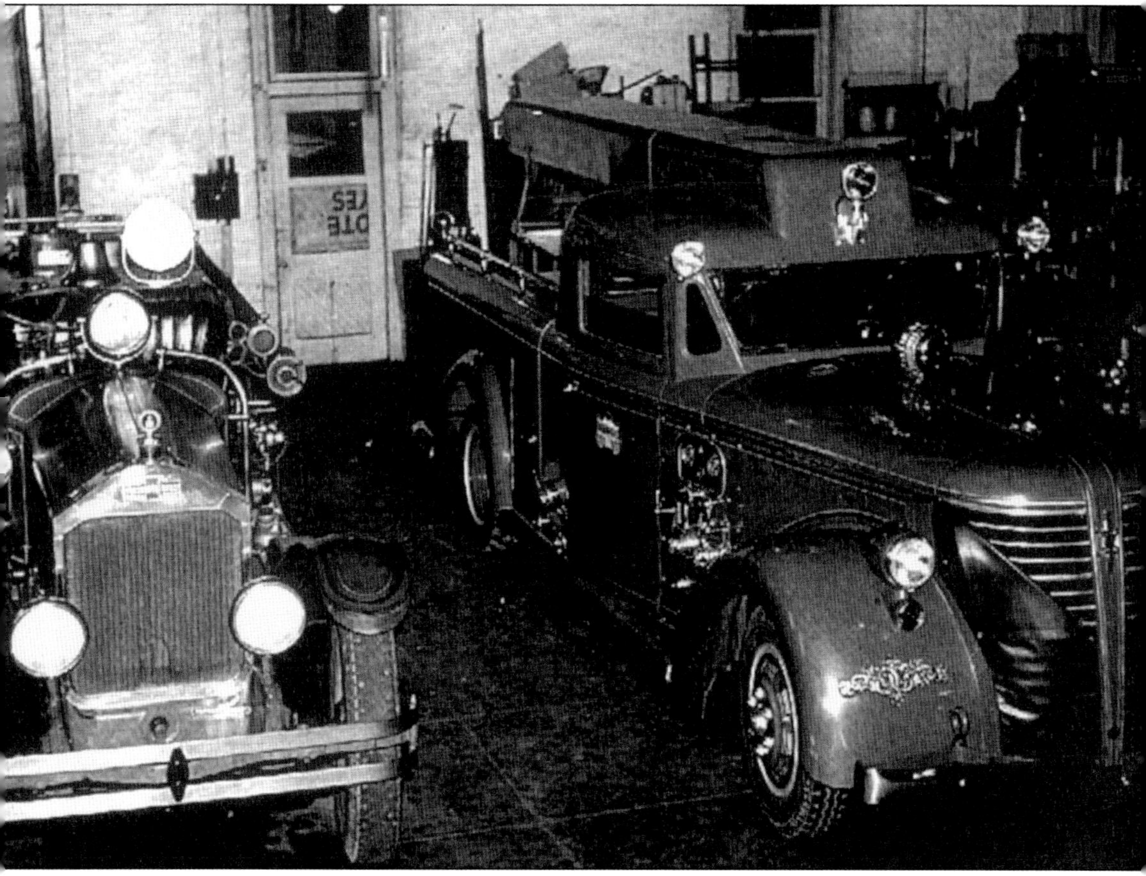

In the early 1930s, the Zanesville Fire Department purchased a new fire truck. The city's first fire truck is shown on the left, and it was replaced with the one on the right. (Courtesy of Wayne Estep.)

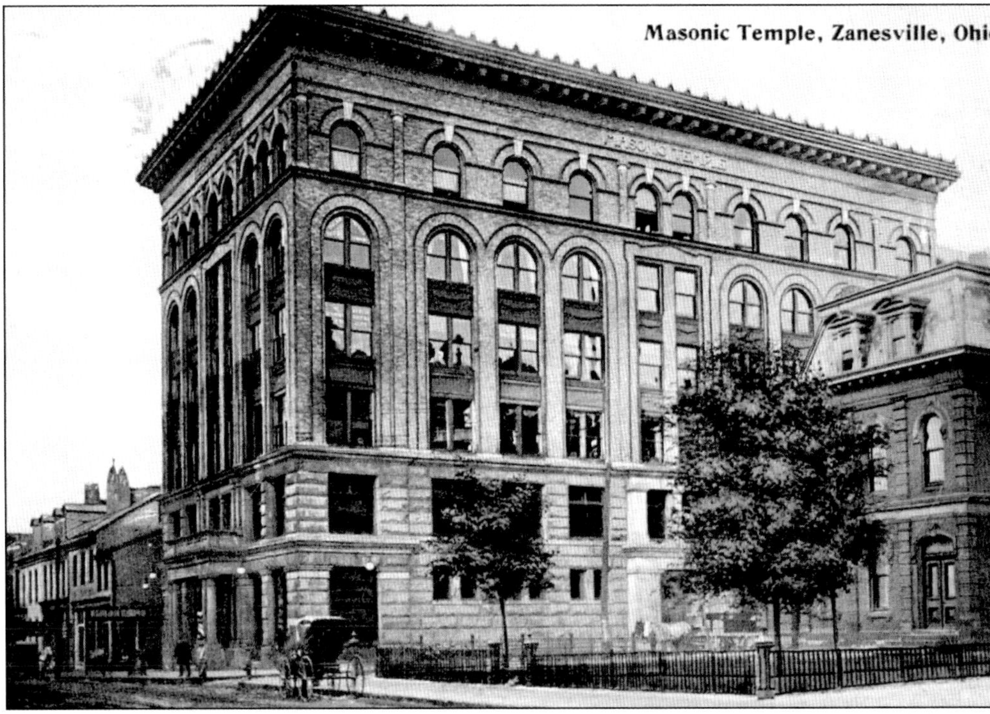

The Masonic temple building, located at 36–42 North Fourth Street, was built and dedicated on June 24, 1903. The six-story building replaced the Masons' former building, on the corner of Market and Fourth Streets.

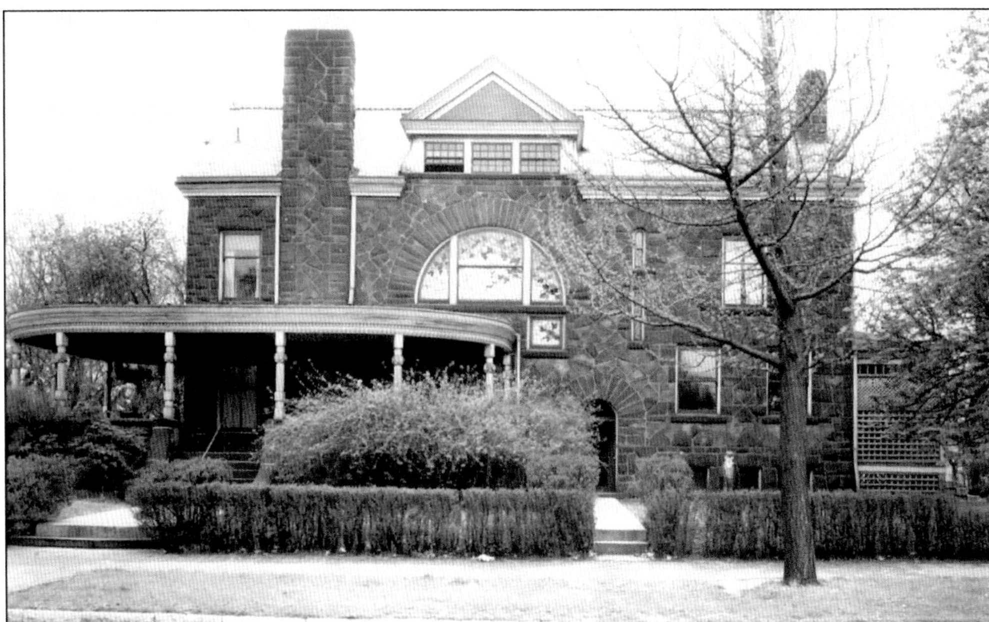

Mr. and Mrs. Edward M. Ayers established the Zanesville Art Institute in 1936. The building was located at the corner of Maple and Adair Avenues and housed the city's permanent collection of art and artifacts. (Courtesy of the Zanesville Art Center.)

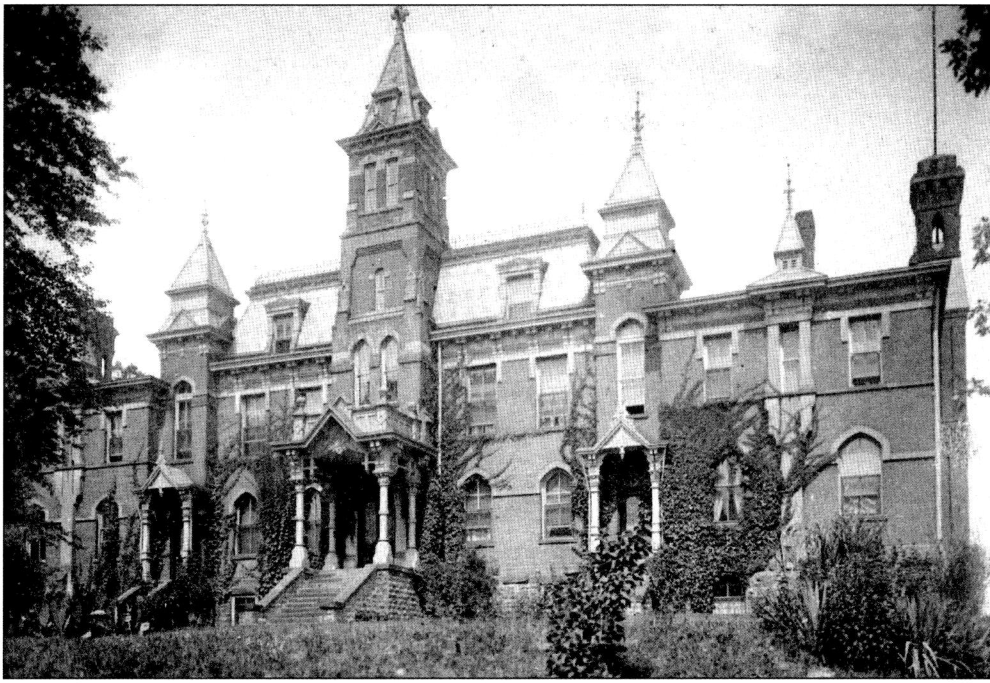

The John McIntire Children's Home was established with funds from the McIntire Estate for Disadvantaged Children by local churchwomen in 1865. The facility was housed in several locations before a permanent site was selected. A large building, located at the north end of Blue Avenue was erected in 1880. The facility closed in 1942, and the building was razed in 1944. (Courtesy of Tom Brown.)

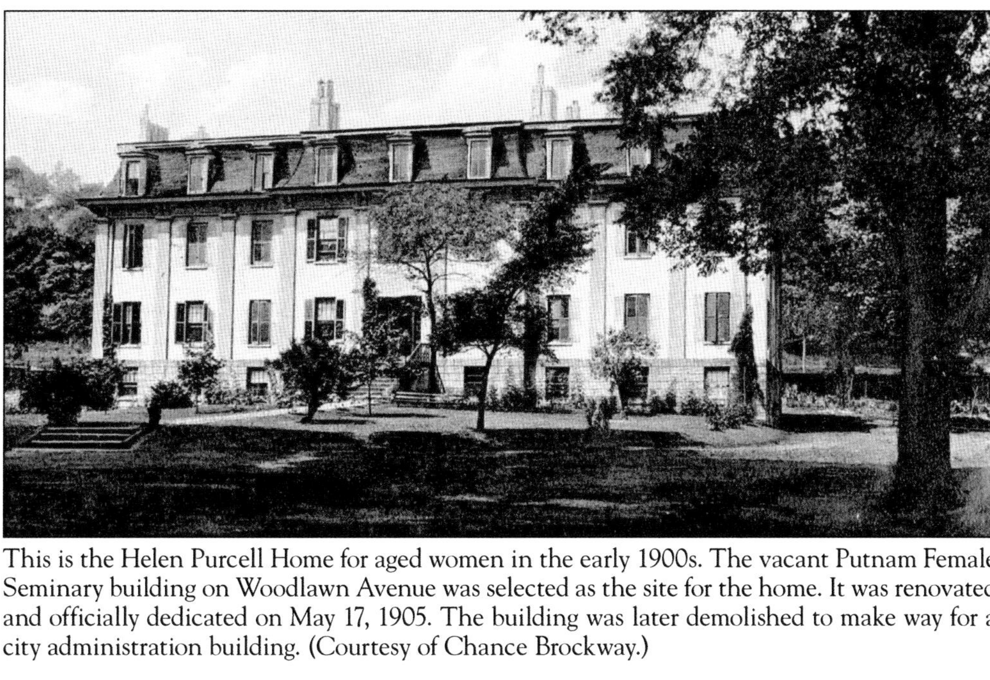

This is the Helen Purcell Home for aged women in the early 1900s. The vacant Putnam Female Seminary building on Woodlawn Avenue was selected as the site for the home. It was renovated and officially dedicated on May 17, 1905. The building was later demolished to make way for a city administration building. (Courtesy of Chance Brockway.)

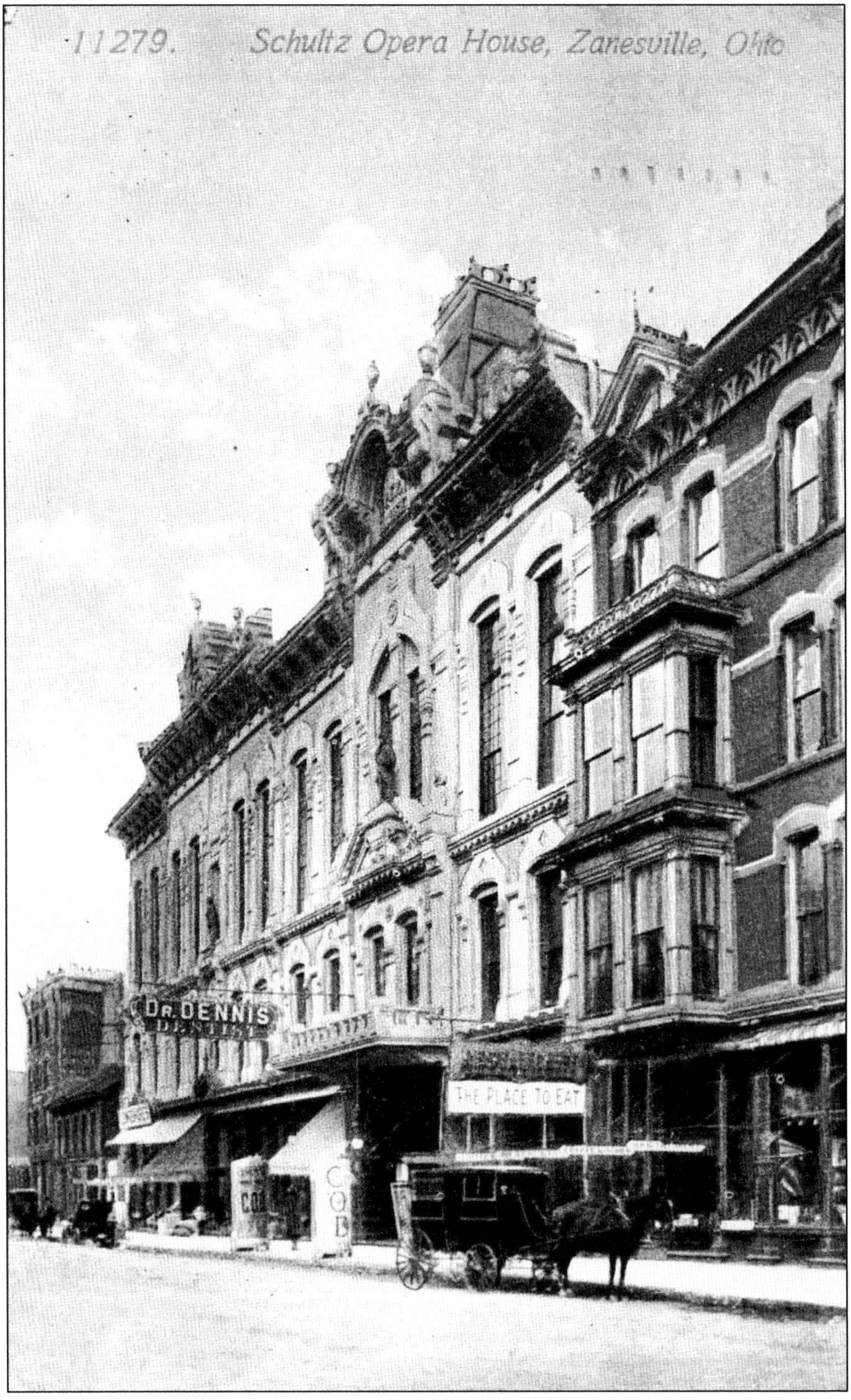

Businessmen Robert Schultz and John Hoge commissioned a performing arts building worthy of their wealth and status in the community. On January 20, 1880, the Schultz Opera House opened on Fifth Street. The building housed two elegant halls on the third floor, while the opera house auditorium occupied the entire first floor. (Courtesy of Chance Brockway.)

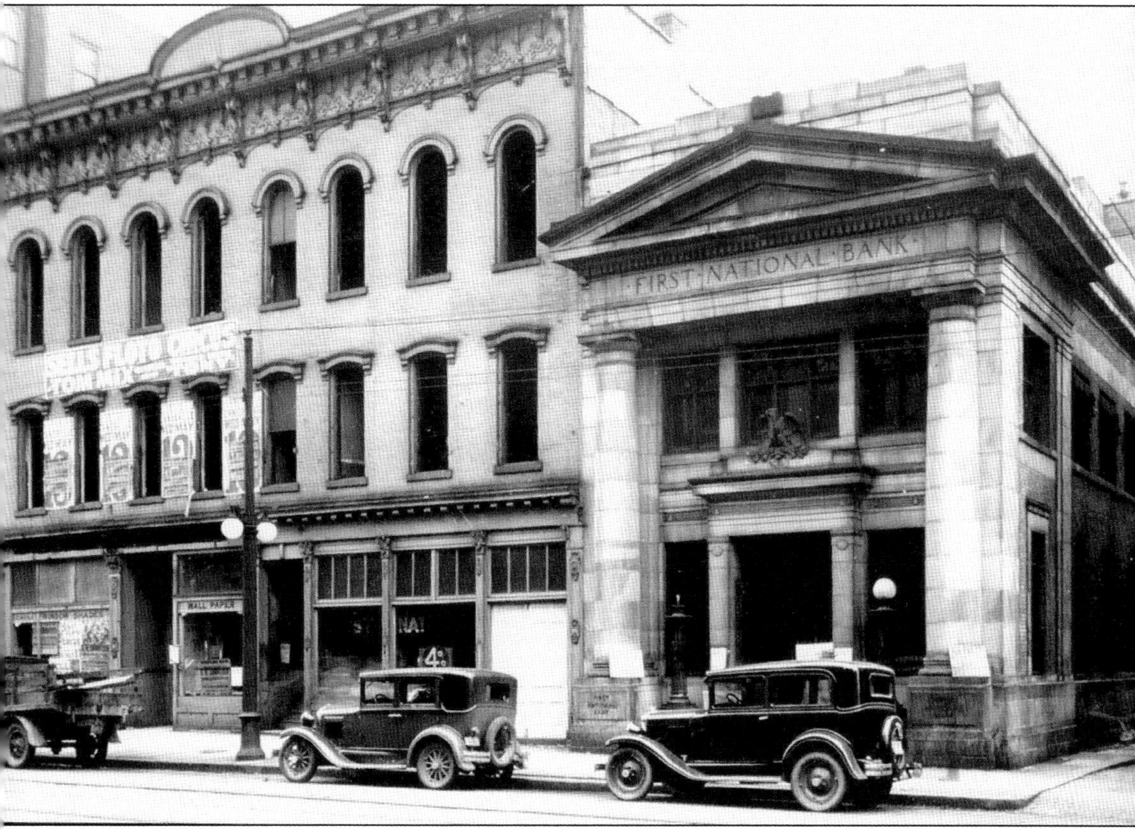

This is the First National Bank located at 422–428 Main Street in the 1930s. (Courtesy of Wayne Estep.)

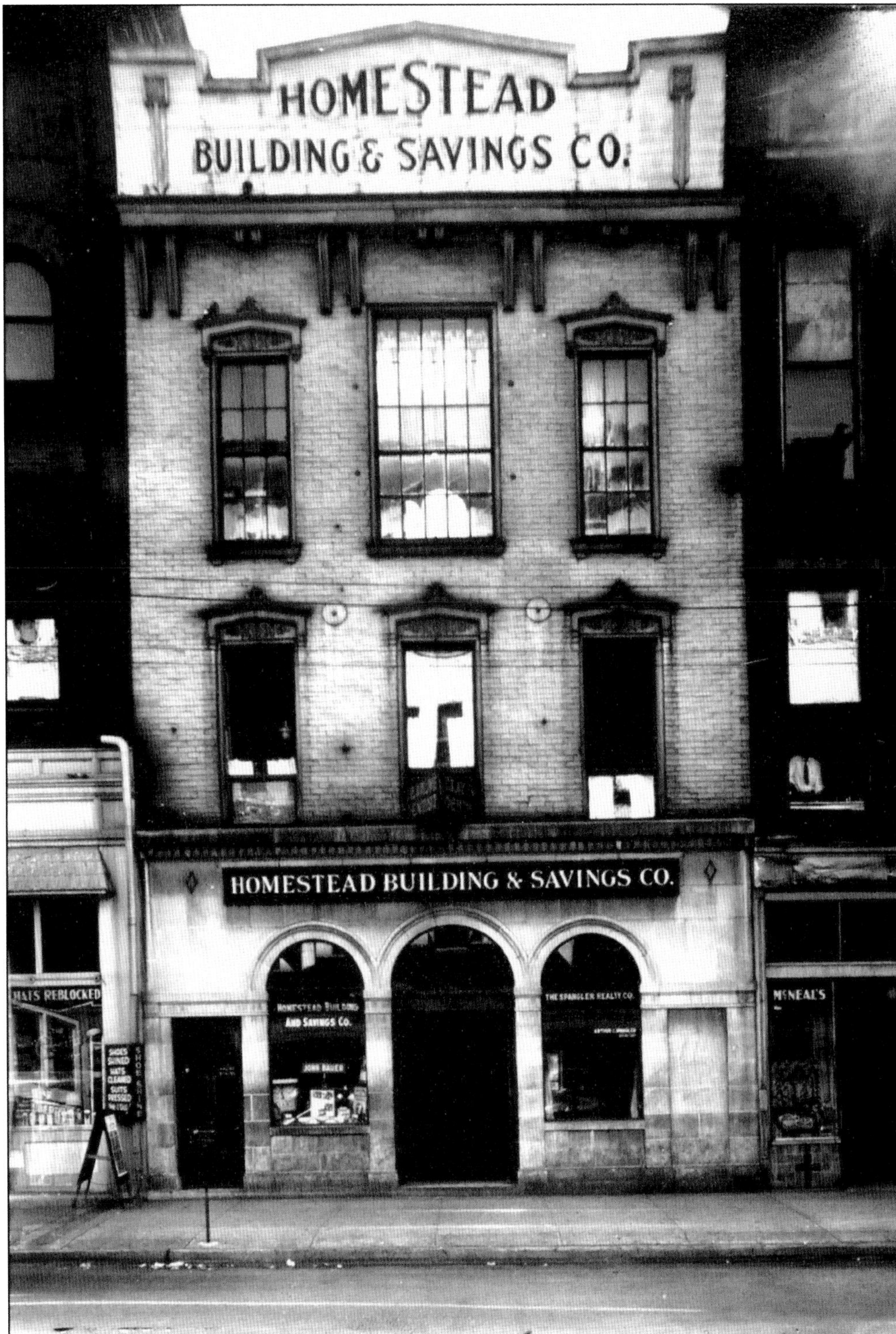

The Homestead Building and Savings Company was located at 155 Main Street. It was organized in 1886 with an authorized capital stock of $1 million. (Courtesy of Wayne Estep.)

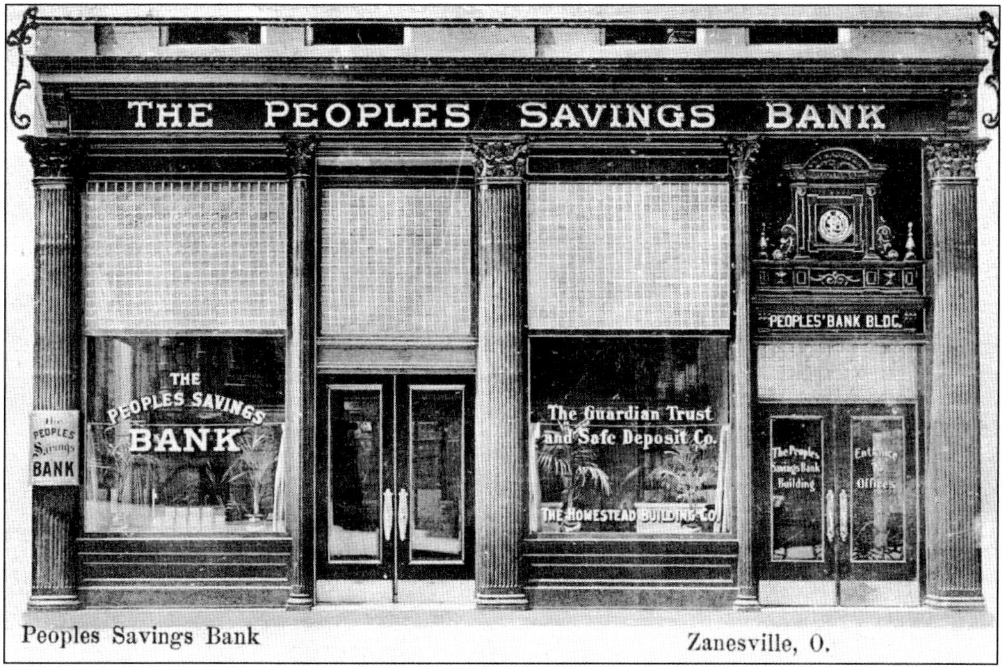

The People's Savings Bank was organized in 1889. It was located in the Clarendon Building at the corner of Fourth and Main Streets. The bank was the first strictly savings bank established in the state. (Private collection.)

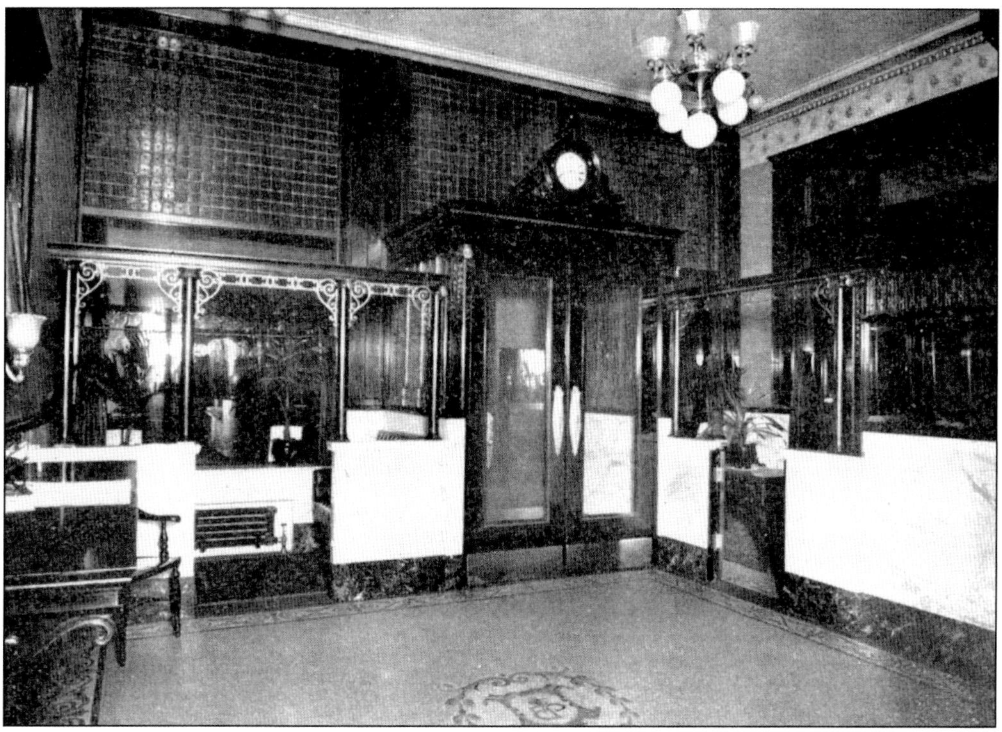

The interior of the People's Savings Bank as it appeared in 1906. Note the locally produced tiles throughout the building.

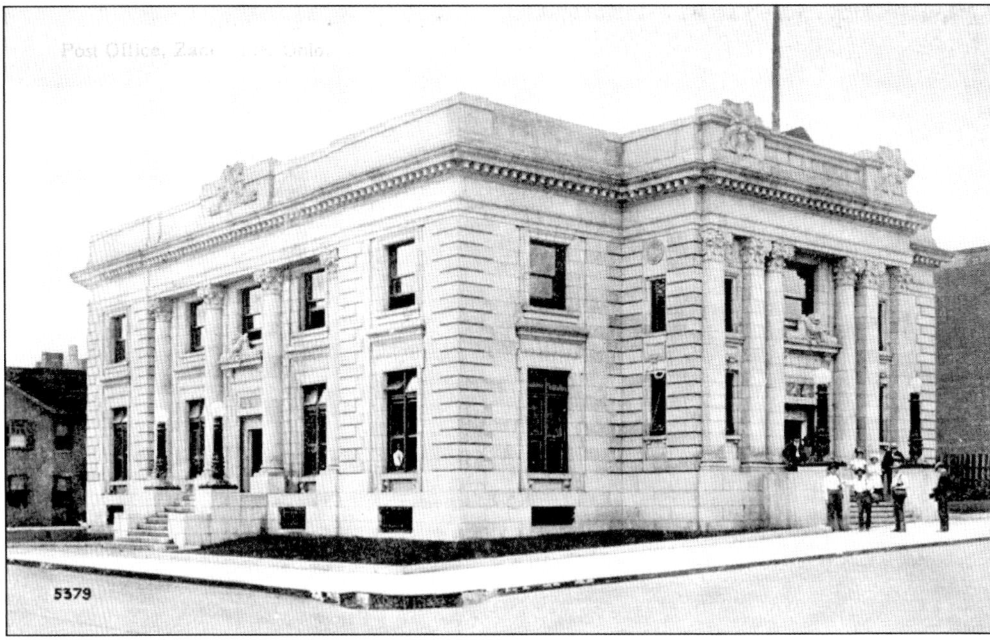

Zanesville's postal facilities were housed in various locations downtown before moving into this newly constructed post office in 1906. The Beaux-Arts building was erected at the corner of Fifth and South Streets at a cost of $110,000. (Courtesy of Chance Brockway.)

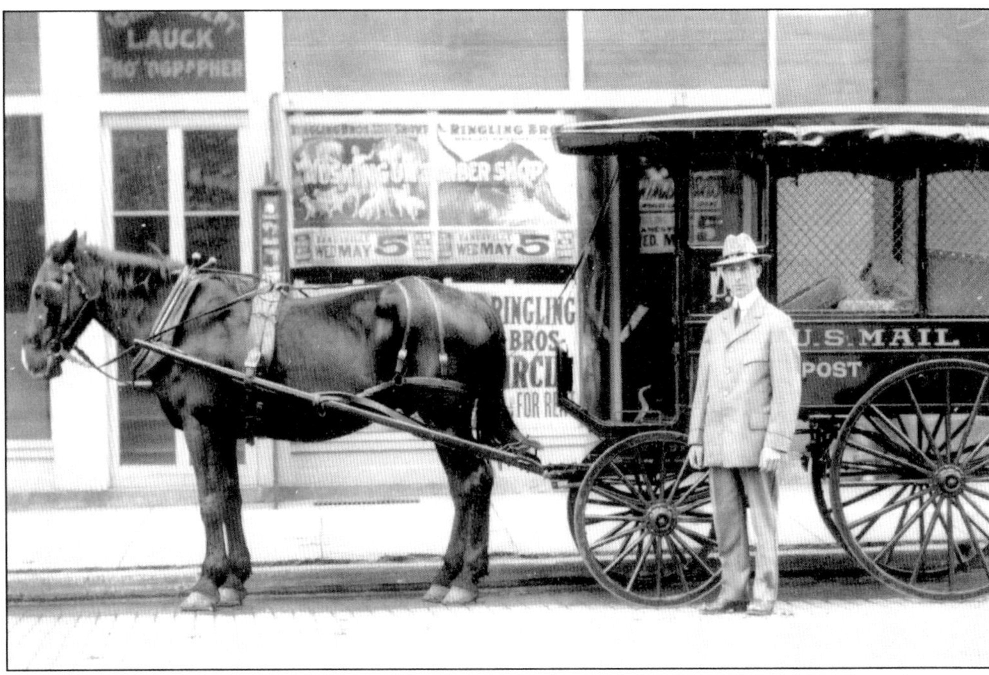

Joseph McCarty is shown beside the city's first parcel post delivery wagon. Note that the wagon is parked outside of John Gilbert Lauck's photography studio. (Courtesy of Wayne Estep.)

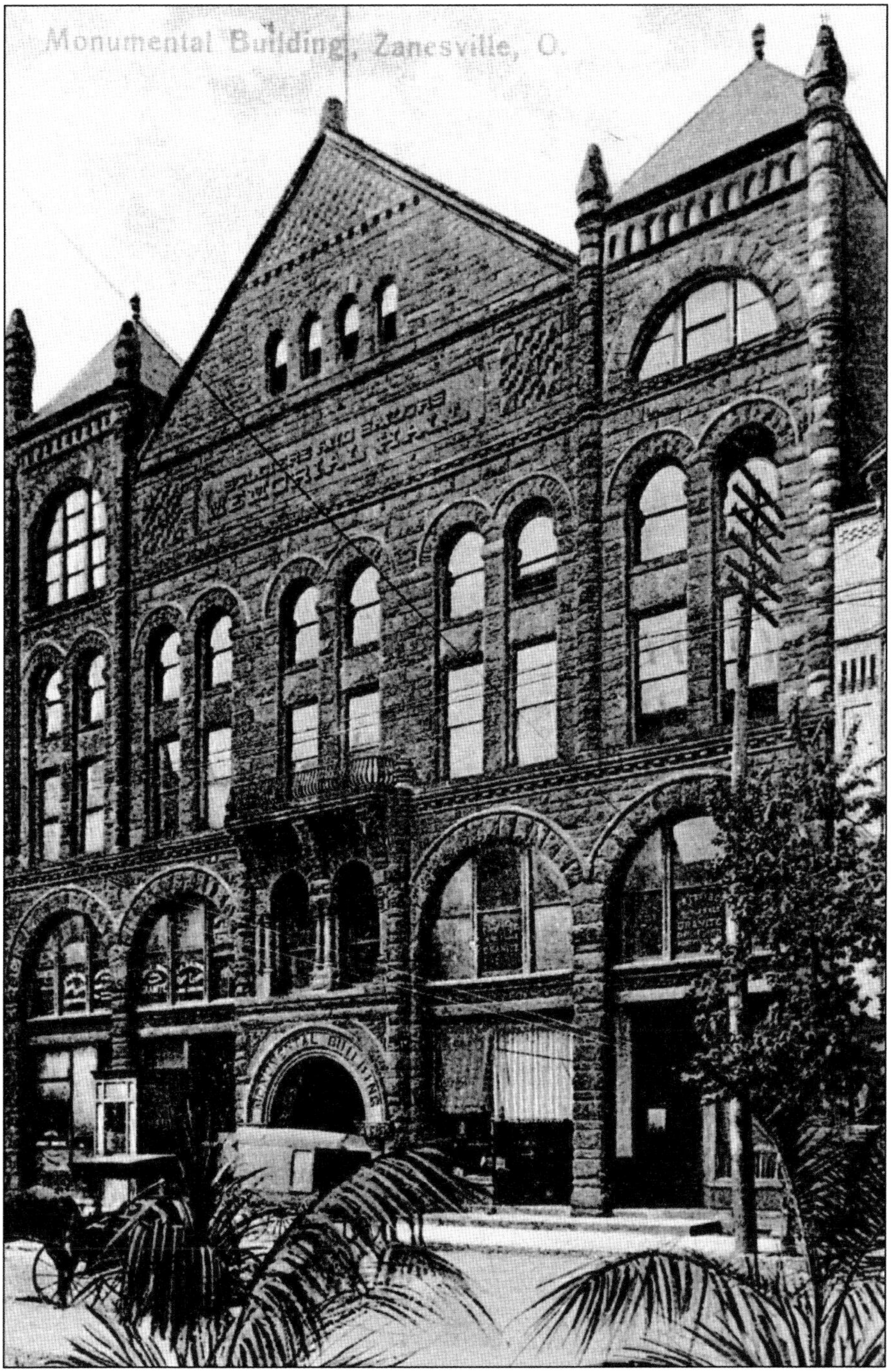

The Soldiers and Sailors Memorial Hall was erected in 1888 to serve as a combined armory and memorial hall for those killed in the Civil War. The grand Romanesque-style building was located on Fifth Street. The armory occupied the basement and rear of the first floor. Businesses occupied the rest of the first floor and the entire second floor. An auditorium, which occupied the third and fourth floors, had the capacity to seat 3,000 people. It was the site of the Republican Convention in 1895. The building was razed in 1937. (Courtesy of Chance Brockway.)

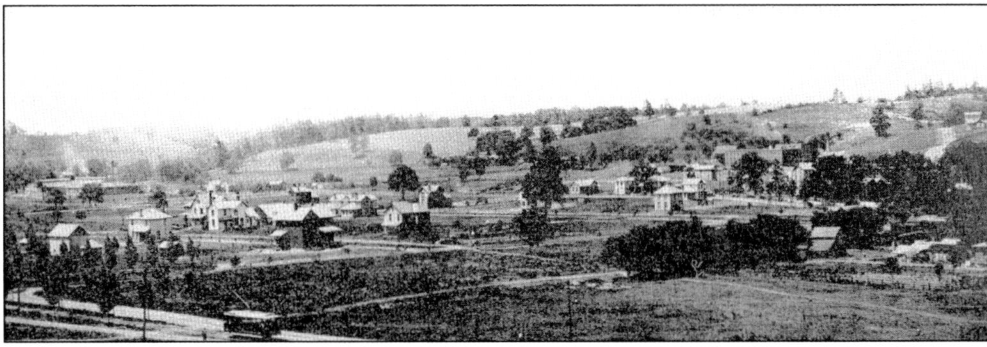

This is the newly established Brighton subdivision in 1895. Note the streetcar making its way up Brighton Boulevard. The subdivision was considered state of the art at the time because of the availability of gas, electric, and water lines as each new home was built.

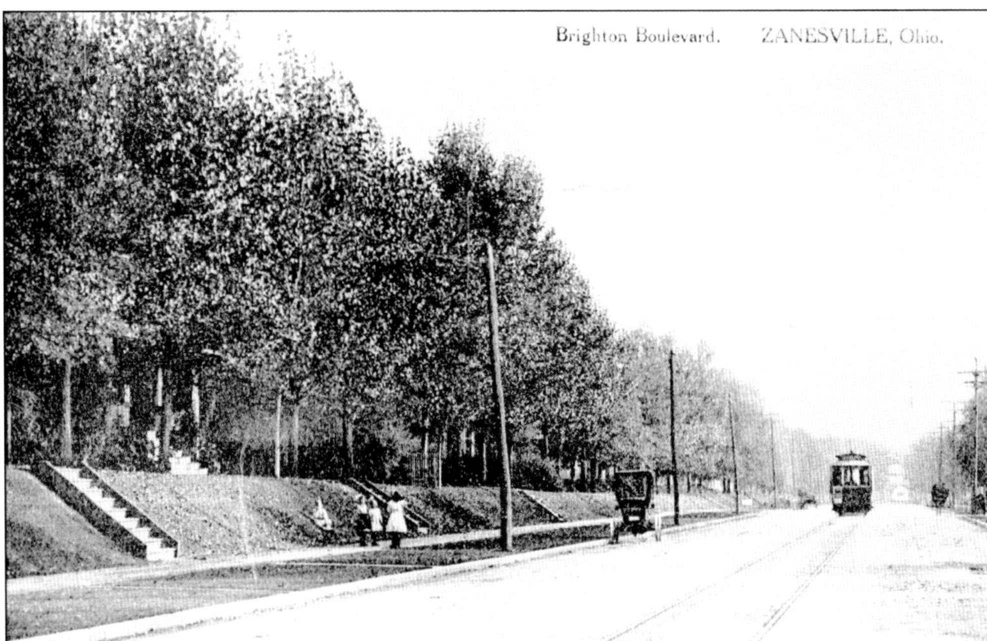

This is a view of Brighton Boulevard in the early 1900s. A streetcar and an automobile are shown on the boulevard. (Courtesy of Chance Brockway.)

Eight

Neighborhoods, Schools, and Parks

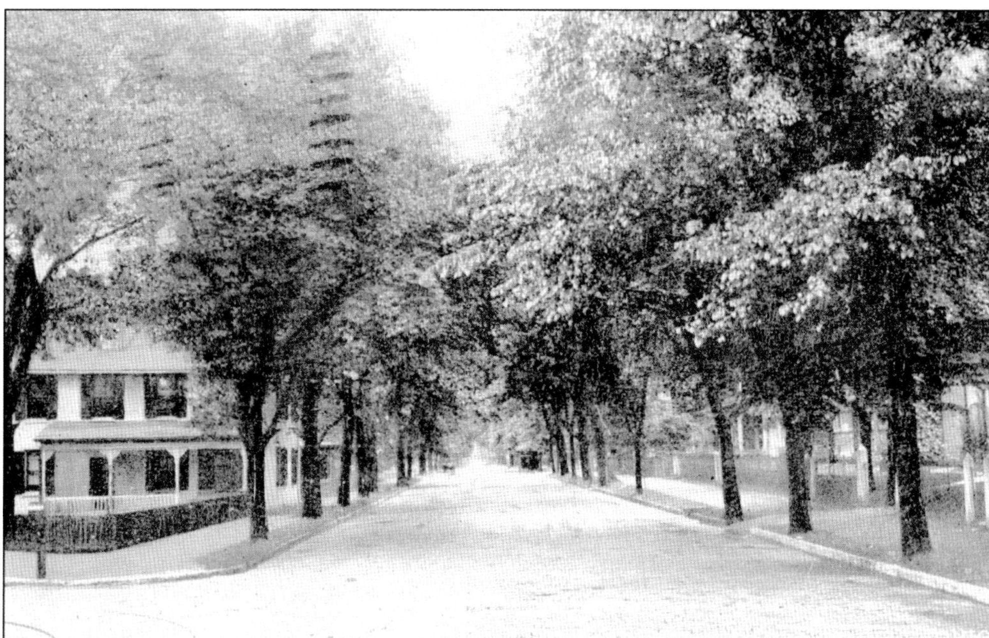

This is Putnam Avenue in the early 1900s. Many of the neighborhoods established in the late 1890s were laid out with wide tree-lined streets and homes set back from the road. (Courtesy of Chance Brockway.)

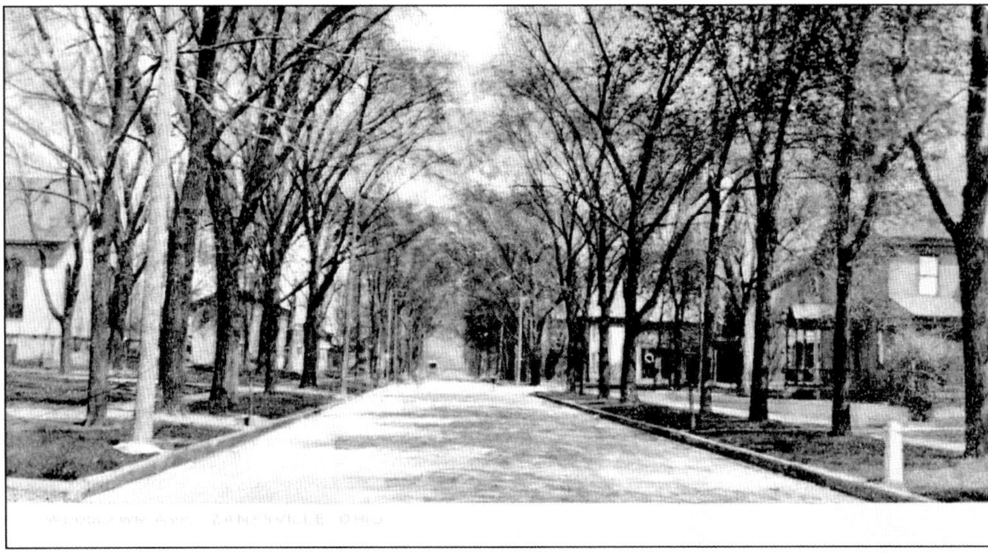

Woodlawn Avenue is one of the oldest streets in the Putnam District. Note that the street is paved for automobile traffic. (Courtesy of Chance Brockway.)

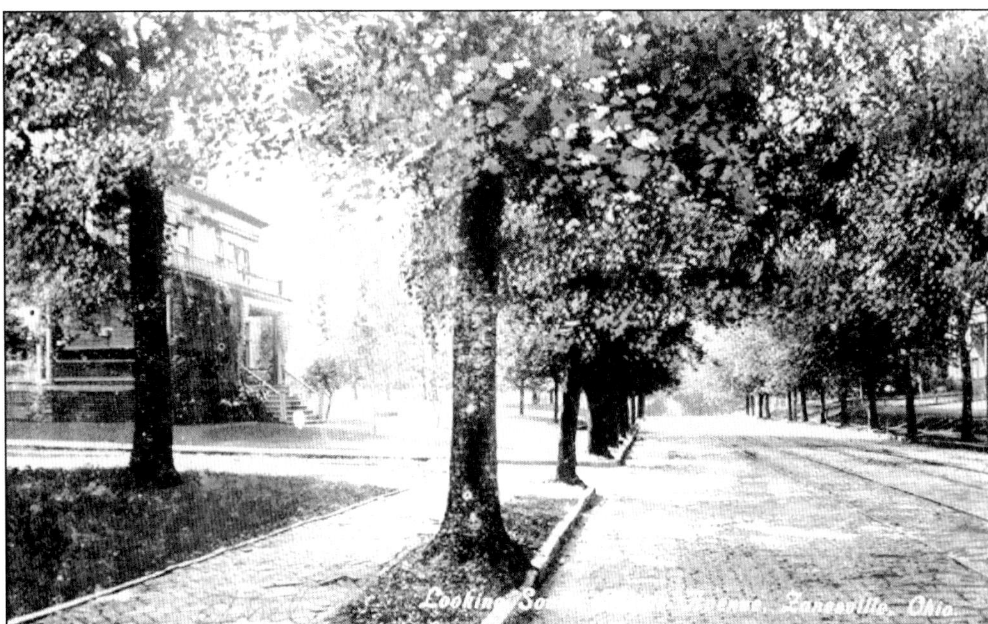

This is a typical streetscape on Maple Avenue in the early 1900s. Note the carefully laid out brick sidewalks and brick-lined street. (Courtesy of Chance Brockway.)

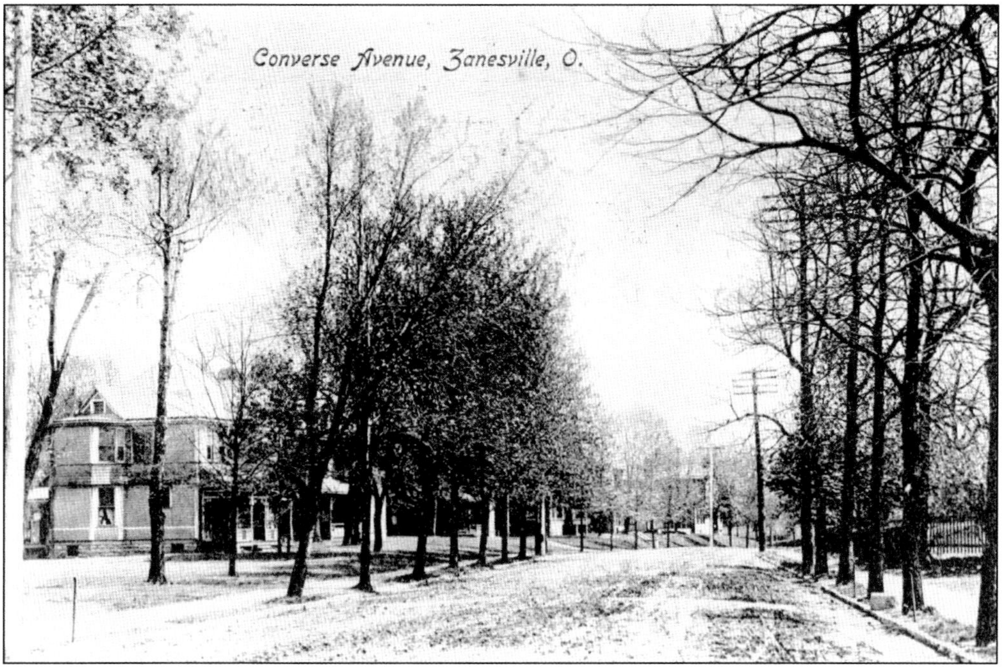

Convers Avenue is located in the McIntire Terrace on the northwest part of the city. The street does not appear to be paved. (Courtesy of Chance Brockway.)

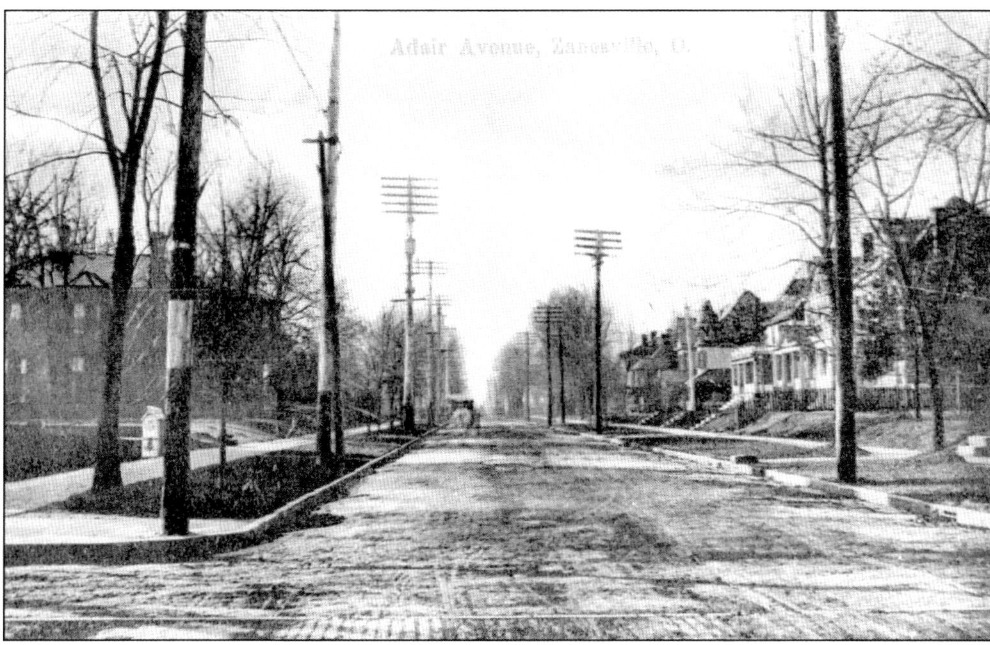

Adair Avenue is also located in the McIntire Terrace part of the city. The street appears to be paved with bricks. (Courtesy of Chance Brockway.)

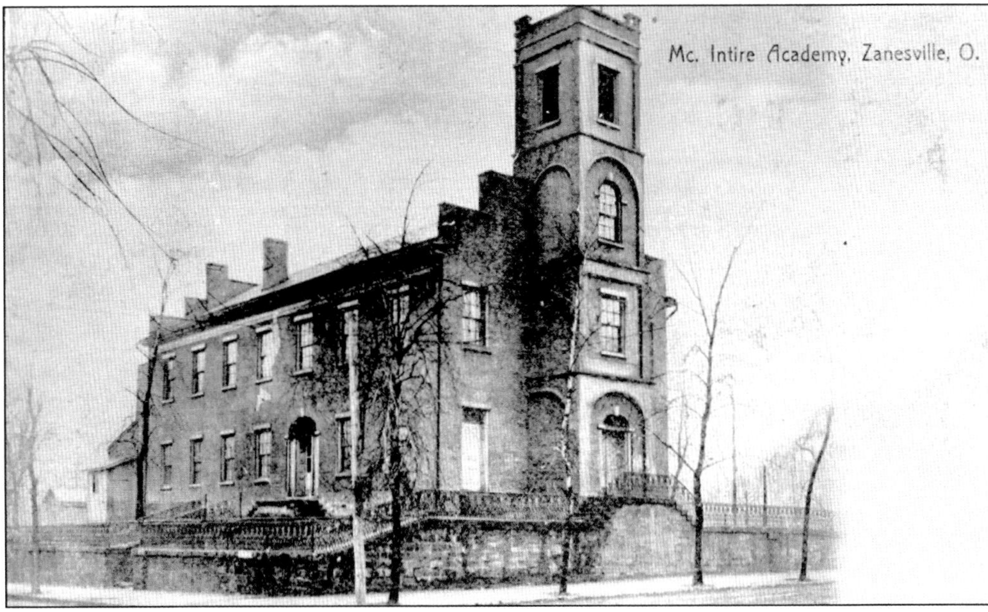

The McIntire Academy was established in 1836 as a school for the less privileged, as stipulated in the will of John McIntire. The academy was located on the north side of Shinnick Street between Fifth and Sixth Streets. It was razed in 1906. (Courtesy of Chance Brockway.)

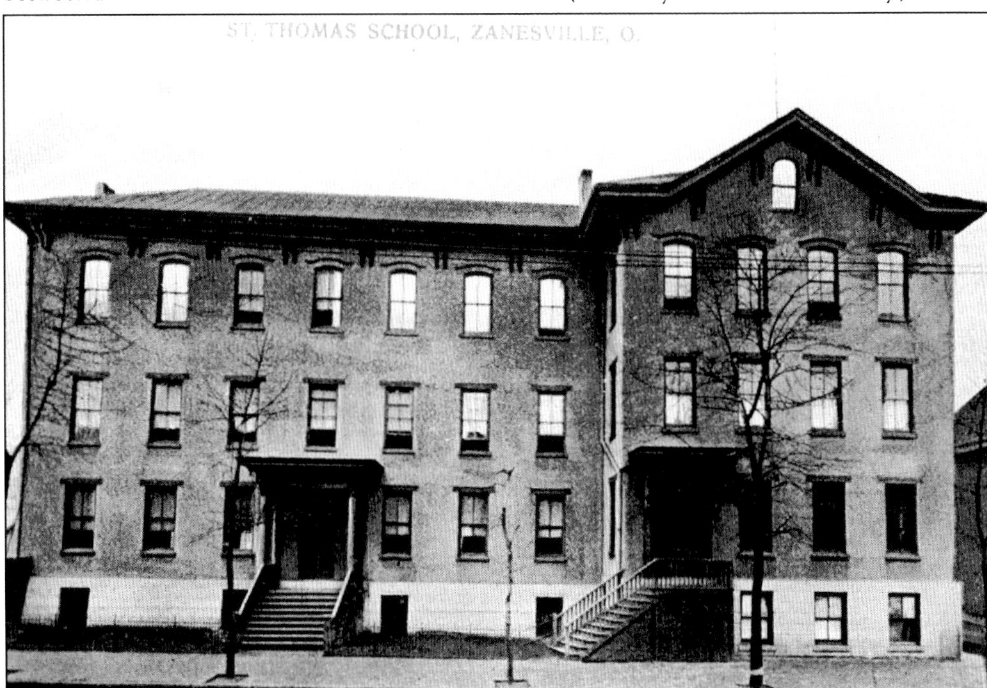

St. Thomas Catholic Church built two schools on North Fifth Street in 1853 for parochial students. The building on the left, with its entry in the middle, was the boys' school, while the building on the right, with the corner entry, was called St. Columbia's Academy and was the girls' school. The building was razed in 1921 to make way for the St. Thomas school that presently occupies the site. (Courtesy of Chance Brockway.)

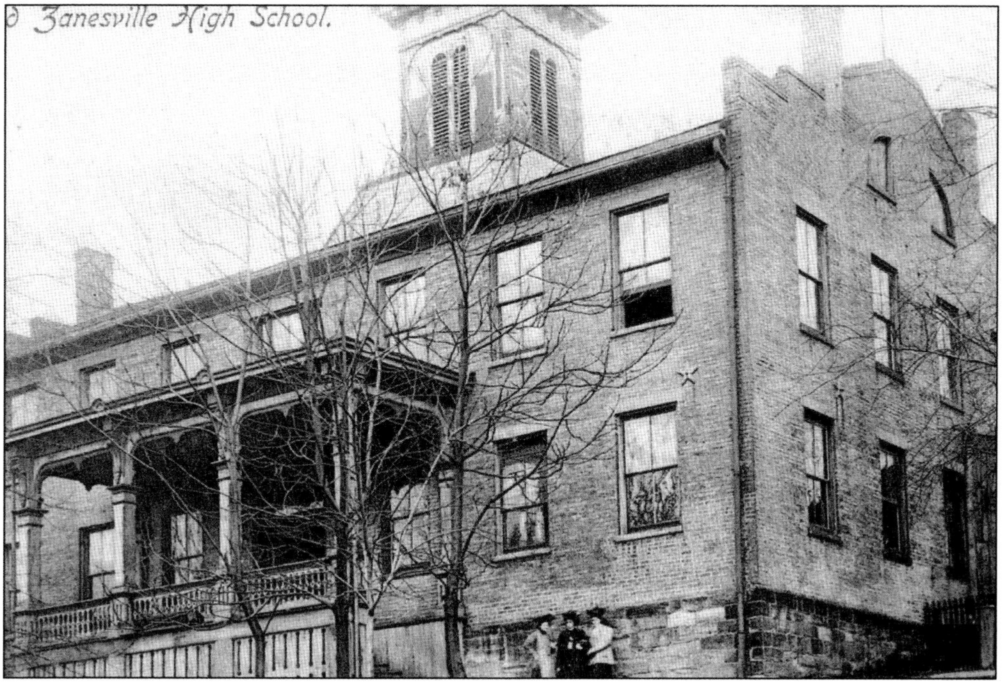

The first Zanesville High School was established in 1855 in the former Boys' Seminary, built on Pioneer Hill in 1840. There were 50 students and two teachers when the school opened. (Courtesy of Wayne Estep.)

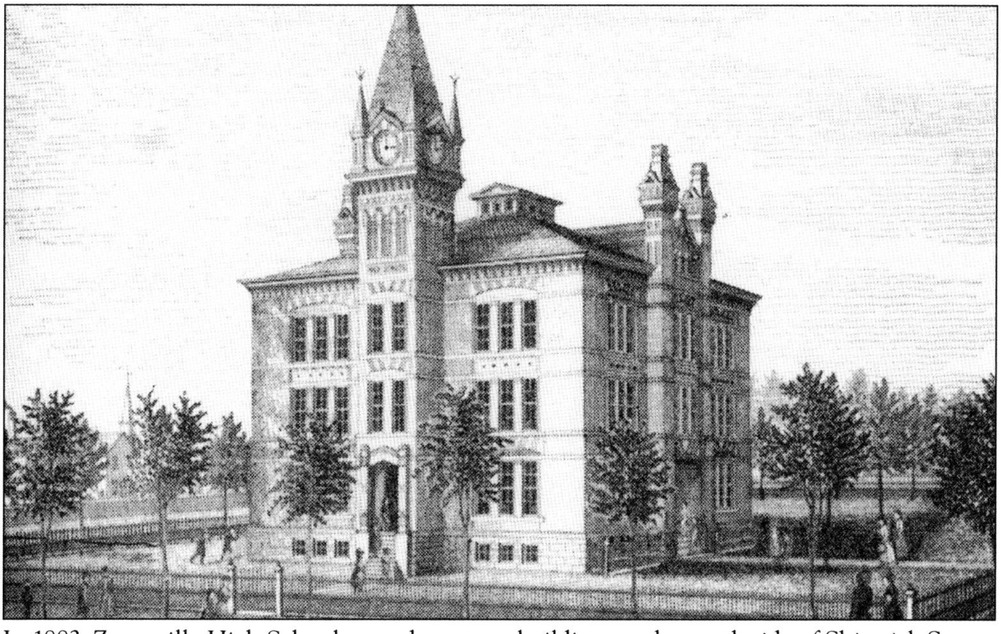

In 1883, Zanesville High School moved to a new building on the north side of Shinnick Street, between Sixth and Seventh Streets. In 1907, Lash High School was erected across the street and the former Zanesville High School building became Hancock Junior High School. In 1953, the Hancock Junior High School building was razed and the students moved across the street into the Lash High School building. (Courtesy of Wayne Estep.)

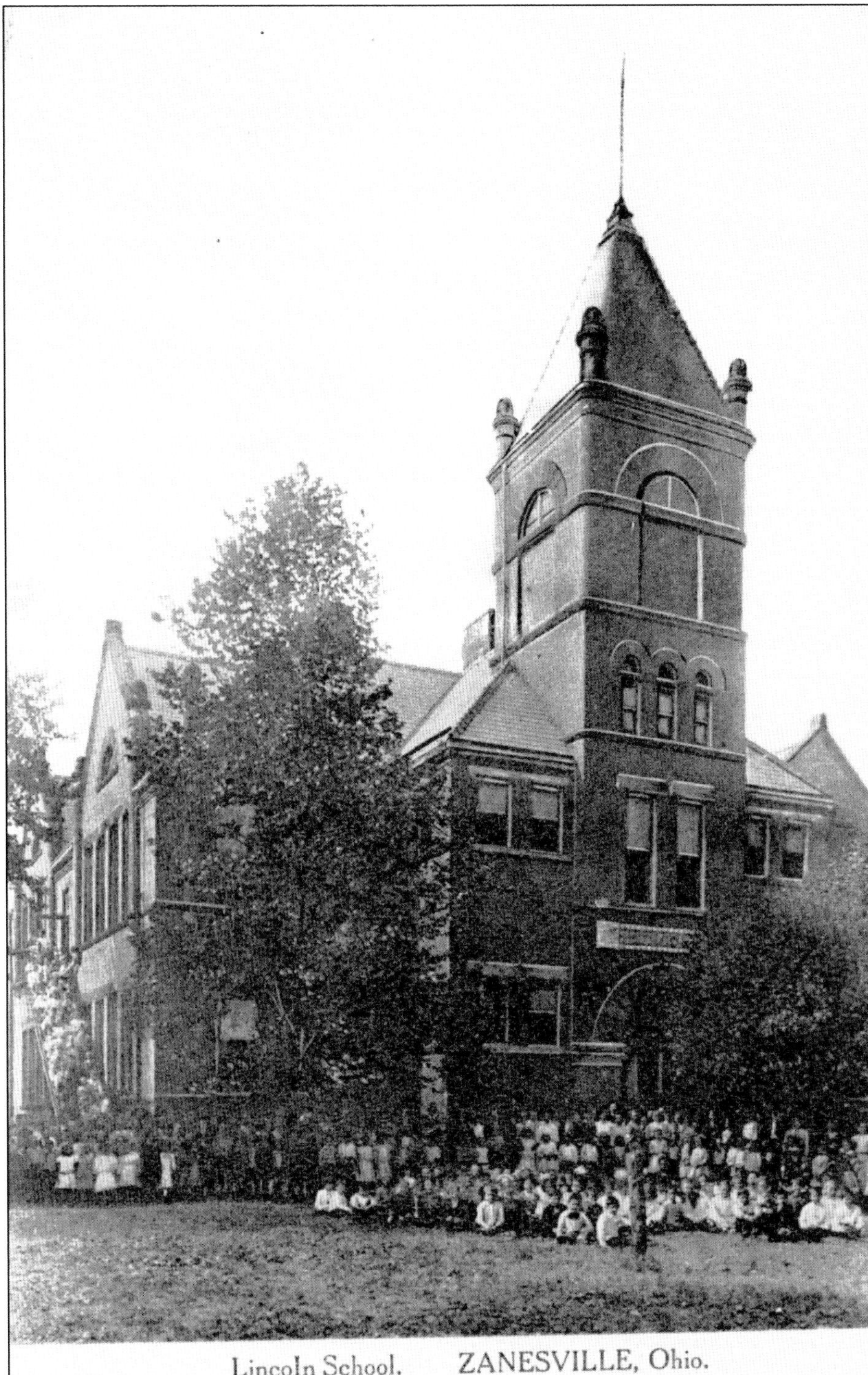

Lincoln School was erected in 1888 on Sheridan Street. It was the first school built in the city's 10th ward. The building survived a fire in 1903 and served as temporary housing for evacuees of the Flood of 1913. The building was razed in 1979. (Courtesy of Chance Brockway.)

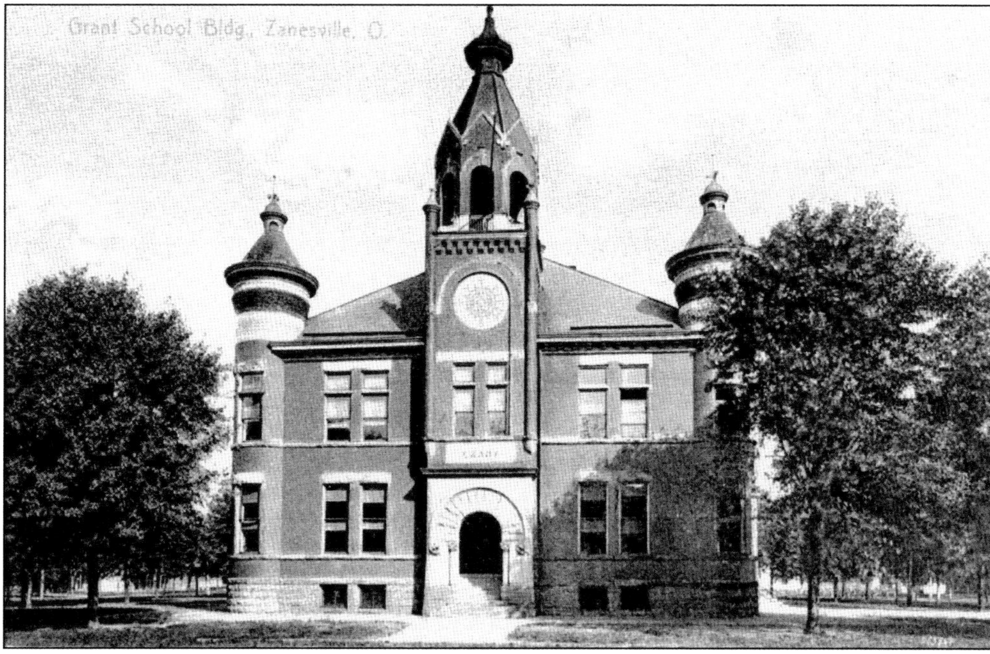

Grant School was designed by local architect Henry Lindsay in an eclectic Queen Anne and Romanesque style and erected in 1896 on Putnam Avenue. Note the turrets of the building were trimmed with Mosaic tile. The building was torn down in the mid-1980s to make way for a new Veterans of Foreign Wars (VFW) building. (Courtesy of Chance Brockway.)

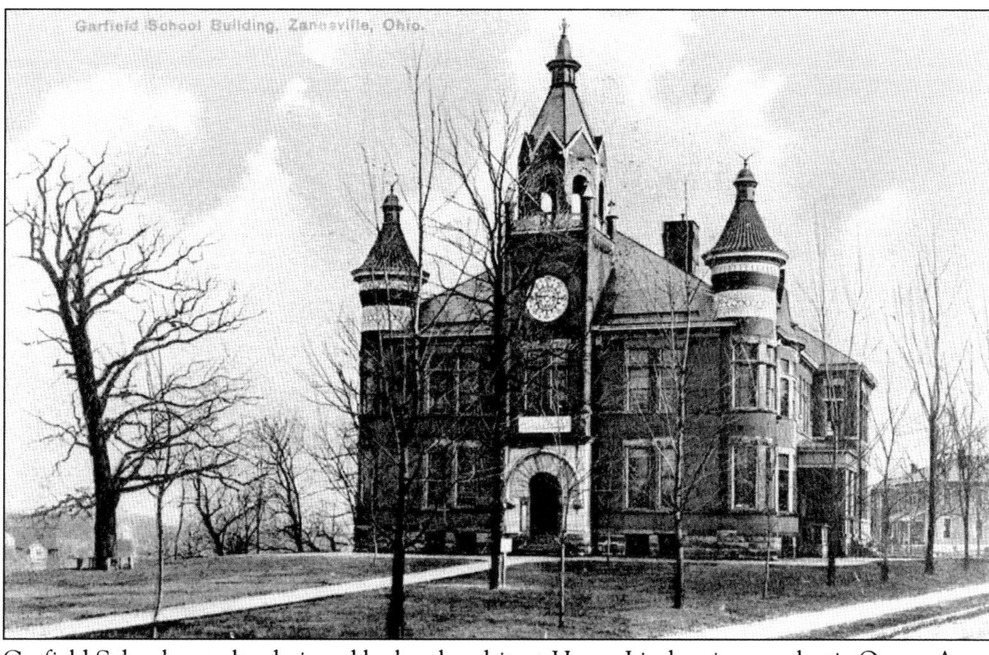

Garfield School was also designed by local architect Henry Lindsay in an eclectic Queen Anne and Romanesque style and was erected in 1896 at the corner of Brighton Boulevard and Dryden Road. The building was similarly trimmed with Mosaic tile. Garfield was torn down in 2001. (Courtesy of Chance Brockway.)

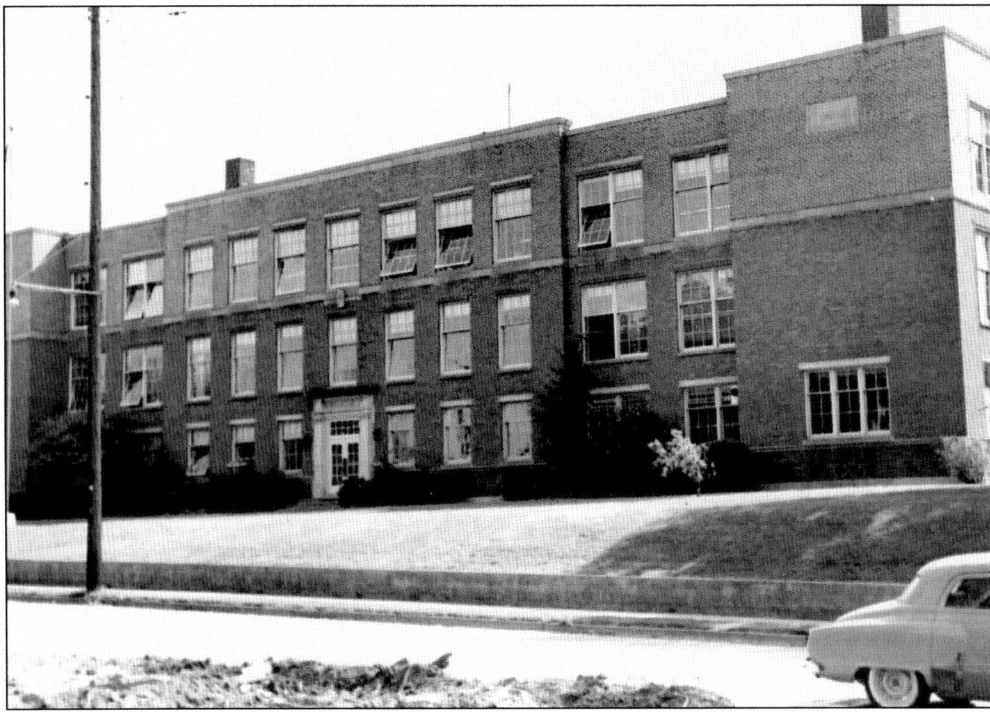

This is Grover Cleveland Junior High School in the 1960s. It was erected in 1924 at the corner of Pershing Road and Pine Street. The building was demolished in 2005. (Courtesy of MCCOGS.)

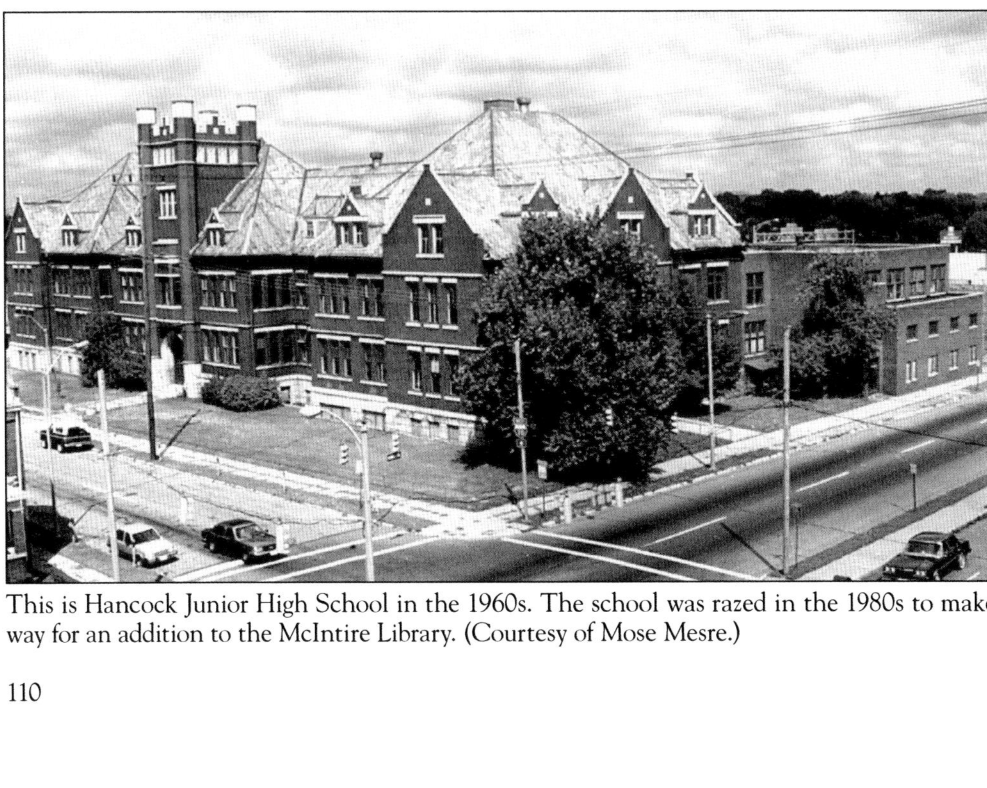

This is Hancock Junior High School in the 1960s. The school was razed in the 1980s to make way for an addition to the McIntire Library. (Courtesy of Mose Mesre.)

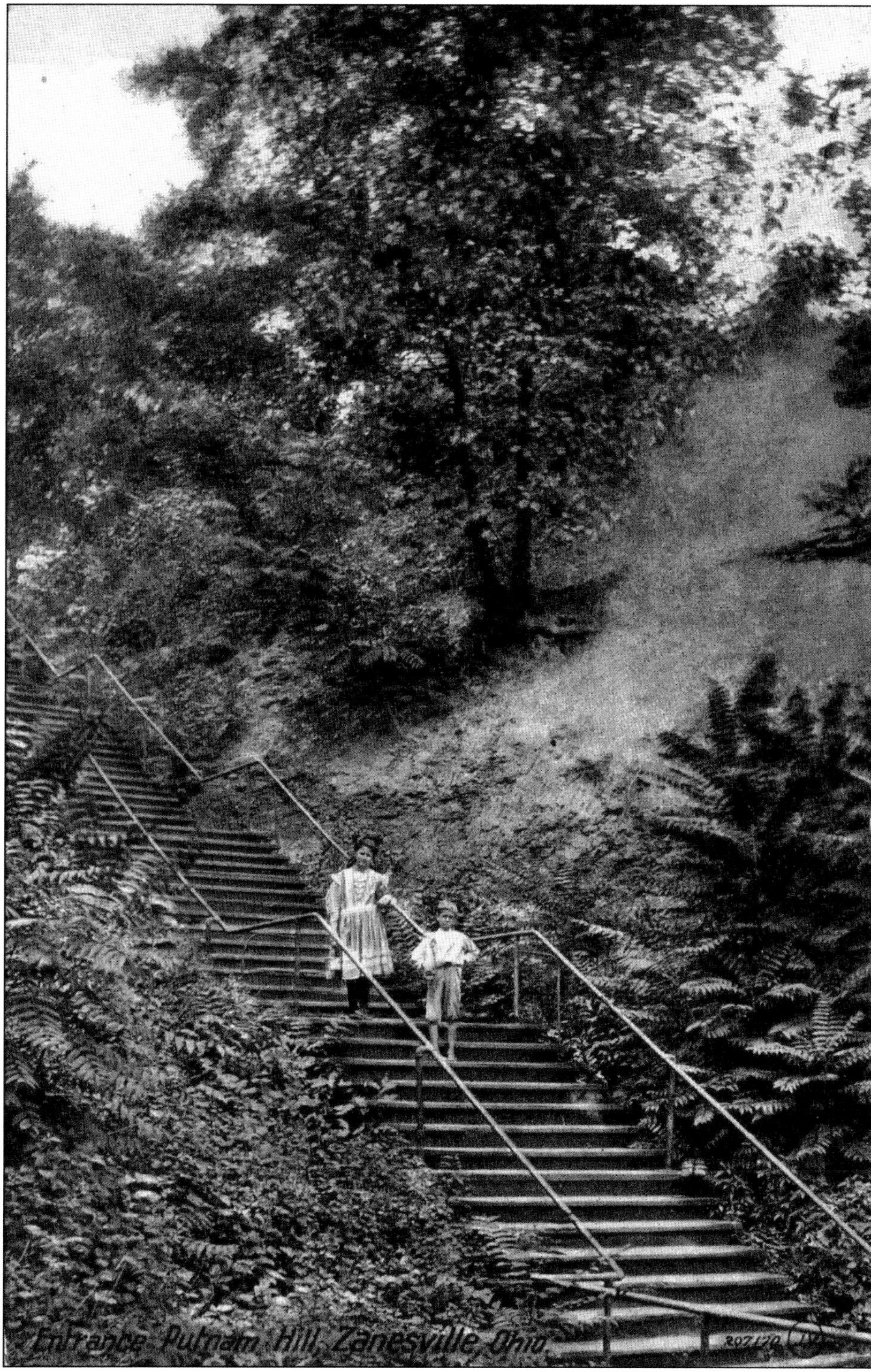

In 1900, a set of wooden stairs were installed leading up to Putnam Hill Park. Between 1913 and 1917, the city added sidewalks, paths, and a shelter house to improve the overall appearance of the park. (Private collection.)

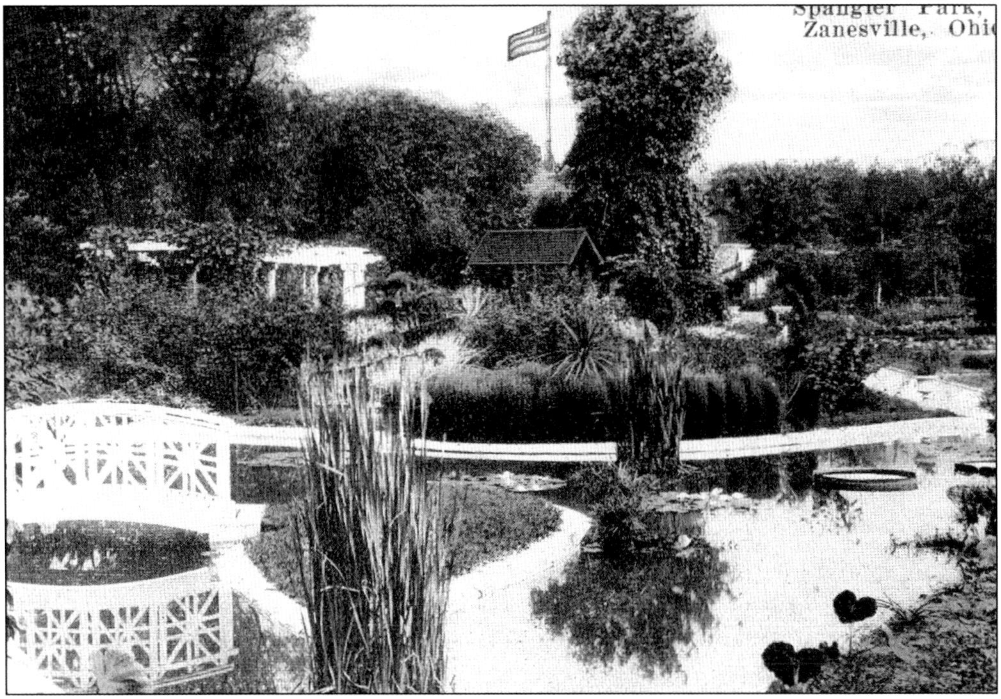

This is Spangler Park in 1899. The park was laid out along Muskingum Avenue with four terraces, ponds, bridges, fountains, and a pergola, all adorned with plants from T. F. Spangler's greenhouse. The park fell into decline following the disastrous flood of 1913. (Courtesy of Wayne Estep.)

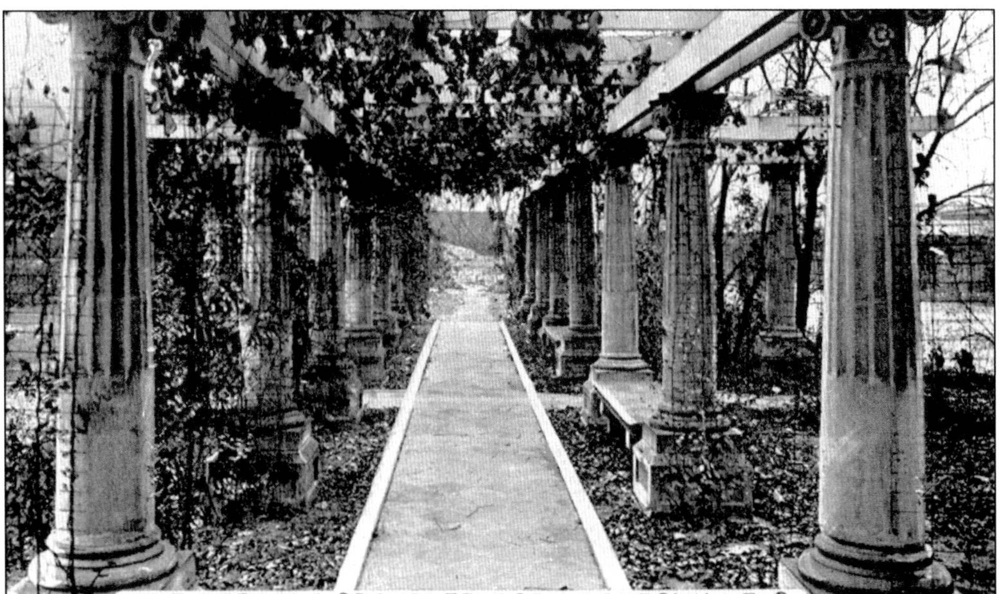

This is the beautiful pergola in Spangler Park. (Courtesy of Chance Brockway.)

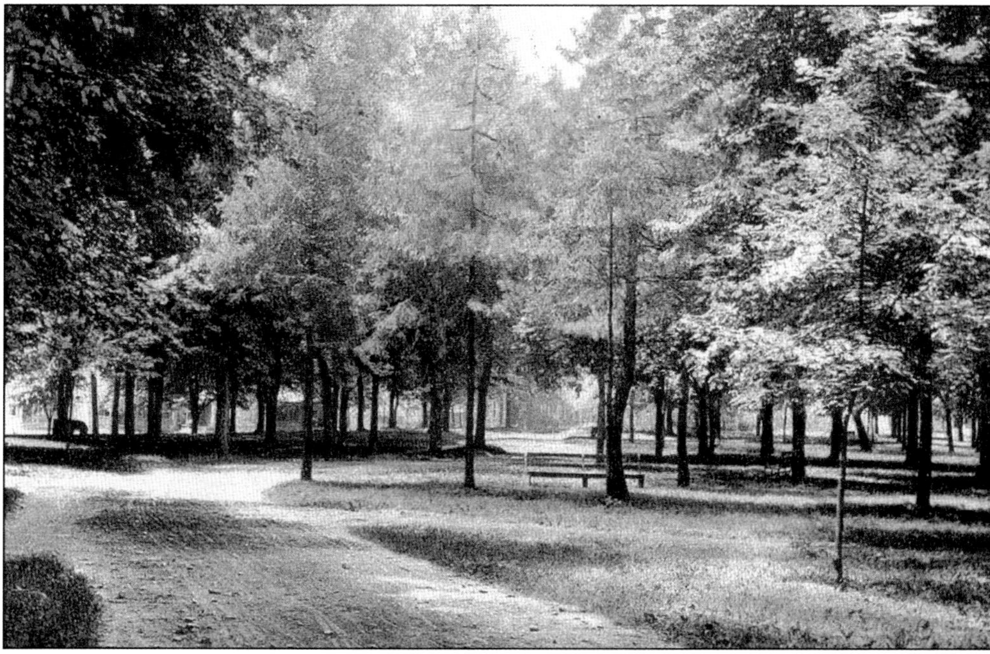

McIntire Park was laid out on a 12-acre site in 1863 by the administrators of John McIntire's estate. The city of Zanesville annexed the property in 1870 and began to improve the appearance of the park by adding sidewalks and paths. (Courtesy of Wayne Estep.)

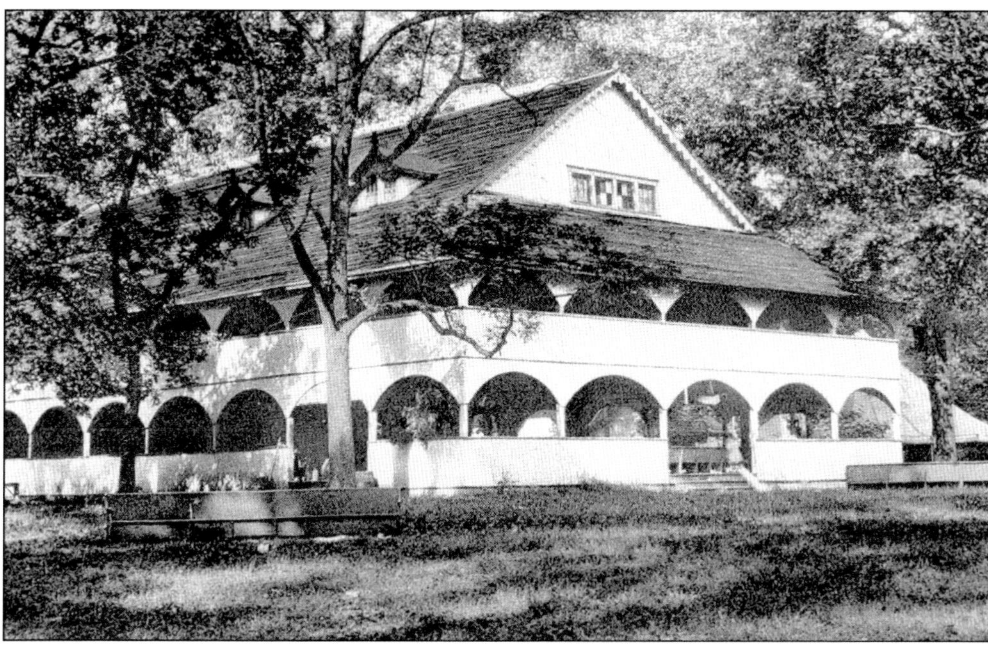

This is the Grand Pavilion at Gant Park in the late 1890s. The park closed abruptly in 1907 when Moxahala Park opened as an amusement park in South Zanesville. The Municipal Stadium was dedicated on the site of Gant Park on September 20, 1940. (Courtesy of Wayne Estep.)

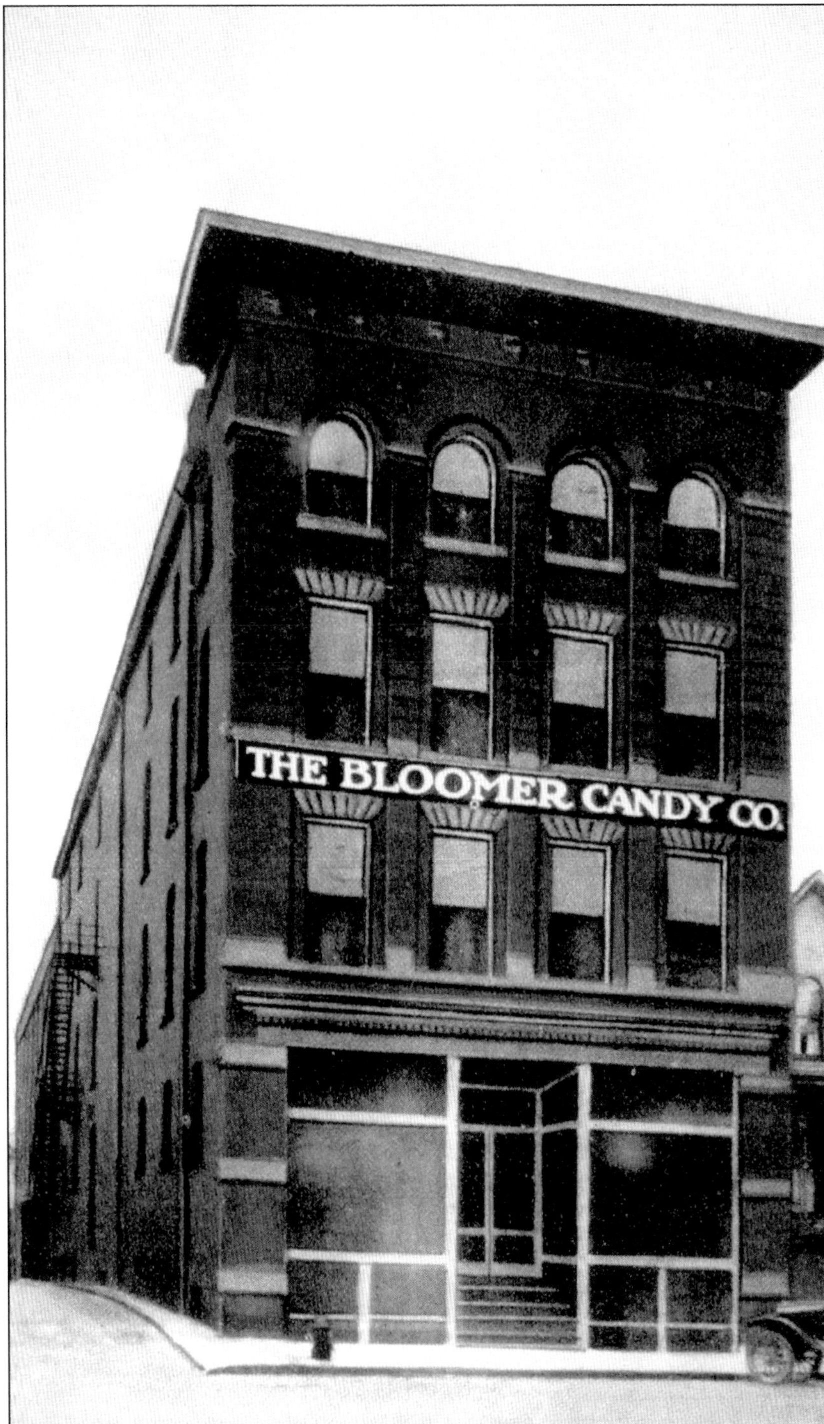

The Bloomer Candy Company has produced delicious chocolates in this building on North Third Street since 1893. The exterior of the building has changed little over the past century. (Courtesy of Wayne Estep.)

Nine

BUSINESSES, HOTELS, AND HOSPITALS

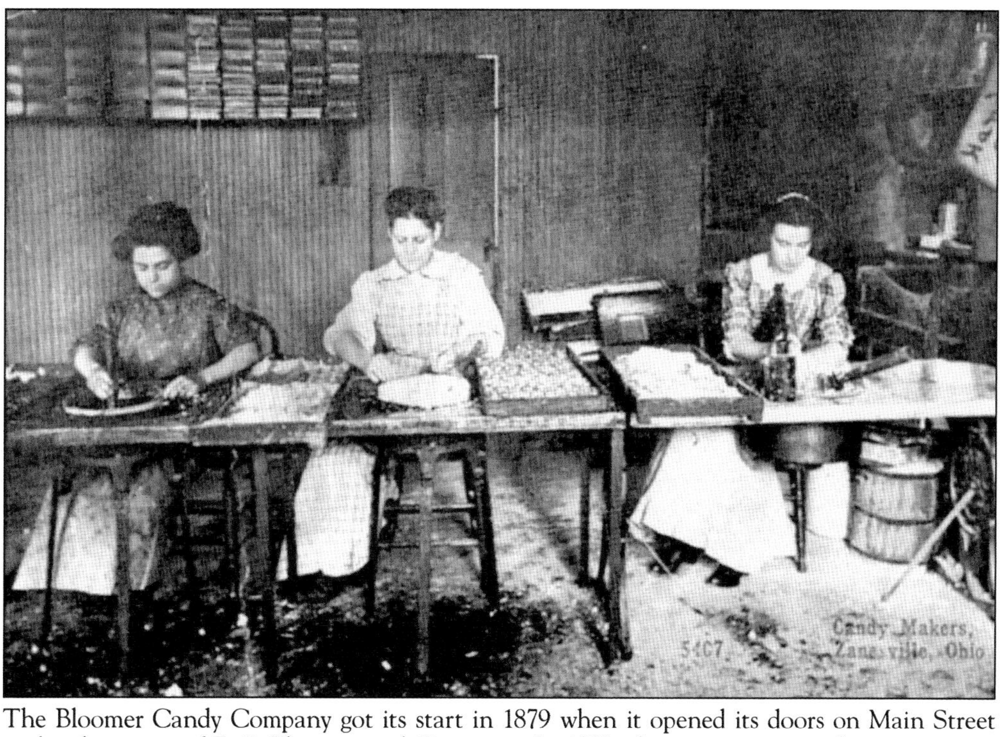

The Bloomer Candy Company got its start in 1879 when it opened its doors on Main Street under the name of E. P. Bloomer and Company. In 1893, the company moved its operations to 39 North Third Street. A group of employees is shown making chocolates. The company is known for its Star Chocolates and bonbons.

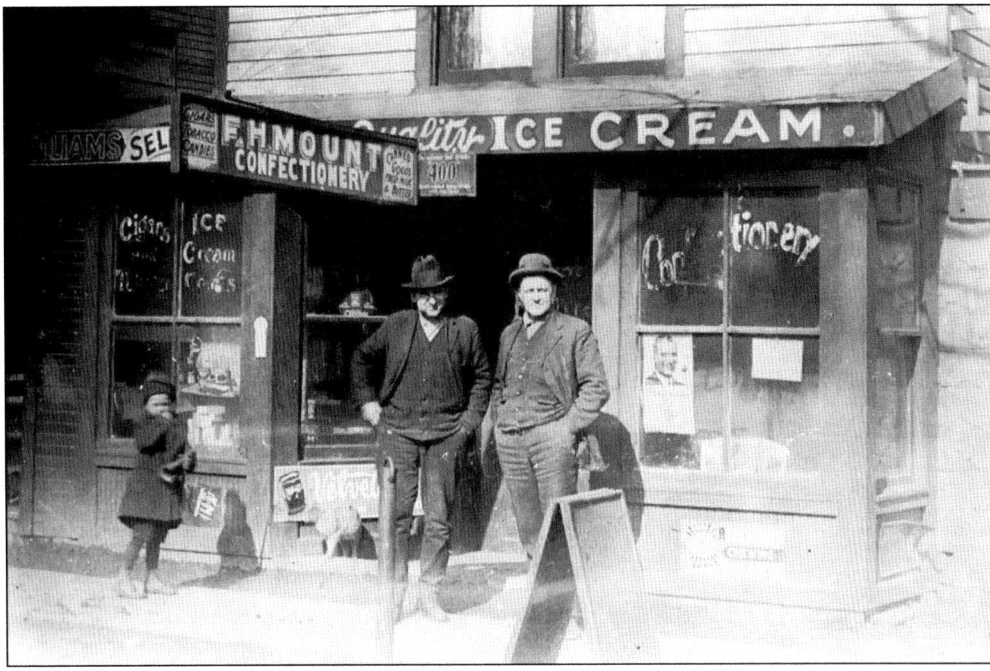

F. H. Mount ran a confectionary at 515 West Main Street in the 1920s. Note the sign over the doorway. Some of the items for sale included cigars, tobacco, candies, canned goods, fresh milk, and butter. (Courtesy of Chance Brockway.)

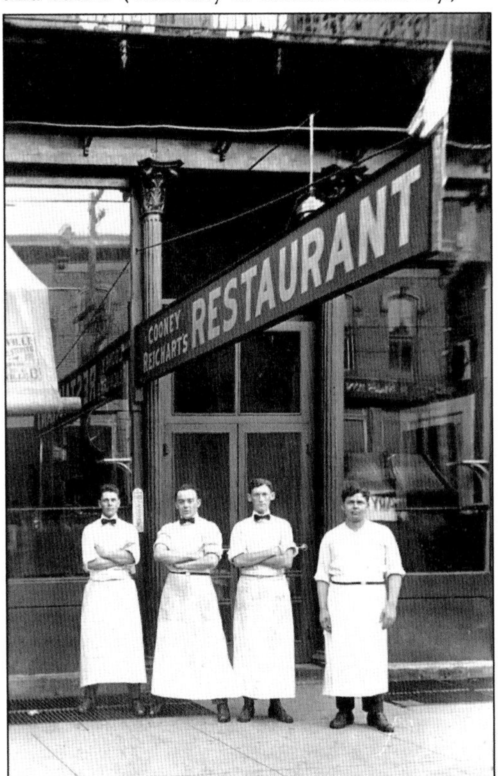

J. C. "Cooney" Reichert and his staff gathered outside his restaurant on Sixth Street in 1919. Reichert relocated his restaurant to 222 Main Street in 1926, and his former location became Hutcheson's Restaurant. (Courtesy of Tom Brown.)

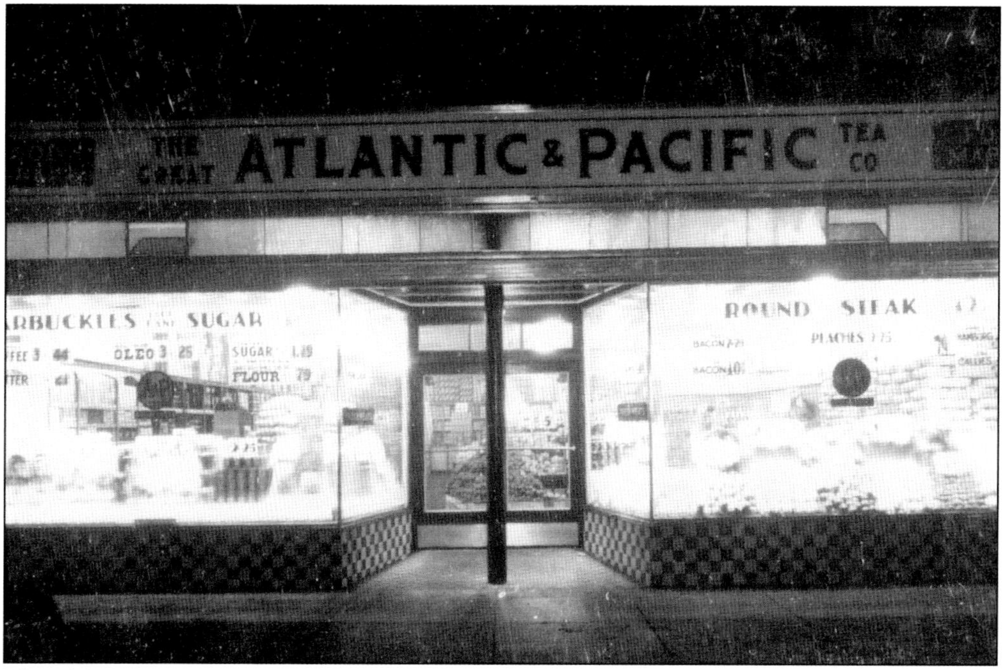

This A&P grocery store was located on North Fourth Street in the 1930s and 1940s. It was heavily damaged in a fire in 1944. (Courtesy of Wayne Estep.)

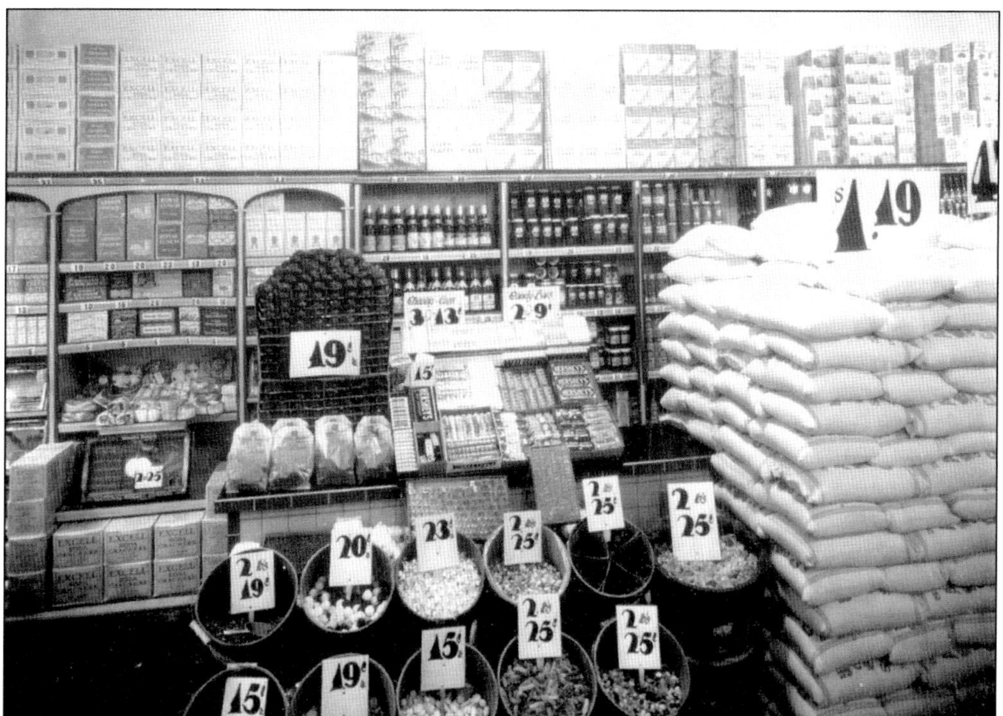

This is the interior of the A&P grocery store. Note the prices of the items throughout the store. (Courtesy of Wayne Estep.)

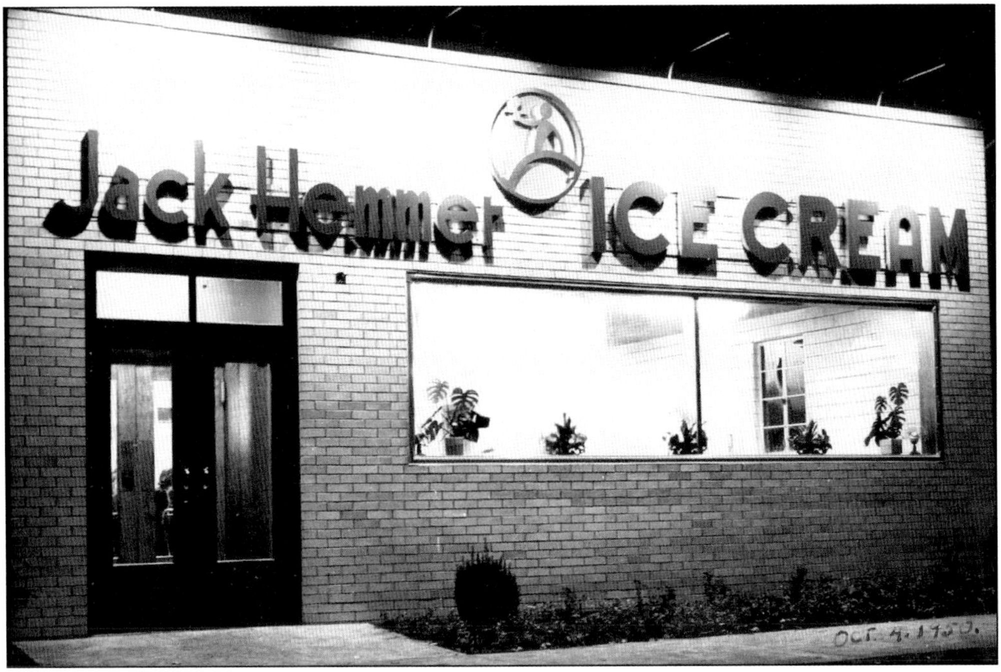

Cousins Jack Hemmer and Tom Mirgon opened the Jack Hemmer Ice Cream store at 532 McIntire Avenue on October 4, 1950, after having quickly outgrown their original location on Linden Avenue. (Courtesy of Bill Sullivan.)

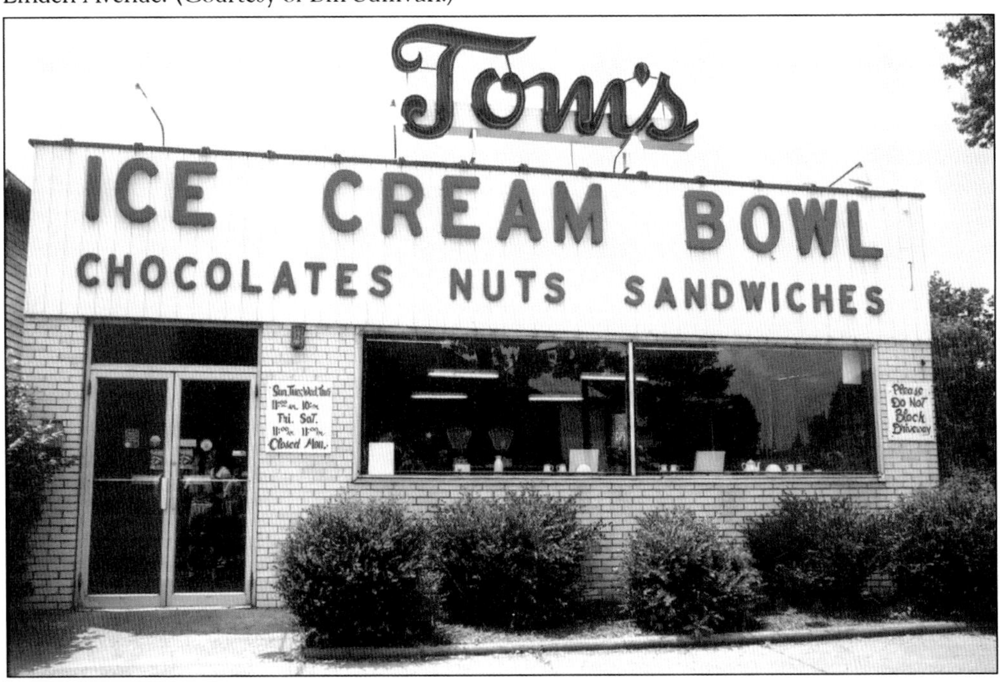

In 1953, Tom Mirgon bought his cousin Jack Hemmer's interest in the business and in 1957 changed the name of the store to Tom's Ice Cream Bowl. Mirgon retired in 1984 and sold the business to Bill Sullivan. Note that, in addition to delicious ice cream, Tom's is also famous for its chocolates, nuts, and sandwiches. (Courtesy of Bill Sullivan.)

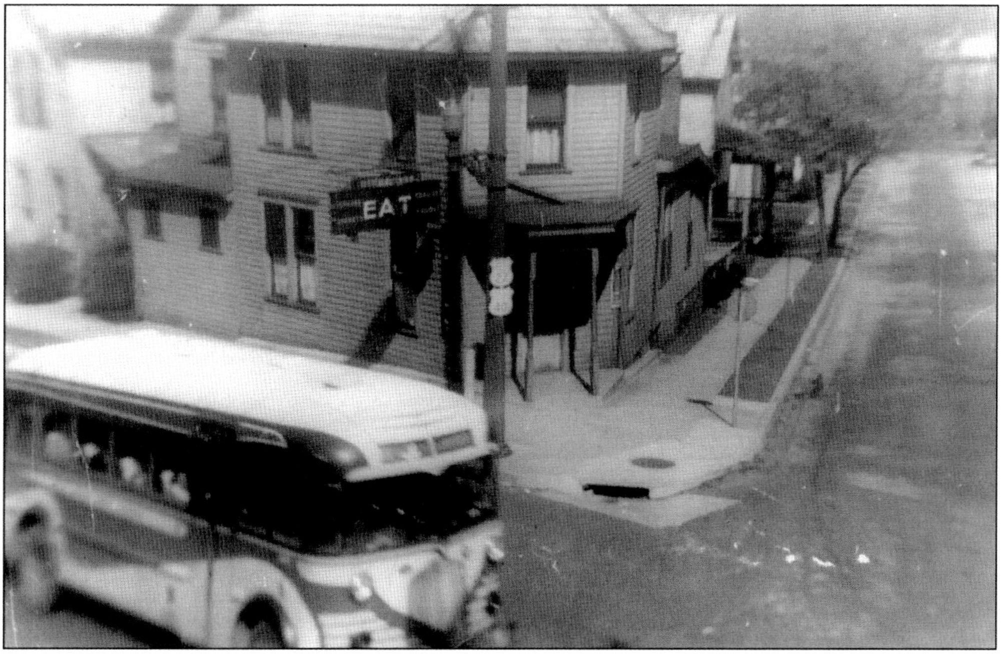

The Adornetto family has operated an Italian restaurant on Market Street since 1937. Over the years, a variety of entertainers have appeared at the restaurant including Henny Youngman, the Four Freshmen, and Burl Ives. (Courtesy of Vincent Adornetto.)

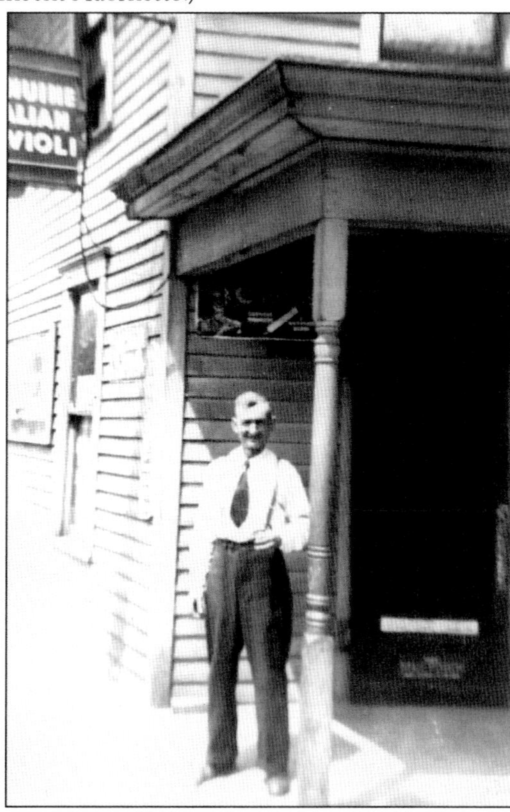

James V. Adornetto, shown here in the 1940s, and his wife, Marie, arrived in Zanesville in 1912 from Sicily. After a few years of farming, the Adornettos decided to open a restaurant. It was originally called the Point Café, but in 1940, the name was changed to Marie Adornetto. (Courtesy of Vincent Adornetto.)

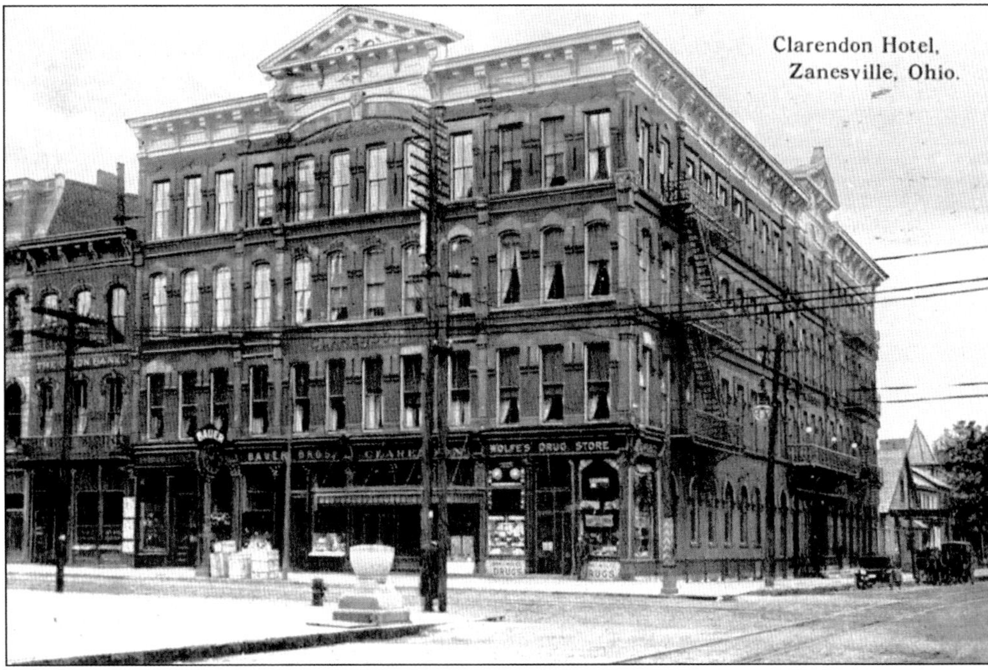

The Clarendon Hotel was erected at the corner of Fourth and Main Streets in 1877, across the street from the Muskingum County Courthouse. The 88-room hotel, known for its sumptuous dining, was considered one of the finest hotels in the state. The hotel was razed in 1972. (Courtesy of Chance Brockway.)

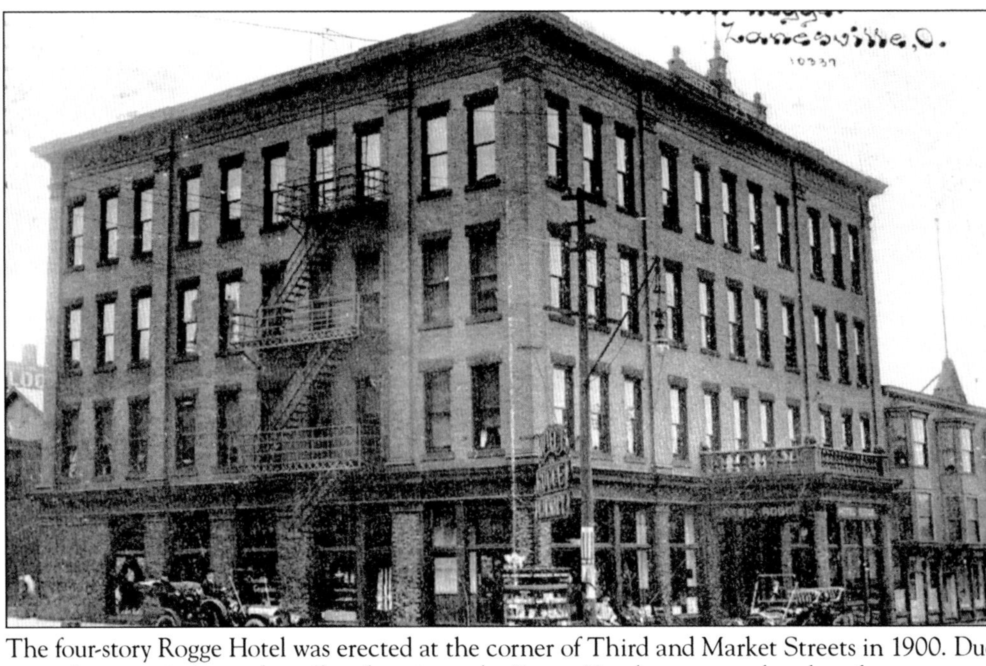

The four-story Rogge Hotel was erected at the corner of Third and Market Streets in 1900. Due to its close proximity to the railroad stations, the Rogge Hotel was a popular place for passengers to stay. The hotel was razed in 1974. (Courtesy of Chance Brockway.)

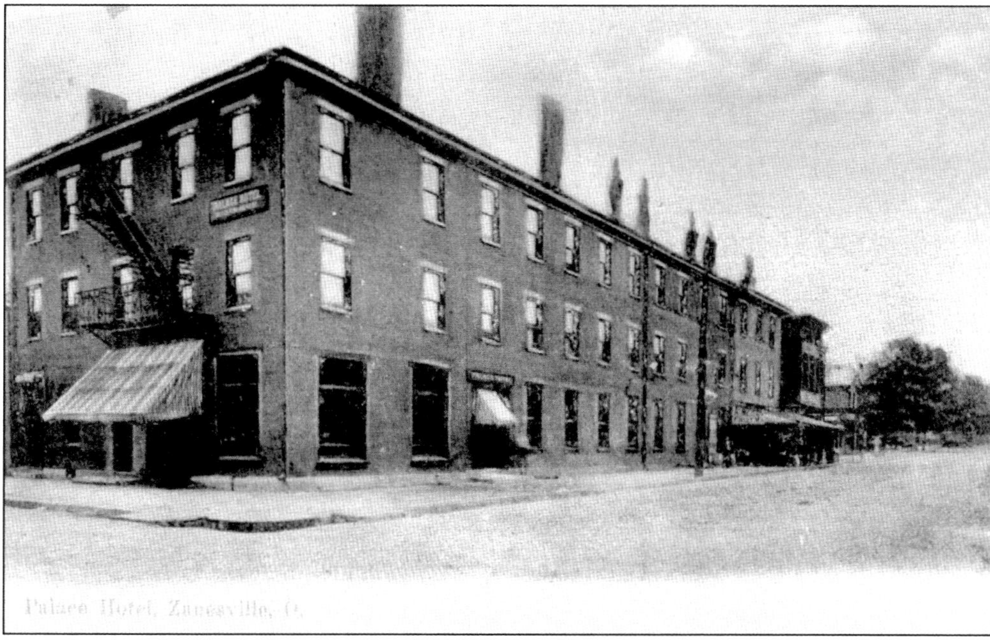

Robert Kirk opened the Palace Hotel in 1893 at the corner of Fifth and Market Streets. Various hotels, including the Stenger, Clifton House, Culbertson, Windsor, and American House, had previously occupied this site. The hotel was torn down in 1957. (Courtesy of Chance Brockway.)

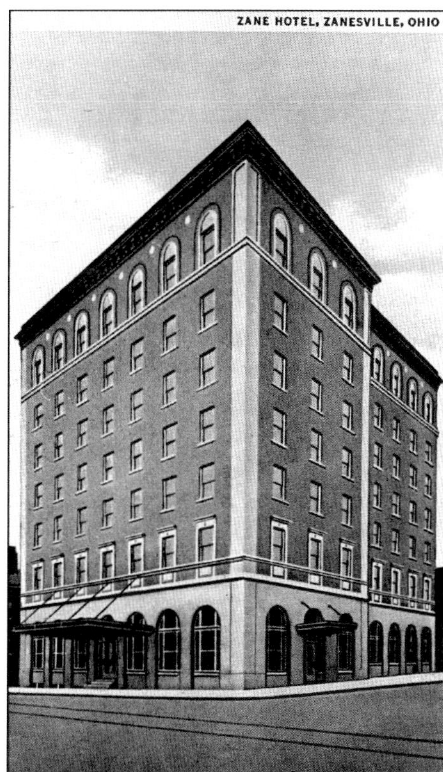

The Zane Hotel was erected on North Fourth Street in 1925. The site of the Zane Hotel had also been previously occupied by a variety of other hotels as early as 1823. The seven-story hotel was torn down in 1974 to make way for a new office building. (Courtesy of Chance Brockway.)

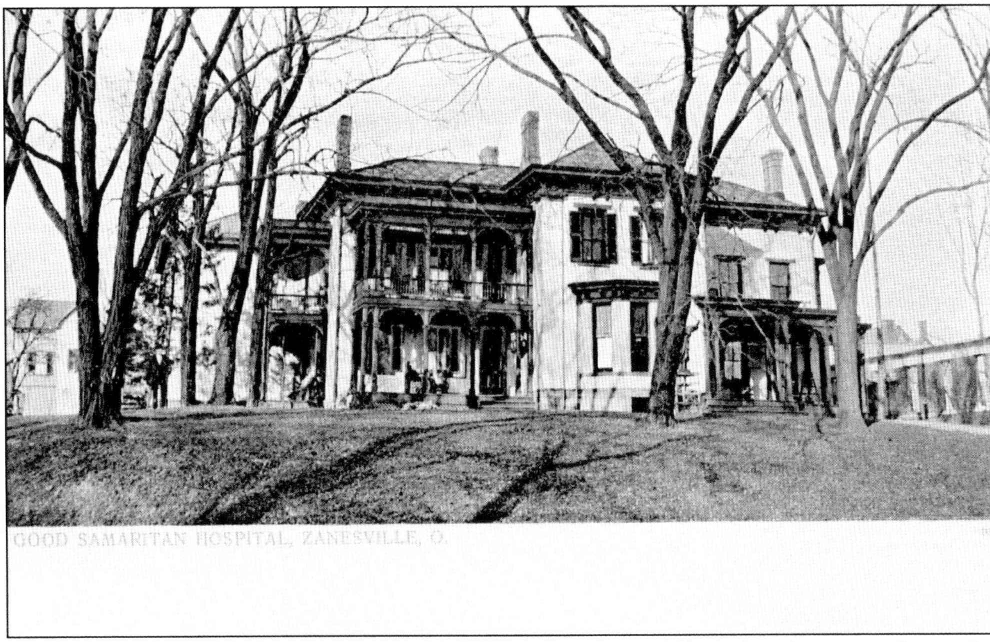

In 1902, the Edmund Brush house on Ashland Avenue was purchased and converted into the Good Samaritan Hospital. (Courtesy of Chance Brockway.)

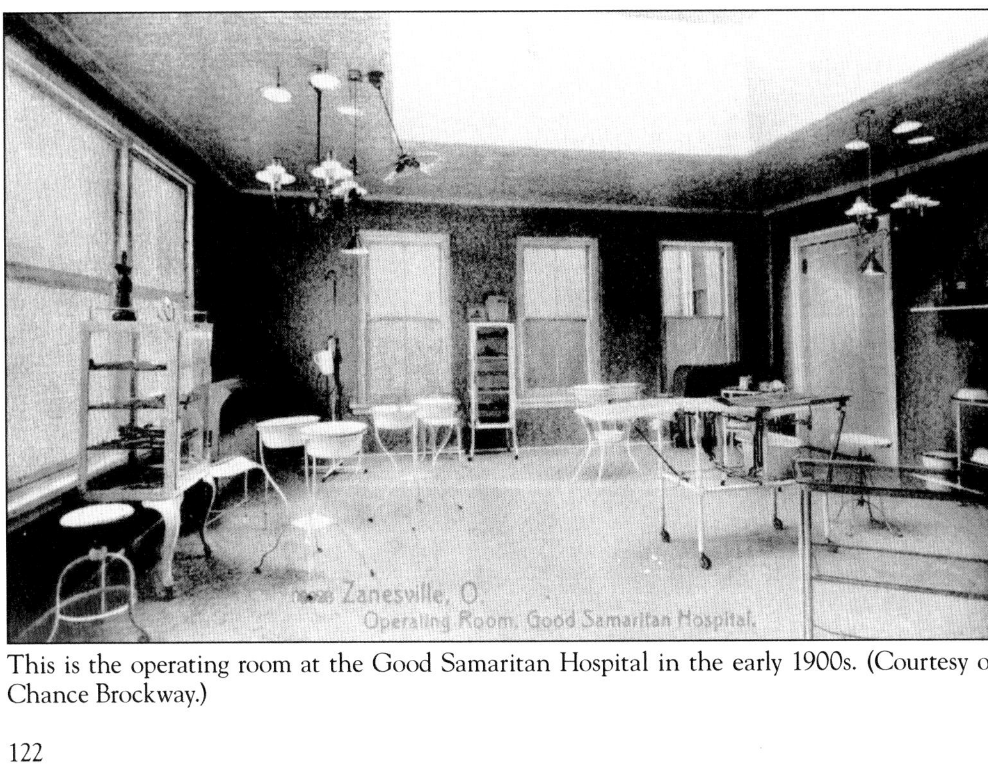

This is the operating room at the Good Samaritan Hospital in the early 1900s. (Courtesy of Chance Brockway.)

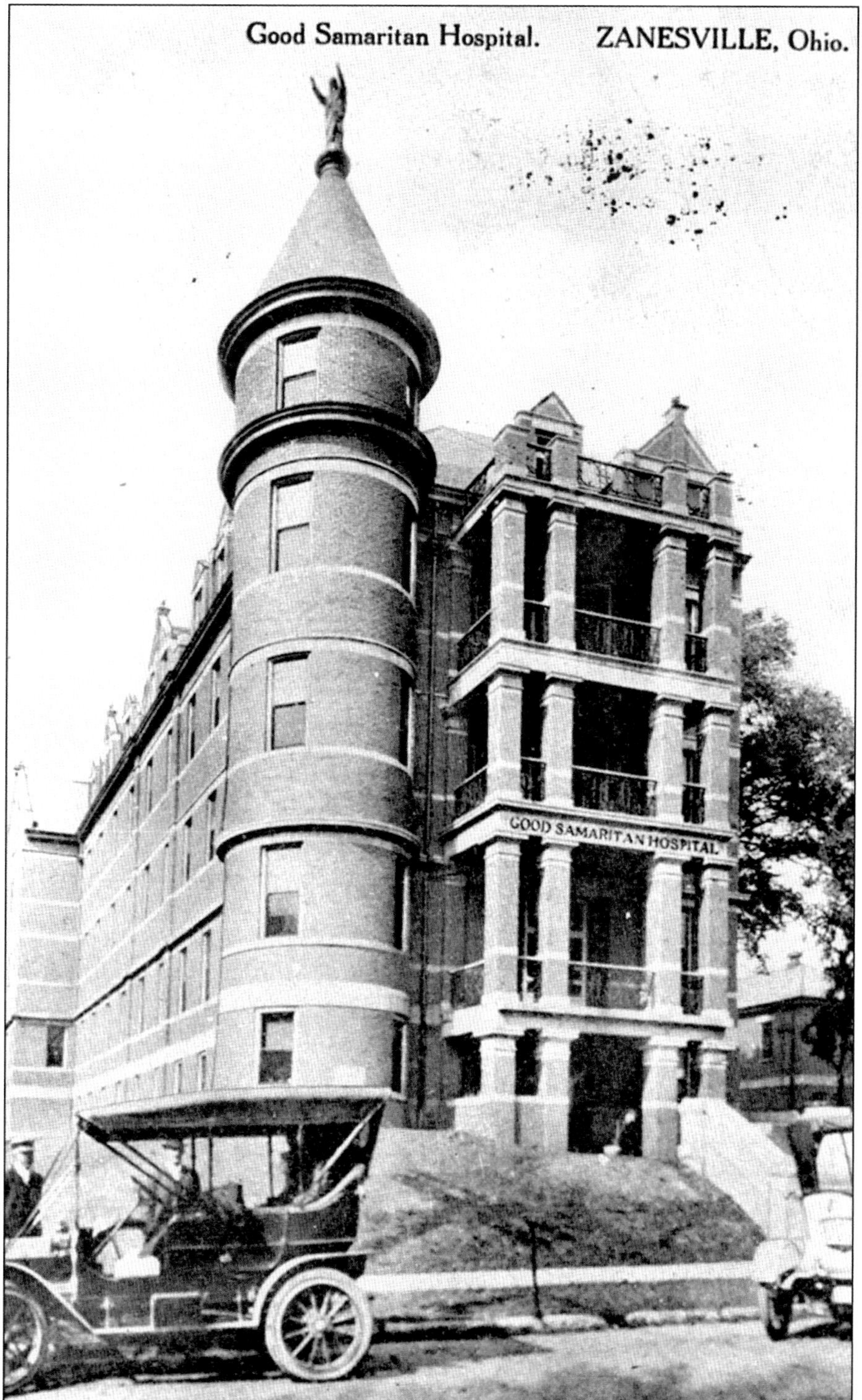

After just four years in the former Edmund Brush house, Good Samaritan Hospital relocated to a new building across the street. The first part of the new building was completed and occupied in 1906. The rest of the building was finished soon afterwards. (Courtesy of Chance Brockway.)

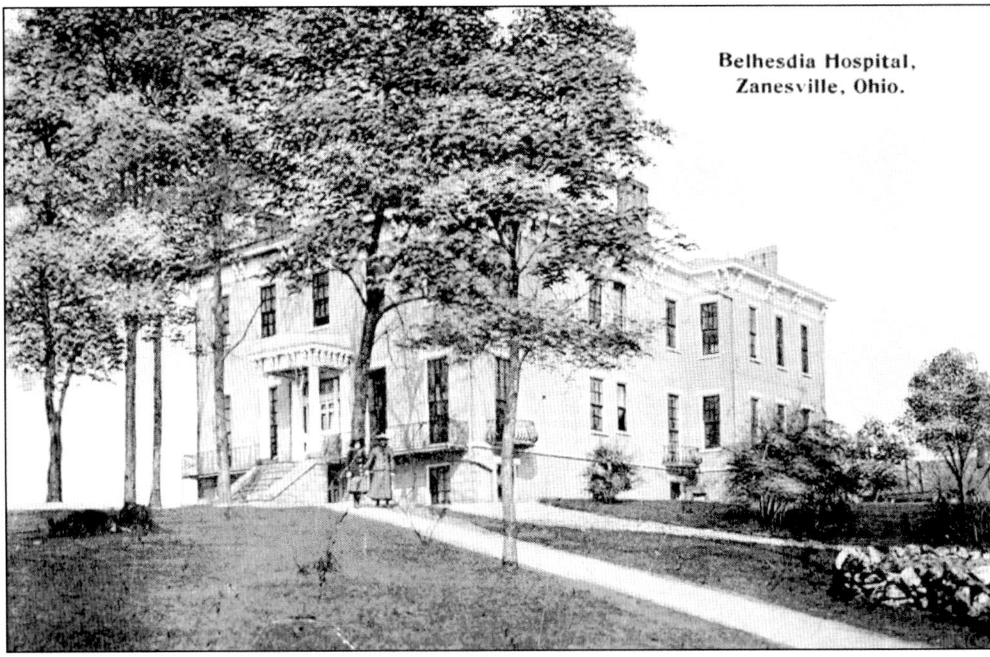

In 1891, the old Peabody house on Eastman Hill was renovated and converted into City Hospital. In 1907, the hospital changed its name to Bethesda Hospital. (Courtesy of Chance Brockway.)

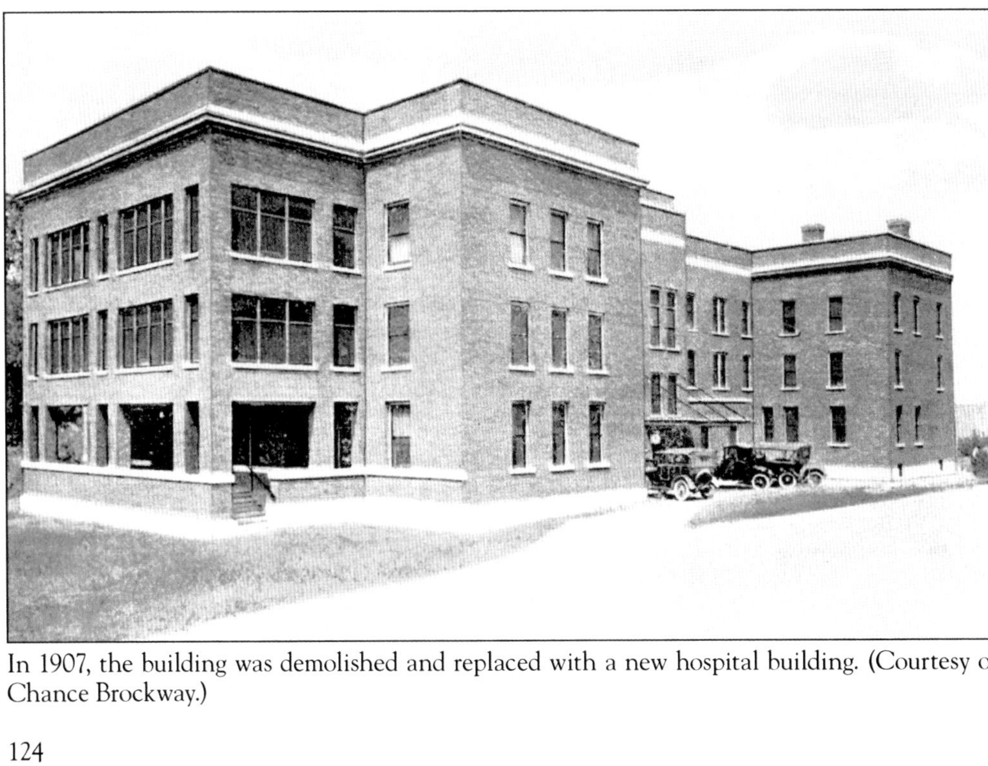

In 1907, the building was demolished and replaced with a new hospital building. (Courtesy of Chance Brockway.)

Ten

Urban Renewal

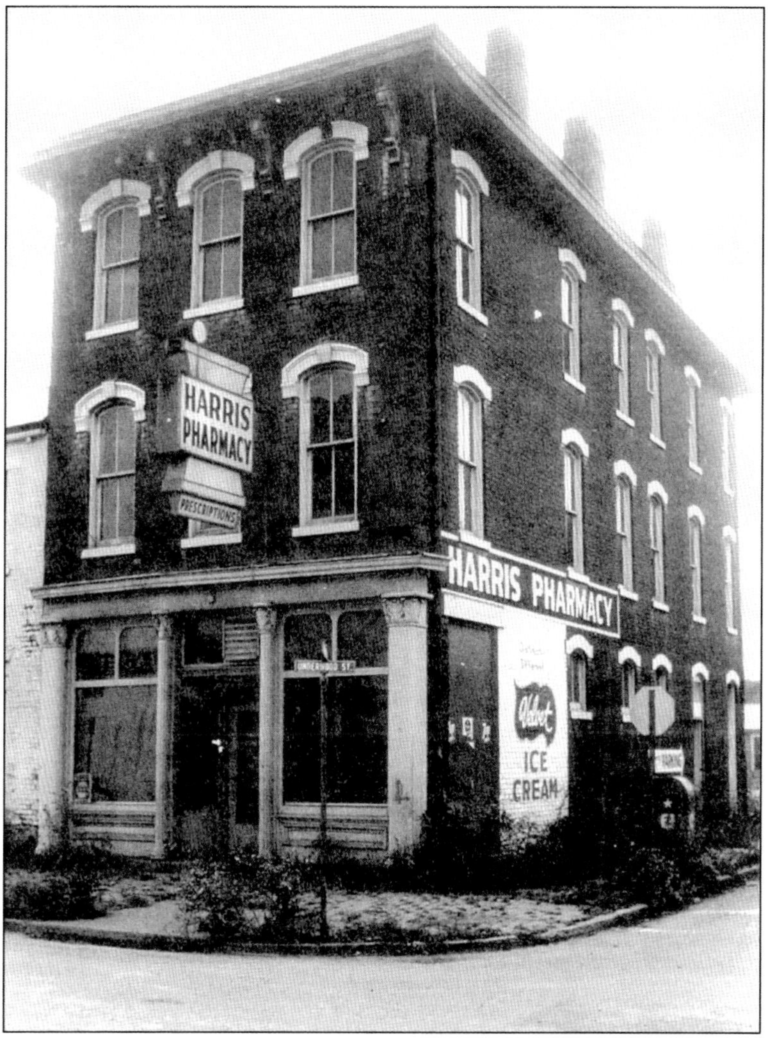

The Harris Pharmacy was located in a three-story brick building on Underwood Street. The building was among those lost to urban renewal in the early 1960s. (Courtesy of MCCOGS.)

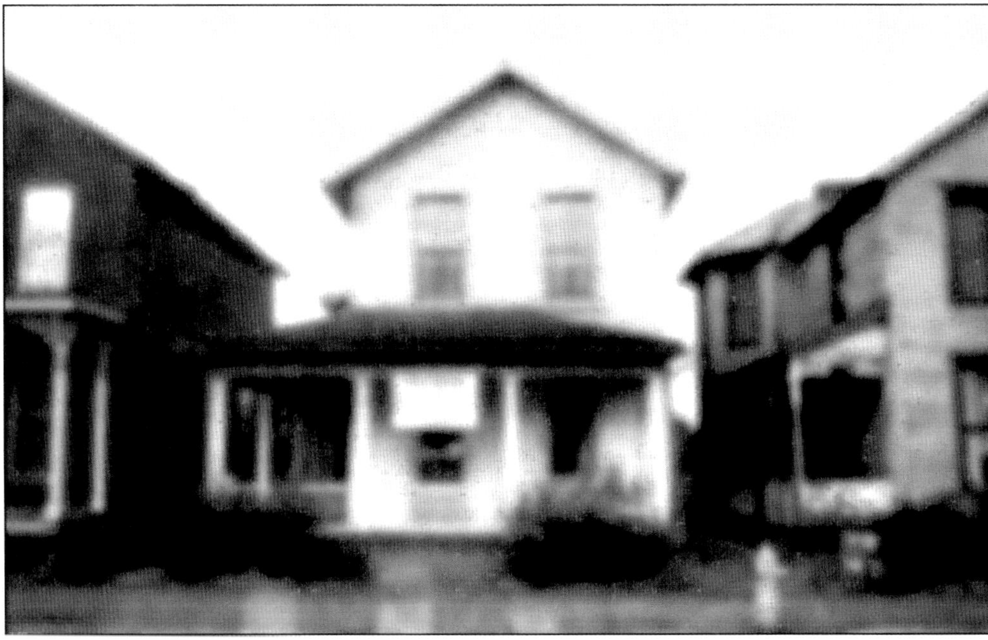

Houses on Underwood Street, like the ones shown in this image from the early 1960s, were torn down to make way for Interstate 70. (Courtesy of MCCOGS.)

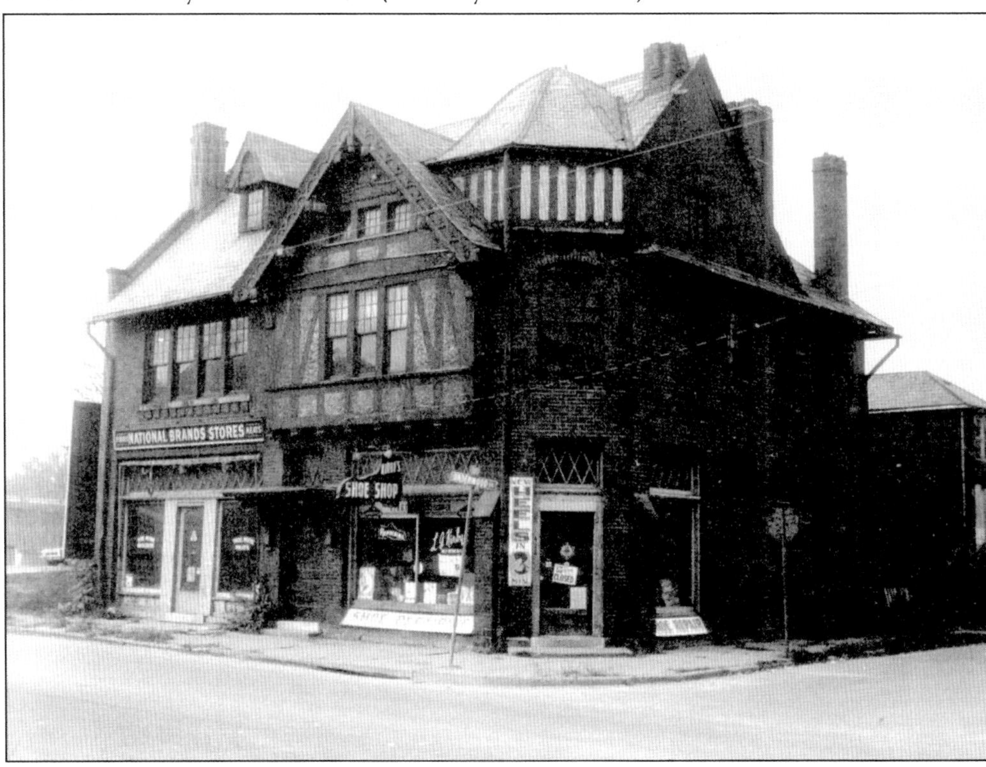

Several small businesses like National Brand Meats and Kirby's Shoe Shop were forced to close during the early 1960s. These businesses were later replaced with new businesses like Bob Evans and the Olive Garden. (Courtesy of MCCOGS.)

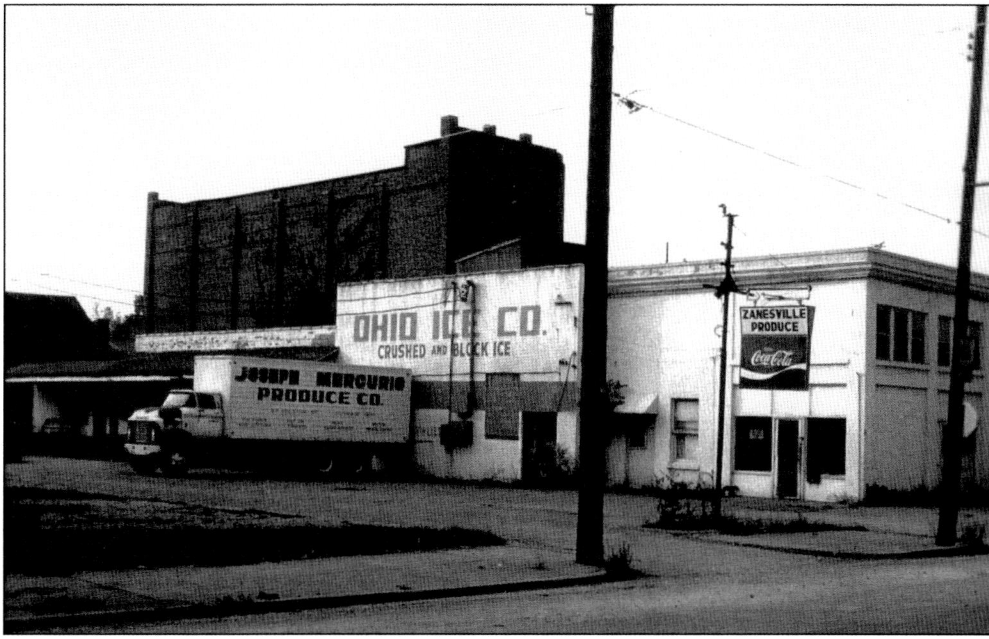

The Ohio Ice Company operated on Underwood Street from 1925 to 1970. It was a popular neighborhood business in the community and was often the first stop for weekend picnickers. (Courtesy of MCCOGS.)

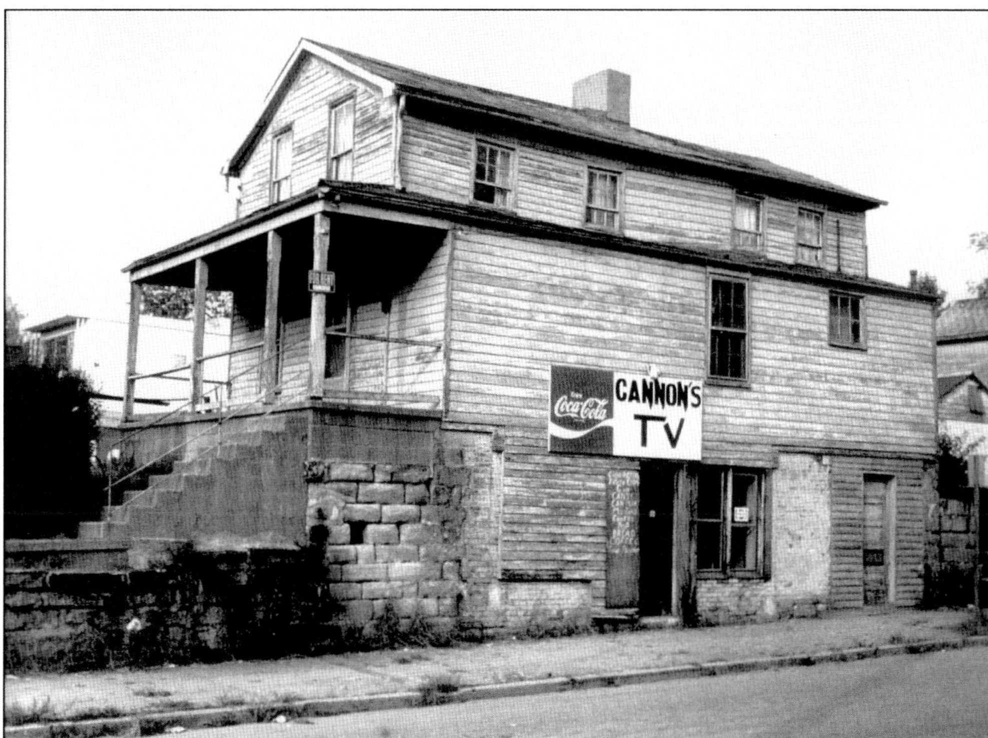

Cannon's TV was another business forced to close during the urban renewal efforts of the early 1960s. (Courtesy of MCCOGS.)

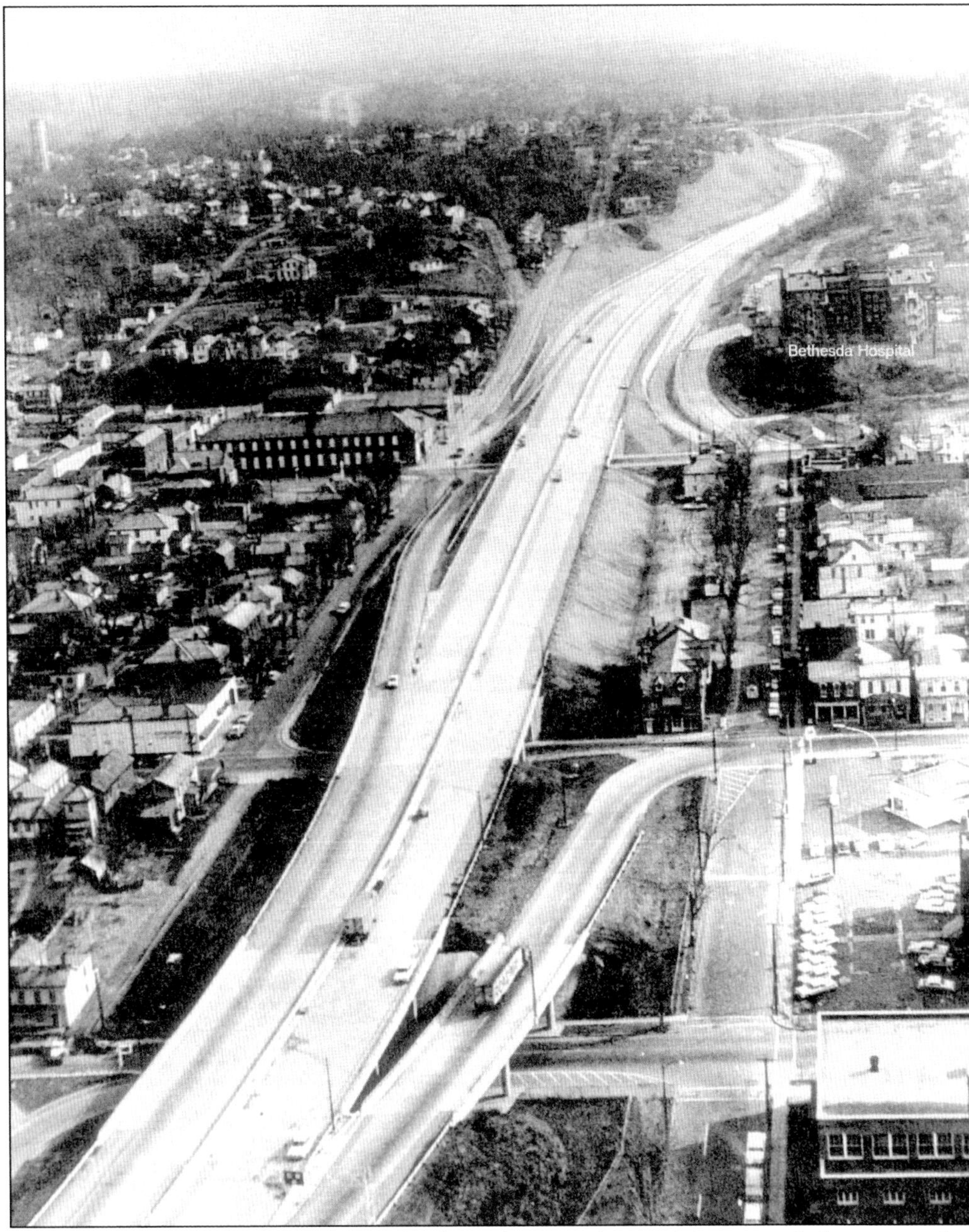

An aerial view of Interstate 70 clearly shows how Underwood Street and the surrounding neighborhoods were changed by urban renewal in the early 1960s. (Courtesy of MCCOGS.)